*OMM 365*

# ONE MINUTE MEDITATIONS
## FOR
# OLDER WOMEN

JENNIFER WESTROM

ISBN: 979-8-218-17391-3

I know well enough that every word I utter carries with it something of myself–of my special and unique self with its particular history and its own particular world. Even when I am dealing with empirical data I am necessarily speaking about myself. But it is only by accepting this as inevitable that I can serve the cause of humanity's knowledge of humanity…Knowledge rests not upon truth alone, but upon error also.

*Carl Jung, CW 4 para 77*

# Introduction

Use this book however you find it most useful.

I've written fifty-two weeks of meditations, affirmations, and writing prompts. My intention was that each day you would read one meditation, use the daily affirmation, and write very briefly in response to the writing prompt. On the seventh day of each week, I ask that you take a break and circle back to review and reflect on what you've written in the previous days.

You will do deep work over the course of this year if you commit to reading and writing for just a few minutes each day.

You can read the text more quickly or more slowly if you like. In my imagination, the later sections build on the former, so skipping around might not work as well your first time through.

Pay attention to where you disagree with the text. This is an important space of exploration where you can bring in something that is missing. You are in a living conversation with this text. Speak your story back to it.

You are welcome to use this book for any kind of discussion group. I've included an addendum showing how I facilitate my groups using *OMM 365*.

I hope *OMM 365* is helpful to you.

# *You've been sold a bad story.*

From your earliest moments to the end of your life, you are drawn to stories. Real and imaginary tales of the world, your family, and yourself help you organize and understand who you are and how you can be in your community.

Storytelling is our most ancient human art. It was the sacred way we passed down our traditions, our values, and our understandings of how to live, love, lose, and grow old. This innate and imaginative connection to stories continuously and creatively weaves the fabric of your identity and your connections.

Have you explored the stories that make up your sense of self and your world? Do you know where these stories come from? I am going to tell you. And you are not going to like the answer.

You've been sold a bad story.

Because with the rise of the consumer age, we changed our storytellers. We moved from listening to the ancient and sacred tales of mystics and medicine women to listening to the stories of for-profit storytellers.

Instead of hearing the paradoxical and confusing wisdom myths of our elders, we now buy easy stories from story-dealers who will provide whatever we want. It is as if instead of providing our children with nutritious food, we allow them to choose the candy they want to eat instead.

Our contemporary stories are like quick sugar fixes. Whether it is the perpetually frightening (yet paradoxically transfixing) news stories that offer no resolution, shallow romances that suggest an easy love that conquers all, or the popular self-help that feeds superficial ego needs of early life (and ignores the developmental needs of late life), we aren't filling our souls with the enigmatic and nurturing stories that hold and allow us to imagine the true complexities of a whole life.

This year, you are going to stop listening to them and start exploring, discovering, and telling your own truest tales.

You are a more complicated story than you know. And it's time we told the tale.

## TODAY'S AFFIRMATION

I pay attention to the stories I engage with.

## TODAY'S JOURNAL PROMPT

The stories of women I grew up on are...
The stories I watch/read/hear today are...

# DAY 2

## *Responsibility, not rescue, is my way forward.*

As you start this new *OMM 365* journey, I'd like to remind you of the one story that will change everything for you–you are responsible. Not for what happened to you. Not for other people. You are responsible for your interpretations of and your actions in this life. Taking radical responsibility for these two facets will powerfully change how you experience your life this year.

Facing this existential truth of responsibility is both empowering and terrifying. There is a rush in realizing that you have some measure of control in our uncertain world. But there is a terror that arrives with the burden of your responsibility for your own path.

You grew up on stories of women being rescued–by princes, knights in shining armor, or superheroes. These dangerous stories of passivity and rescue seep into your soul and lure you away from the truth that you must save yourself.

When you take responsibility, you can't blame anyone. When you take responsibility, you can't wait for anyone or anything to do your work.

We will be together for at least a year. Starting today, make a commitment to take full responsibility for your journey.

Embrace the fear and freedom this brings you.

## TODAY'S AFFIRMATION

I take responsibility for my actions and my interpretations.

## TODAY'S JOURNAL PROMPT

The idea of radical responsibility for my journey makes me feel...

# DAY 3

## *Your healed self is your greatest gift to this world.*

So many women learned to put others before themselves. They feel like they are being selfish or self-absorbed when they take the time to focus on themselves, but the truth is exactly the opposite. The wisdom of older women, who have walked and survived a hard path, is exactly what we need more of in our wounded world.

Throughout the history of humanity, it was the wise women who passed healing on to the next generation. We lost that passing of old women's wisdom as popular media took over our narratives. If you are like most older women today, you've had few mentors and only glimpses of this ancient wisdom as you tried to make your way in the world.

So, please remember, your work on yourself is not just for you. Your work on yourself is also your task of bringing healing to the people around you. This is not a selfish or self-absorbed act, but ultimately, your most selfless one.

Today, pay attention to where you are prioritizing the needs of other people or things over your own journey. Reflect on how one healed woman can start a culture of wisdom and healing in the circle of people around her. Imagine yourself becoming that woman.

You deserve the joy this selfless giving will bring you.

### TODAY'S AFFIRMATION

Investing in my own healing is my first step of healing this world.

### TODAY'S JOURNAL PROMPT

When I imagine dedicating time for myself, I feel…

# DAY 4

## *I embrace the changing seasons of my life.*

As we explore the stories of your growth and development this year, I am going to ask you to think about your life in a new way that returns you to more ancient ways of understanding.

Your life includes four seasons, *Receptivity, Responsibility, Reflection,* and *Return.* You have a year (or more) to reflect on this, but, as an introduction, I will start with a very abbreviated overview of the forgotten four seasons of a woman's life.

> *Receptivity :* As a young girl, in the spring of your life, you were open and receptive to the ideas and stories of those around you. As you engaged with your community (whether positive or negative), you constructed your own interpretations of yourself, others, and your world.

> *Responsibility :* When you went into the world, you started the summer season of responsibility. Maybe you were a mother or a worker, or both. Laden, with the responsibilities (or chaos) of this season, you didn't have much time to think deeply about your stories and your journey.

> *Reflection :* In the fall of your life, something happened. You discover some shortcoming or experience some failure (a divorce, death, or just inexplicable despair). Now starts the season of turning inward. In this third part of your life, you are forced to reflect in ways you've not reflected before (This reflection after a fall can start in any decade of life.)

> *Return :* And finally, you return. With the wisdom you've gained from your reflection, you become a teacher. You are a wise woman in the winter of her life, stepping into an invisible world and learning how to completely let go.

This year you will gain a greater awareness of why you made the choices you made in your earlier seasons. You will stop blaming yourself and start intuitively knowing that the way you were was exactly how you needed to be in that moment.

Over the course of this year, we will return to these seasons and the stories that remind us. But today, hold them loosely and reflect briefly on how you've lived them in your life. Recognize where you still put unrealistic expectations on your younger self. Embrace the purposeful change that comes up with aging into the wise woman you were always meant to become.

You will love the full circle knowing this will bring you.

### TODAY'S AFFIRMATION
I embrace the changing seasons of my life.

### TODAY'S JOURNAL PROMPT
I do/do not recognize the different seasons of my life and
the differences in what I could do and know in each season…I notice…

# DAY 5

## *Your coping skills need review and revision.*

As a little girl, you likely faced psychological challenges that were confusing to you. Whether it was the simple fact that mom had to go to work or that someone in your family was truly dangerous, your young mind had to strategize how she could keep herself psychologically (and maybe physically) safe.

These were necessary adaptations to your environment, constructed by a very young girl. If you didn't adjust, you would have ended up with deeper psychological wounds.

The problem arises when we are older, out of that dangerous (or just confusing) environment, and still using the stories (coping skills) of our childhood selves. Maybe you learned to shut people out (to stop feeling hurt). Maybe you learned to read people's needs and to do what they want (to be safe). Maybe you learned to turn to food or other distractions to find temporary psychological comfort.

There are an infinite number of coping skills you could have developed at that stage of life that are unique to you and the environment you were trying to live in.

Your job today is to reflect on those old coping skills. What are you still doing to protect yourself? Does it still make sense to do that? When you think about the psychological goals of this stage of life, how might you change some of your earliest stories that are still hanging around and holding you back?

Today, see if you can unearth some of these old patterns that aren't working for your new goals.

You will love the growth and transformation this opens up for you.

### TODAY'S AFFIRMATION

I reflect on my old patterns and let go of habits
that no longer work for me.

### TODAY'S JOURNAL PROMPT

As a child, I probably learned to be...
This might still be present in my life in that...

# DAY 6

*When our ways of being have failed us,
it is time to be open to new ways of being.*

We all get trapped in our thinking loops. We may be frustrated with some aspects of our personal life. We may feel discontented with some parts of our spiritual growth and development. We have ideas about what we need to do, but our plans to make change never seem to work out.

The problem is often that we are turning to the same resource that failed us–our ideas. If your thinking could get you there, you'd be there by now. It hasn't. This is when we know it is time for you to be open to radically different ways of being. But how?

When you are out of ideas, stop trying to solve your problem in your own head. Instead, start looking outside of your own paradigms. Explore people, thinkers, and approaches that are totally different from your own. Find role models who achieved what you are seeking. Read the books they read (or wrote).

This sounds like such a simple bit of advice, but I see this rigid thinking loop most frequently in smart women. They know they haven't gotten where they want, but they are still depending upon their own ideas that have repeatedly failed them.

Today, notice where you've felt stuck (in any aspect of your life). Explore where you might find radically new ways of being (not in your own head!). Don't rush for resolution, but start practicing being open to something outside of your thinking brain.

You will love the new paths this radical openness brings to you.

## TODAY'S AFFIRMATION
I am open to radically different ways of being.

## TODAY'S JOURNAL PROMPT
Areas where I feel repeatedly stuck are…

# DAY 7

# *Rest, Review, and Reflect*

Over the course of this year, we will move forward and then circle back each week.

On the seventh day of each week, I'd like for you to review what you explored the previous six days. Switch hats and become a compassionate listener to the woman who wrote this week (it is very important to not be critical; show the compassion you might show to someone you feel protective of). Explore your writing however it feels right to you. Here are some options if you'd like some help (don't try to write in response to all of these questions, as that is too much; they are just intended to provide some guidance if you feel stuck).

1.  Review what you wrote, listening with compassion to the woman writing.

2.  Did you realize anything new about yourself this week? What insights came up for you?

3.  Which OMM did you connect with most? Least?

4.  Was there anything in the OMMs that you felt was not quite right for you? Or even completely wrong? Explore what would be more correct for you (this can be a very productive exploration).

5.  Did any unexpected stories or memories pop up for you this week? Reflect on why these stories might be surfacing for you now.

6.  After reviewing the writing, what would you like the woman who wrote this week to know or feel?

## *Your resilience is your key to your contentment.*

The Western story of happiness is built upon youthful and superficial values, so it was a shock when researchers studying mental health discovered a truth antithetical to the story most Westerners believe.

What they stumbled upon was the unexpected paradox of aging. Despite our idea that we would be happier if we got what we wanted, they saw that many older adults score better on reports of mental health and well-being than young people–despite living with much more significant losses. How could they make sense of this discrepancy?

What later research proved was that the key to our well-being, especially in our last decades of life, is resilience. Resilience is not a quality you either have or don't have; it is a skill that you can always develop. And you must develop this skill.

Today, instead of imagining what you need to feel better, imagine how you can adapt to not having what you want. Instead of focusing on your losses, focus on improving your ability to cope. Instead of retreating into despair, see if you can persevere in reconnecting with your healthiest practices.

Your resilience is your key to aging well.

You deserve the contentment this skill will bring you.

## TODAY'S AFFIRMATION
I am resilient.

## TODAY'S JOURNAL PROMPT
My response to crisis or loss tends to be...
Some practices I can incorporate to improve my ability to adapt might be...

# DAY 9

## *You can heal with your imagination.*

We've lost awareness of the role of our imagination in our healing. We get so fixed in our ideas, perspectives, and beliefs that we lose our ability to imagine alternatives or the perspective of the other. This is where the transformative power of your imagination is most needed. In your imagination–in that playful space between you and your stories of other people and your world–you create something totally new that can heal you.

We see this truth in the foundational work of famed psychologist Donald Winnicott and his discovery of the healing power of play. Winnicott reminds us that children's play doesn't even need interpretation for it to have a healing effect. The play alone is healing.

But where do older adults find imaginative play? One place we evoke our imagination is when we read or hear stories that elicit our creative engagement. This would be a story that has enough space to let you fill in the color, detail, and bits of the story (think cryptic myths, simple fairy tales, or confusing parables). Your imagination is naturally evoked in your creative imaginings, where you unconsciously fill in the blanks in the story. Between you and that story, you create something totally unique and totally new. This is what the ancient tales of wise storytellers used to do for us.

Classical era writers recognized that something important happened when we witnessed or heard a story. When real life is imitated (the fancy term is mimesis), this elicits a weird response in the listener. She suspends her disbelief in the fictional nature of the story (experiencing the story 'as-if' it were true), and she is affected on an empathetic and emotional level. If you've ever cried at a movie, you know this is true for you.

This is the magical space of your healing–this space between you and the stories you encounter. As you project your inner world into a story (imagining the thoughts, feelings, and beliefs of a character, for example), you are creating a new reality between your world and the world of that story. You connect and create new truths about yourself, others, and our world.

This is why your stories and the stories you hear and tell matter. Pay attention to the stories. Because the imaginative space between you and these stories is where you live and heal–yourself and our world.

### TODAY'S AFFIRMATION

I am open to the imaginative spaces of healing.

### TODAY'S JOURNAL PROMPT

The stories I love most are...because...

## *Your unexpressed pain is expressing itself somewhere.*

If you are like most women, you probably learned to suppress your pain. This coping skill was critically necessary when you first developed it. When hard things happened, you were so overwhelmed that you couldn't make sense of it in that moment. Later, deep in the responsibility season of your life, you were so busy working, taking care of people, or responding to life's never-ending obligations that it was impossible for you to find a moment to reflect.

But now, in this later season of life, you do have moments to reflect. And what was necessary for you then is not working for you now.

When you ignore your pain, it doesn't disappear. Like the ancient Scylla and Charybdis that tormented Odysseus, these underwater sea monsters lie in wait, indefinitely, to suck you back into your story.

Our unexpressed pain reveals itself in our addictions or obsessions (e.g., shopping, drinking, eating, or gossiping). It shows up in our dislike of others (what I deny in myself, I project onto them). It shows up as physical symptoms (I see so much stored trauma in the body in my EMDR therapy sessions).

So you may think you pushed this pain out of your life, but it is still very much here.

Today, pay attention to the habits you struggle with. Notice the physical pains in your body. Ask yourself if these are related to unexpressed emotions. Ask yourself, through writing, painting, or some other creative exercise, what these old feelings might be trying to tell you.

Your younger self deserves to be heard. Your older self deserves the healing.

**Note:** Not all physical symptoms/pain/illness are related to unprocessed pain. An aging body can hurt, so don't take personal responsibility for this universal process.

## TODAY'S AFFIRMATION

I am resilient enough to process my old pain.

## TODAY'S JOURNAL PROMPT

When I imagine allowing my unexpressed pain to come up, I…

# DAY 11

## *Your dark night of the soul is not the death of Spirit. It is the death of your false ideas about Spirit.*

It is so painful when you feel spiritually abandoned—angry at "God" or whatever is out there that won't relieve your suffering. This spiritual crisis can feel like a death and a terrifying moment of feeling completely forsaken by an indifferent universe.

You feel uniquely alone in that moment, but the dark night of the soul is a theme that recurs again and again in our greatest spiritual literature. Your dark night isn't the death of the spiritual world. It is a death of your ideas about the spiritual world that aren't working anymore. You had an idea about God or the supernatural, and it turned out to be wrong (e.g., God won't let bad things happen, etc.). Instead of concluding, "Maybe my ideas were wrong," we jump to more grandiose conclusions like, "The idea of any spiritual reality is wrong."

This is a death—and a rebirth. A tale of defeat and resurrection found in any ancient tradition you choose—from Phoenix out of the ashes to the Eastern teaching that we need to "die before we die" to the rebirth of baptism in the Christian faith. These ancient stories remind us that an experience of spiritual defeat isn't unique to you but is part of our universal spiritual journey.

Ultimately, we can't understand the mystery that surrounds us. But we can look to our ancient traditions and teachers to learn that all of us are in a life-long process of death and rebirth—constantly gaining and then letting go of things, expectations, and beliefs.

So, remember, when you find yourself again in that long, dark night, know that you have not stepped off your path; you are on your long journey of letting old things die away so that something new has room to come in.

Be patient with your process. You are worth it.

### TODAY'S AFFIRMATION
I can let go of old ideas.

### TODAY'S JOURNAL PROMPT
My beliefs about God or the supernatural are...
These beliefs came from...

## *Stop waiting to feel ready.*

We have a lot of misunderstandings about what it takes to do the things we dream of doing. An obstacle that is usually overlooked is one I see too frequently in my work with women–waiting for the perfect state of being to arrive in order to take action on something. Maybe she is waiting to feel confident enough, strong enough, less fatigued, or no longer afraid.

This is a very common and dangerous form of psychological paralysis because that perfect state never arises in our lifetime. Getting started is always scary. Waiting for a future moment where you aren't afraid to take the first step keeps you stuck indefinitely; you are trapped in a delusion that your work will only begin when you reach a state of being that will never arrive.

Remember, none of us ever feel strong enough, brave enough, or capable enough. We all start our journey feeling (and being!) weaker, more afraid, and less capable than we wish.

Today, notice what you feel you want to do but are not yet ready to do. Ask yourself if you are waiting until you *feel* ready. Promise yourself you won't allow this misunderstanding to paralyze your need to get started.

You deserve the momentum this brings into your life.

### TODAY'S AFFIRMATION

I can take action, even if I don't feel ready.

### TODAY'S JOURNAL PROMPT

I might be trapped in this idea of 'waiting until I feel ready' with...

# DAY 13

*Practicing gratitude brings you more peace.*

The old platitude that we need to be grateful can grate on our nerves when we are not feeling it. But the problem with this old saying is not with the advice; the problem is that that advice is so frequently misunderstood. The fact is, research proves, again and again, that practicing gratitude causes a measurable and dramatic improvement in our mood.

The misunderstanding is that too many people hear, "I *should feel* more grateful." Then they feel worse because they don't. That is not practicing gratitude.

The practice is not about how you should feel. The practice is a very specific technique. When we force ourselves to say, "I am grateful for…" or "Thank you," in response to some situation, even (and especially!) when we are not feeling it, we change our brain.

Today, see if you can work on some daily habits of gratitude. When you get your morning tea or coffee, get into the habit of saying, "Thank you." (I don't care to whom or what, it doesn't matter). On a hot or cold day, notice your air conditioner or heat and say, "Thank you."

This does something to our brain, and it makes us feel better. So, remember, I am not suggesting you should feel more grateful. I'm teaching you a cognitive trick that will make you feel better.

And you deserve that.

## TODAY'S AFFIRMATION
I am thankful.

## TODAY'S JOURNAL PROMPT
I am grateful for…

# DAY 14

## REST
## REVIEW
## REFLECT

# *Your Season of Receptivity.*

What are some of your earliest memories? I'd like to make a guess that when you wander back to the earliest stories you can remember, you will find a young girl trying to interpret a new world. In those memories, you were probably in a world that didn't completely make sense, but you were constantly gathering information and weaving it into something that did.

This was your receptive season of life. You were confused. Maybe you were safe. Maybe you were unsafe. What was actually the case doesn't really matter for this exercise. What I want you to recognize is that you were like a little receiver that was taking in an extraordinary amount of new information and trying to make sense of your world.

This is where you built the first provisional stories about yourself (e.g., your value, your safety, how others viewed you, etc.). You weren't a responsible adult. You weren't a reflecting older woman. You were a receptive little girl, trying to make sense of this world she found herself in. You started constructing your first stories.

Today, reflect on that little girl and how different she is from you today. See if you can remember what it was like to be in that space. Hold her with compassion and protection as you remember her and her attempts to make sense of a confusing world.

## TODAY'S AFFIRMATION

I can hold my youngest self with compassion and understanding.

## TODAY'S JOURNAL PROMPT

My earliest memories are…

# DAY 16

## *Believe in something beyond yourself.*

When life gets overwhelming, we feel a crushing sense of not being able to keep up with anything. But your feeling of overwhelm is actually trying to communicate something important. It is a message that you shouldn't be trying to do this alone. It is a call for you to reach beyond your ego's story that imagines you should be in control of everything.

The story of individualism in the West has you steeped in a myth that we all should be able to do all things by ourselves. But this ridiculous story is actually a very recent (and naive) idea. All of our ancient and sacred tales remind us that we are completely interconnected and interdependent. This modern demand for such absolute individual accountability is a self-constructed suffering that you can dismantle.

You don't have to believe in anything specific for this to work for you. Whether you develop faith in a transcendent reality or construct a commitment to ethical humanism that connects you to your community, know that you can embrace this practice within any spiritual or secular belief system.

Today remember that the most ancient and true story is that we all need help. See if you can ask for help from someone, or if that doesn't work, from some transcendent reality. I am not guaranteeing that help will come, but this practice of remembering you can't and shouldn't try to do this all on your own will bring you more peace.

You deserve the relief this brings to your life.

## TODAY'S AFFIRMATION

I was never supposed to be able to do all of this by myself.

## TODAY'S JOURNAL PROMPT

Needing help makes me feel…
I probably feel this way because…

# DAY 17

## *Through success or failure, we all end up lost.*

At different paces and via different routes, we all arrive at the same crucible–the shocking discovery that the outside world won't save us. We get there whether we are 'successful' or 'unsuccessful' in reaching our external goals. Some of us fail to achieve any of our ambitions and find ourselves miserable. Some of us achieve all of our aspirations and discover we are still miserable.

This critical psycho-spiritual crossroads of moving into our reflective years is a space where many older women get stuck. We hit this important bump on our track and end up completely derailed. We can't get back on the old track but are now lost in an unfamiliar wilderness. This is where the story of the wise woman begins. You let go of the old path laid out for you by your community and culture and head into an invisible, inner wilderness where you discover your own.

Yes, it is scary. Yes, you wish someone could provide guidance on exactly where you should go and what you should do. But this is your quest. Your task is to traverse this internal wilderness and find your own way. Like Virgil and Beatrice assisting Dante, mentors, and guides can help, but ultimately, this is a journey only you can take.

Today, notice if you are still focused on getting the outside world to fulfill some goal, milestone, or expectation so that you can finally be content. Recognize that this is the naivete of a younger woman dependent upon an external world. Step into your wise woman journey and allow yourself to wander inward.

You will love the discoveries this journey brings you.

### TODAY'S AFFIRMATION
I turn inward and find my own way.

### TODAY'S JOURNAL PROMPT
When I imagine letting go of my expectations of the world, I...

## *Mother Nature will heal you.*
## *Go outside.*

Many of the things we do in an effort to bring ourselves comfort actually increase our suffering. Over the last hundred years, we've moved farther and farther away from the natural world. We seek the comforts of enclosed buildings. We look to technology and screens for our entertainment. We protect ourselves from the messy, natural world and all of her unexpected difficulties and delights.

You do these things in a sincere effort to soothe yourself, but the research shows that you are doing exactly the opposite of what helps you. Studies repeatedly prove that the more we are away from our buildings and our technologies and in a natural environment, the happier we become.

We make these mistakes because we don't know that going outside works. A research study had a group of students predict how happy they would feel after a walk; one group was assigned to walk inside, another was asked to walk outside. Both groups of students incorrectly predicted the emotional impact of their walk. The indoor group *overestimated* how much they would enjoy the indoor walk–it didn't make them as happy as they had predicted. The outdoor group *underestimated* how much they would enjoy the outdoor walk–it made them happier than they had predicted.

The research proves that nature makes you happier. The research proves that we don't know this.

Today, try to find a few minutes in a natural environment–whether it is just looking more closely at a tree or a patch of grass, watching birds or bugs, or feeling the wind on your face, see if you can remember how to connect with your natural world.

You deserve the contentment this will bring you.

### TODAY'S AFFIRMATION

I find time each day to be in a natural environment.

### TODAY'S JOURNAL PROMPT

My feelings about being in nature are…
I tend to be in a natural environment…(how frequently?).

# DAY 19

## *There are more ways of knowing than we know.*

In the West, we are dominated by one story of knowing. In philosophy, the study of what we can know has a fancy term–epistemology. The fact that this is an advanced topic of scholarship that has interested the greatest thinkers for millennia should humble us when we think we know what we can know. There have been big debates by big thinkers about this for centuries.

But, even so, ever since the Enlightenment, the West has told us only one story of knowing. In the seventeenth century, the rise of rational inquiry and empirical science abbreviated our beliefs to things that are concrete, causal, and repeatable (remember when you learned the scientific method to discern what was 'true?'). In this new understanding, things are caused by other material things, and if you can't repeat it, it isn't true.

We've lost so much in this paradigm shift. The stories of spiritual experiences, intuitive knowing, and meaningful coincidences are ridiculed as naïve.

I am not saying that the story of empirical truth isn't true. I am saying that there are more ways of knowing what is true than the short story you've been told–logic has its place, but so do intuition and feeling. They all belong in your repertoire of knowledge.

Today, reflect on these different ways of knowing. Pay attention to how each of them plays a role in your life.

You deserve the expansive truths this brings you.

### TODAY'S AFFIRMATION

I trust all of my ways of knowing–my feelings, my intuition,
and my logical thinking.

### TODAY'S JOURNAL PROMPT

My experiences with knowing or experiencing things beyond the rational include
(e.g., spiritual experiences, meaningful coincidences, etc.).

# DAY 20

## *We are dying of safety. Embrace risk.*

Somewhere in the last few decades, we changed our story about risk and safety. Clearly, early settlers in the West embraced risk, with many dying, or nearly dying, as they explored and settled on the lands of Native Americans.

But today, many women see any risk as a non-negotiable stop sign. Or, at least, as a warning that she should not tread in such dangerous waters lest she be found blameworthy for her foolish treks.

This idea that we should prioritize safety, at all costs, over the rough and tumble reality of a life with risk is one of the most dangerous psychological stories that have recently arisen in our culture. Because of this, we lock up our elderly–denying them their freedoms in order to keep them perfectly safe. We keep our children in our homes for fear that they will be hurt if they are outside and unobserved. We avoid the adventures and follies that enrich our own lives.

We see the pathology of this new tale in the demand for psychologically 'safe places' in learning environments. We see it in our litigation. When someone is hurt, we look for someone or something to blame rather than remembering that risk is an inevitable companion in all of our lives.

No one enjoys the experience of being hurt, rejected, or of failure. It is normal to want to avoid these. But we get into real trouble when we prioritize avoiding these experiences over pushing ourselves to grow.

Your true journey requires serious risks. To say to yourself, "I am going to write my memoir," or "I am going to move to a foreign country where I can afford help and live on $1,000 a month." You have something like this that is nagging you. What is it?

Yes, you might fail. Yes, you may be hurt. You are too old to naively assume that you will be granted the success and safety that you seek. But you are old enough to know that you will be grateful that you tried–that you didn't let your fears keep you from doing the things you always hoped you would do.

Today, ask yourself where you are imprisoned by this new story of safety. See if you can take one small scary step with the reality of risk today.

You will love the thrill, terror, and battle scars this will bring you.

### TODAY'S AFFIRMATION
I can tolerate risk.

### TODAY'S JOURNAL PROMPT
If I increased my tolerance for risk, I would…

# DAY 21

# REST
# REVIEW
# REFLECT

# Use your senses to connect with the present-moment.

Staying present can seem like an incredibly elusive spiritual skill. We are so lost in our busy lives and thoughts that we think we either forget or never knew how to stay in the present-moment.

But you used to be able to do this with ease. Staying present is something you could do at birth. As you got older, your thinking grew more complicated (worrying about the future, ruminating on the past, etc.). Then, as you got even older, your thinking probably got less precise (memory problems, confusion). But despite these changes, your ability to stay present has never changed.

You are literally built for this task. Any one of your five senses pulls you out of your thinking and brings you into this moment.

You've come across this ancient truth in various sayings and advice–*smell* the roses, *feel* the warm water as you wash the dishes, *taste* your food, *watch* a candle, or *listen* to the sounds of nature. All of these different sayings are the same message of bringing you back to your senses because your senses are always in the present-moment (your thinking almost never is).

It doesn't matter if you can't remember the recent past anymore or feel too confused to figure out the future. You don't need those thinking and remembering skills for your most critical spiritual task of staying present.

Today, use your senses to bring yourself to the present-moment. You can't find your glasses, but you can enjoy your meal. Pay attention to which sense is most grounding to you. See if you can use that sense to bring yourself back to this moment more often (and write yourself reminder notes if you can't remember to do this!).

You will love the present-moment awareness this will bring you.

## TODAY'S AFFIRMATION

I stay present with my senses.

## TODAY'S JOURNAL PROMPT

When I think about my experiences of trying to stay present, I…

# DAY 23

## *The problem is not that you are invisible. The problem is that they cannot see.*

You've undoubtedly heard an older woman say, "I've become invisible!" She might speak of a time when she was younger when she believed she was 'seen.'

What part of that woman was visible that is no longer visible? Her intelligence? Her compassion? Her amazing perseverance through the difficult trials of life? No. The only thing no longer visible is her usefulness as an object of superficial sexual desire.

Laura Mulvey coined the phrase 'male gaze,' which speaks to this paradigm in which women are only seen through the lens of male sexual desire.

When we, as older women, describe ourselves as invisible, we are choosing to speak from the perspective of this oppressive lens. You know you are not invisible, so how can we be convinced to say such an absurdly false thing about ourselves? Your grandchildren can tell you this is nonsense.

You can only call yourself invisible if you are looking at yourself through the lens of someone who doesn't see you.

The best news is that when this oppressive gaze inevitably falls away, you have an opportunity. It is time to ask yourself, who am I outside of their lens? Instead of feeling despair, use these years to learn how to finally see yourself in all of your complexity. You are not disappearing. You are developing into a wise woman, stepping into an invisible and mysterious world that not everybody can see.

There are decades of enriching experiences for older women, but our culture doesn't see or tell this story. Don't feel bad for yourself that you are invisible to them. Feel bad for them that they cannot see you and this magical, invisible world.

See yourself. You deserve it.

### TODAY'S AFFIRMATION

I am moving into a mysterious world that not everyone can see.

### TODAY'S JOURNAL PROMPT

My experiences of feeling seen and feeling invisible are…

# DAY 24

## *Notice the stories that capture your imagination.*

As you pay attention to our stories, I'd like for you to pay a little extra attention to the specific stories that attract your attention. When I am working with a woman, sometimes I will ask her, "What are you watching on TV these days?" or "What are you reading?" Because, for me, this almost always opens up an imaginative thread of where she is trying to heal.

We can get so confused about where we are supposed to go with our inner work, but I want to remind you that you do have guideposts. When your imagination is feeling drawn to a particular type of story, play with that story almost like a dream you actually had. Who do you feel connected to? Why does their story matter to you (and I really don't care how 'stupid' the story is! I hear this so frequently, so please don't stop your creative exploration with that negation).

Your creative imagination is like a little plant reaching for the places that will help it grow. If it feels drawn toward stories of heroic (or rescued) characters, to stories of survival, to stories of romance, or something else, notice why you feel drawn. Play therapist to yourself and ask, "Why is this meaningful to me?" and "What does that reveal about my own imagination's desire to grow and heal?"

You are in a constant relationship with stories. Sometimes they are put upon you, but sometimes you seek them out. The stories matter. Discover why.

You deserve the self-discovery this will bring you.

### TODAY'S AFFIRMATION

I notice the creative stories that I feel drawn to.

### TODAY'S JOURNAL PROMPT

The stories I am feeling drawn to are. I might be feeling connected to…

# DAY 25

## *Train the muscles of your patience.*

As you develop the psychological and spiritual practices of aging, there is a foundational skill you should work on now that will support all of your later progress.

Practice being patient. Patience is not a quality but a skill. Because it is a building block for so many other late-life developmental tasks, it is no surprise you see this extolled as a spiritual virtue in every faith tradition, from East to West.

Developing patience is easy to start practicing because I am just asking you to do nothing. I am asking you to wait. You will be astounded by the power of this simple non-action.

This seemingly simple act of learning to wait is the first step for learning to be reflective rather than reactive. It is the first step in learning how to endure your hardest moments. It is key to embracing the uncertainty that growing and aging will demand of you.

Today, practice your patience. Whether you are waiting in line, wishing someone would finish up some task, or on hold with customer service, see if you can say to yourself, "I am using this moment to practice my patience." Like training a muscle, you will get stronger. And you need this muscle for your journey.

You deserve the calm energy this brings into your life.

### TODAY'S AFFIRMATION
I practice being patient.

### TODAY'S JOURNAL PROMPT
When I think of being patient or impatient, I realize I am probably…

# DAY 26

## *Let go of your pursuit of happiness. Real life is far more interesting than that.*

As we've lost touch with our ancient storytellers, we've ended up with superficial stories that are literally making us suffer. One of the modern stories women tell themselves is that they should be happier (or that if they were only doing things better, they would be happier). A wise woman knows better.

This modern myth of perpetual happiness is the degradation of a much wiser ancient story we don't tell anymore. Thomas Jefferson, a follower of the ancient Greek philosopher Epicurus, wrote in the *Declaration of Independence* that everyone had a right to the "pursuit of happiness."

Jefferson's original idea was a good one, but our later stories dumbed it down. When we look at the Epicureanism that inspired his declaration, we find a philosophy that purports happiness to be the result of living modestly with limited desires. This would result in a feeling of tranquility and freedom from fear.

The happiness that Jefferson is referring to sounds a lot more like the simplicity of Jesus or the Buddha. And nothing like our modern story of consumption and conquest.

Let go of our degraded and misunderstood story of the pursuit of happiness; it is making you sick. Pursue this ancient idea of finding tranquility in limiting your desires and in present-moment simplicity. It will heal your soul.

And you deserve that.

## TODAY'S AFFIRMATION

I will find peace in simplicity, not stuff.

## TODAY'S JOURNAL PROMPT

My beliefs about life and happiness are…

# DAY 27

## *You are connected to the Divine.*
## *Your task is to find the spaces where you feel it.*

I meet so many women who believe they have abandoned all faith because they walked away from a particular one. I meet even more women who believe they are not spiritual because they don't gain spiritual nourishment in a space where so many others do.

If you didn't find a spiritual connection in the faith of your childhood or in the faith of your friends, your journey requires a bit more work. Because you have to keep searching until you find that space where you feel your connection.

The best way to do this is to reflect on the places and activities where you feel most connected to yourself. It might be painting, yoga, nature walks, or service work. It might be poetry, dancing, or working with animals. It might be a traditional faith practice or a nontraditional one. Your job is to be open, to explore, and to pay attention to how you feel.

You are connected to the divine. Your responsibility is to find the space where you feel it. Today, reflect on where you feel most connected. Visualize yourself in that space or activity. Notice how it impacts you to go there in your mind.

You will love the spiritual connectedness this will bring you.

### TODAY'S AFFIRMATION
I am connected to the Divine.

### TODAY'S JOURNAL PROMPT
I feel most connected to something larger than myself when…

# DAY 28

# REST
# REVIEW
# REFLECT

*You don't need to know how to do every step.*
*You just need to know how to do the next step.*

When you listen to women who feel stuck, you hear the typical angst about moving forward with a big change or lifelong dream. The idea is impossible, she will insist, because she doesn't know or understand any of it. How can she become a writer? A painter? Or try to move and live somewhere else?

This is the story of omniscience undermining your goals. You think you are supposed to know everything, and that story has you trapped. When a young person wants to start something new, do you expect her to know every nuance of what it will require over the course of the whole journey? Or do you expect that she will start out as a complete novice?

The permission you grant others is the permission I ask you to grant yourself. Let yourself start new things without having any idea what you are doing. You don't need to know every step; you just need to know the next step.

Today, reflect on the things you put off for yourself because you don't believe you know enough. Remind yourself that you simply can't know what you haven't done yet. Don't get trapped in a story that you should be an expert in when you are a beginner. Imagine taking one step toward a goal, tolerating your novice status.

You will love the change this will bring into your life.

## TODAY'S AFFIRMATION
I can take the first step.

## TODAY'S JOURNAL PROMPT
The thing I want to do but won't because I don't know how is…

## *Practice observing without judgment.*

One of the first things we learn as young children is to make judgments about our world. This starts with a very rudimentary ordering of things (e.g., good/bad) that gets increasingly complex as we move through our life.

It is not a bad thing that we form judgments; we need this cognitive capacity to construct our stories and to fit into our communities in the first seasons of our life. But it is important to remember that we are doing it–that we are constantly narrowing our worldview through our increasingly particular lenses of judgment.

It can be a profound spiritual practice to step back and observe this habit–to move from our evaluative judgments to a more neutral observation. When you practice neutral observing, you are less reactive as you attempt to see the world without ascribing any particular value. For example, you can notice that a person is honking and shaking their fist at you on the road without jumping to any evaluative judgments about her or you. You can just observe her doing it without judgment.

I'm not suggesting that you should (or even could) live without any judgments. I'm suggesting that the practice of stepping back from your constant judgment of your world can open you up to new ways of imagining, thinking, feeling, and being.

Today, take a minute or more to watch your mind watch the world. See if you can observe without judgment. If you are just starting this practice, step back from that goal and see if you can notice that you are making evaluative judgments.

You deserve the bigger world this will bring you.

### TODAY'S AFFIRMATION

I can observe the world without judgment.

### TODAY'S JOURNAL PROMPT

If I were more neutrally observant and less evaluatively judgmental...

# DAY 31

## *Exercise your Eros.*

You've seen the workshops and retreats–women dancing or drumming together in ways that either attract or annoy you. That practice may stir a desire to participate, a sense of horror, or something in between. There is no correct response to that particular method, but what I want you to know is that there is something in what they are doing that you also need to learn how to do–practice connecting with your eros energy.

If you feel drawn to dancing and/or drumming, then go for it. If you don't, keep exploring to find where you connect with a surge of inner energy. This is something that rises up within you. It is a feeling that, "It doesn't matter if this activity has a purpose. I am feeling it and loving it."

The most important aspect is that you do not subject the activity to your rational (e.g., logos) scrutiny. The activity doesn't have to 'make sense' in any way. It might be much cheaper to buy a quilt than to make one, but the way you feel when searching for new fabric connects you to that eros feeling.

Music can help here, but you don't have to dance or drum. Put on the music that moves you and see if you can master that sourdough starter, get that old engine to rev up again on the car you are restoring, or see the buds emerge on your latest planting.

This eros energy is your life force. It is beyond words, beyond logic. But it is the healing energy of desire that allows you to continue to imagine and grow.

Today, see what activities elicit this feeling from you. Put on your favorite music and go.

You deserve the feeling.

## TODAY'S AFFIRMATION

I exercise my eros.

## TODAY'S JOURNAL PROMPT

The activity that would probably excite me the most is...

# DAY 32

## *Spiritual health does not promise health or wealth.*

So much of our current spiritual self-help is focused on physical and material gain. From the prosperity gospel of the Christian faith to *The Secret* of the New Age, contemporary spiritual gurus suggest that, if only we are spiritual enough, we will gain the fruits of our physical and material world and, thus, the happiness we seek.

This strange new story, a combination of our protestant work ethic, capitalism, and materialism, is a particularly American degradation of the story of how spiritual practices bring us more contentment (ironically, no one seems to notice that Jesus, the Buddha, and Mother Theresa are all failures within this new prosperity-gospel-secret standard).

No sacred story tells this tale. The earliest followers of the prophet Mohammed sanctified poverty. The Buddha renounced the wealth of his family. Jesus blessed the poor.

I am not asking you to take a vow of poverty, but I am reminding you that, unlike what most gurus are telling you, spiritual growth does not correlate with physical comfort and material gain. As you age, your spiritual development demands that you contend with loss, not acquisition. You are learning to let go. You are learning to be okay when your world doesn't validate you as being okay.

You are not practicing spirituality in order to find material comfort. You are practicing spirituality because you know the material world can't bring you the comfort you need.

Today, explore your beliefs about the connection between spiritual growth and physical and material comfort. Reflect on our most ancient stories. Imagine your own.

You deserve the spiritual wealth this brings you.

### TODAY'S AFFIRMATION

I seek spiritual wealth.

### TODAY'S JOURNAL PROMPT

My beliefs about spiritual health and physical and material comfort are...

# DAY 33

## *We are making stories out of everything.*

It can be a strange idea to consider that we are not perfectly seeing and interpreting our world but that we are actually constantly constructing (and deconstructing) stories to create our world.

We know we have too much data coming at us to process. If five women were in your space, all five would report different things about the environment and the experience. But it isn't simply that we notice different things. Each of us is always constructing the objects and actions into a unique story.

Studies show that when people watch the movement of digital objects, they will infuse those digital images with their interpretations. Colored circles moving on a screen will eventually be interpreted as objects that are pursuing, playing, or fighting with each other.

We know these graphic circles are not doing any of these things, so the important point is not about what the simple digital images are actually doing. The important point is to remember that we are always taking the (often overwhelming) data of our world and constructing it into meaningful narratives that are infused with our own stories. The narratives we experience as true are always a mix of what we are experiencing on the outside and the inside.

Today, remember that you are always creating stories out of the experiences you encounter in your world. See if you can start to notice that space of creative construction between what you see and the story you tell.

You deserve the space for more stories.

### TODAY'S AFFIRMATION

My stories are my creation between me and my world.

### TODAY'S JOURNAL PROMPT

When I imagine that I am not perfectly seeing the world in its absolute truth,
I think/feel…

# DAY 34

## *Your mid/late-life crisis is an unlived part of yourself still trying to grow.*

Mid-life and late-life crises are terribly misunderstood. Most people think of them as a self-destructive break from traditional life and believe the healthy goal is to get the person back to how they were before.

But this is exactly where we get it wrong. Our mid and late-life crises are the markers of important developmental milestones; your mid-life crisis is an attempt from your deepest self to move you into a different orientation toward your world. It marks the end of your *Responsibility* stage and the beginning of your *Reflective* stage of development. Late-life crises are a harbinger of your movement toward *Return*.

Things are changing, and you are getting uncomfortable. You don't go back to how you were before. Your job is to step into what you are still becoming.

Like adolescence, these phases are often accompanied by changes to your hormones, your body, and your changing feelings about others. Your 'crisis' may be triggered by an external event–an empty nest, a divorce, a diagnosis, a death, or just a new and confusing despair. In mid-life, your long habit of 'doing' is coming to an end. As you enter your *Reflective* stage, it is time to stop and reflect more deeply on your life and what is meaningful to you. In late life, you need to connect more deeply with loss, resilience, and *Return*.

You are on a long, circular journey of moving from an external orientation (toward others) to an internal orientation (toward your deepest self), where you will ultimately reconnect with everything. If you try to return to your old life, you will end up more confused and miserable.

Remember that trying to go back to your earlier identity is like the little girl fretting over her adolescent maturation or the adolescent girl anxious about moving into the adult world. You wouldn't ask them to go back to who they were before, and you can't either.

You are aging and learning to turn inward. Let this 'breakdown' break down the structures in your life that were the tools of a younger woman.

You will love the new ways of being this will bring into your life.

### TODAY'S AFFIRMATION
I embrace my seasons of change.

### TODAY'S JOURNAL PROMPT
If I had a mid-life crisis, it was probably when I...I responded by...

# DAY 35

# REST
# REVIEW
# REFLECT

# *It keeps happening because you still have something to learn.*

So often in my work with women, clients will express a sense of defeat over being ensnared in a circumstance that they've been through too many times before. She feels like a failure as she realizes she is reenacting old patterns again and again.

But this circling through our experiences over and over isn't an error. You are moving through your own healing spiral, and this circling back is the way we all bring our unconscious wounds into our conscious awareness. Our most important stories always repeat. We all perform our psychic injuries (in an effort to heal ourselves) until the act becomes all too familiar and a new insight is finally born.

Like the ancient story of Ariadne, who helps Theseus out of the labyrinth with her ball of thread, your job is to continually find new ways out of the seemingly impossible riddle.

So, remember, you are not irreparably wounded because it is happening again. It is happening again because that is how we all heal.

Today, pay attention to the patterns that have repeated in your life. Your responsibility is to engage with these stories to see what you can discover about yourself and your world. Try exploring them by writing them as a fictional creative story, painting them as an image, or through some other creative task. See if you can bring more consciousness to what these experiences are trying to show you.

You will love the insight this will bring you.

## TODAY'S AFFIRMATION

My repeated experiences are meaningful stories that facilitate my growth.

## TODAY'S JOURNAL PROMPT

The theme that seems to repeat in my life is…
Maybe I need to become more aware of…

## *Resenting catastrophe is a waste of precious time. Accept. Assess. Do the next right thing.*

Difficult things happened to you, and you are still here. I am here to remind you that it isn't the event that is so destructive to you but how you respond to it. This truth is a secret keystone to your psychological survival. What do we do when we are knocked off our feet with grief or pain? How long do we stay down before we collect ourselves and carry on?

**Step one** is to allow yourself the time you need to metabolize the blow. This could be hours, days, or much longer (with grief). If you are numb, try to stay present until you can feel it. Allow it to rock and shock your body. You can handle this. I promise.

**Step two** is to observe your thinking. If you are repeating to yourself, "This shouldn't be this way! I need for this to be different to be okay," then you are stuck in a repetitive thinking loop and need to be proactive with changing your thoughts.

**Step three** is to get yourself to a very <u>provisional</u> level of acceptance. You can still wish this weren't the case. You can still be in shock. But emphatically state to yourself. "It is what it is. What is my next healthy step?"

**Postpone :** In crisis, it's easy to get overwhelmed by the enormity of your new reality. It is critical to postpone decisions that don't have to be made immediately. Only focus on your immediate, next necessary action.

When you get to the point of, "This is certainly not what I would have ever wished for myself. This is so hard. But I'm going to assess and accept and figure out my next healthy move," then you are on your way.

You may not need this guidance today, but please keep this close for when you do.

### TODAY'S AFFIRMATION

I know how to calm down and deal with a crisis.

### TODAY'S JOURNAL PROMPT

When I am in a crisis, I usually…

# DAY 38

## *Your most important relationship is with your own unconscious.*

Relationships with other people are vital. We are hurt in relationship, and we heal in relationship. As a therapist, I've witnessed the power of interpersonal relationships for healing our deepest wounds. But your most important relationship isn't with someone else. Your most important relationship is with your own unconscious.

Whether we acknowledge her presence or not, she is there, always influencing our actions and often running the show.

Freud came up with this idea at the turn of the last century. Jung and others developed it. But we see her in our oldest sayings that predate their theories. I *fell* in love. I was *blinded* by rage. I was *possessed* by jealousy. All of these sayings are making reference to *some other force overtaking us.* This thing that takes over is your unconscious, so she is worth getting to know better.

Your unconscious is where your stories of injury are hiding and where your stories of healing are trying to emerge. None of us can ever fully grasp our unconscious, but we should always be in the process of trying to know her more. What I would ask you to do first is to recognize her ever-presence in your life–know that she is always participating.

A good place to learn more about her is whenever you feel something intensely. Instead of immediately responding to that stimulus, try to move into a space of 'observing self.' Try to watch yourself in this interaction. See if you can see patterns or projections through reflecting upon or journaling about your feeling and fantasy responses in this situation. Explore what your imagination is bringing up. This is how you discover your unconscious stories.

This will bring you more self-awareness and peace. You deserve it.

## TODAY'S AFFIRMATION

I seek a relationship with my unconscious.

## TODAY'S JOURNAL PROMPT

I feel taken over by the feeling of...when...

# DAY 39

## *The story of aging is not a story of failing youth.*

Our stories about aging are exactly backward. If you do any research on aging, you will find hundreds of articles on how to avoid it. This is absurd, as aging is (and must be) an important part of every long life journey. But, instead of teaching you how to step into your wisdom years with curiosity and grace, the message you find is, "Don't age. Stay youthful!"

This story is killing us. Because to grow into the wise woman you need to be–to become the elder who enjoys the last decades of her life–you can't stagnate in their youthful values. Your story of aging is not their story of failing youth. It is still your story of continued development–as you move from trying to conquer and succeed in your outer world to surrendering and flourishing in your inner journey.

Yes, the physical and material aspects of life can get more challenging as you age. But. as you look at your growth so far, where did it come from? The easy parts of your life? Or from the challenges? Just as they were in your younger years, your current and future challenges with aging are a necessary part of your ongoing developmental journey.

Today, notice if you imagine aging as merely a degradation of an idealized youth. Pay attention to your thoughts and feelings around the mandate to "stay young." See if these stories match up to our most ancient tales of becoming the wise woman you are meant to be.

You deserve to discover your wise woman journey.

## TODAY'S AFFIRMATION
The challenges of aging are purposeful.

## TODAY'S JOURNAL PROMPT
When I hear the phrase, "Stay young," my response is...

# DAY 40

## *Practice your courage so you have it when you need it.*

As you move into the late stages of life, you need to know that you can face the big challenges that will come–both difficult and delightful. In the hard or exciting moments that are still ahead of you, you need the confidence that you've cultivated the necessary courage to take them on.

But it will be hard to take on these big challenges if you haven't been practicing along the way. It's almost unfair to think that we'd have it in us if we've been avoiding challenges and not learning to overcome our fears bit by bit.

All of our ancient tales are celebrations of courage in the face of challenges. None are about the contentment that comes when you retreat from your quest. Learn from these stories. Today, practice your courage. Push yourself to do something small that intimidates you. Allow yourself to hold the contrast between feeling afraid and still taking action.

No matter the outcome, it is vitally important that you give yourself words of praise afterward as part of your practice. Like, "Good job! That was scary, and I did it anyway!" It may seem silly, but I promise, it works.

You will love the courage this will bring to your life.

## TODAY'S AFFIRMATION
I practice my courage with small acts.

## TODAY'S JOURNAL PROMPT
I could probably practice my courage by...

# DAY 41

## *Maybe we don't know why.*

The more we learn about our brain, the more humble we should become about anything we believe we 'know.' Some of the most interesting neurological research to come out of the last century is from the work of Michael Gazzaniga and Robert Sperry.

These neuroscientists researched patients who had the connection between their two brain hemispheres severed (often as a treatment for uncontrolled epilepsy). The researchers discovered that when one part of our brain doesn't have access to all of the environmental information, it will create (and emphatically believe!) a newly constructed story that makes sense.

As an example, one hemisphere may get a visual instruction to 'stand up' that the other side cannot see. The participant will stand up and, when asked why they stood, will offer a new explanation such as, "I need to go to the bathroom" or "I need to stretch." Later research proved this construction of meaningful stories to be true in individuals without split brains.

These researchers proved that we all do this–when we don't have all the information, we will construct a story that makes sense to us, and we will believe it to be true.

Today, loosen your hold on what you know to be true. Recognize that we are all making meaning out of a world we can't completely understand.

### TODAY'S AFFIRMATION

I can be less rigid in what I assert to be absolutely true.

### TODAY'S JOURNAL PROMPT

If I imagine myself as a person who would construct such a meaning,
I think/feel…

# DAY 42

# REST
# REVIEW
# REFLECT

## *Pay attention to your dreams.*
## *They are trying to tell you something important.*

When you read ancient literature, you encounter the reverence attributed to the stories of our dreams. As we moved into the rational age, our respect for this sacred, symbolic storytelling space fell away. As you are turning inward in your psychological and spiritual journey, I'd like to remind you of this ancient practice of listening to your symbolic stories.

Your dreams are not the simple recycling of your day. They are symbolic communications (using the material of your day, symbolically) from your deepest self. I can't tell you what your dream means, but I can help you imagine what your own dream symbols might mean for you.

Start with a few cheat sheet methods. First, imagine every character in the dream is a part of you. Explore and imagine the story of each of these parts within you. What are they doing (who is helping, harming, hurting, etc.? Who is heard? Who is silenced? Who is hiding, etc.?)? How might these represent different parts of yourself?

Notice where the dream takes place. Pay attention to the symbolic meaning of such a space. You can use some rough cheats, like, a house might represent yourself. A car might represent your sense of agency (who is driving the car?). Are you in a childhood home or a transitory hotel?

The trick is to play. Ask yourself what that person, item, or place represents in your symbolic world. Let your imagination and intuition guide you to the 'aha' feeling.

The important goal is to not be too literal. This is symbolic language from your deepest self. Your unconscious is trying to tell a story. It may be the opposite of your conscious story. Even if you can't find meaning in the dream (this is very common!), there is absolute value in writing down, listening, and imagining the confusing dream in your conscious life.

Today, make a commitment to try to start remembering and reflecting on the symbolic content coming up in your dreams. You will love the creative, imaginative force this opens up for you.

### TODAY'S AFFIRMATION
I listen to my dreams.

### TODAY'S JOURNAL PROMPT
My dreams are often about...Or, I have had a recurring dream that...

# DAY 44

## *We have too much new information and too little ancient wisdom.*

You are in the midst of the 'information age.' An era where your ability to access almost unlimited amounts of new information has transformed your world.

But this 'advancement' has come at a cost to you. You may have access to unlimited amounts of data, but you don't have unlimited attention or retention. This creates a problem. You are lost at sea in information overload.

Even worse, this access isn't improving your quality of life but filling your mind with more and more information that never circles back around to help us make sense of ourselves, our world, and the lives we are trying to live.

Prior to the information age, we were limited to the repetition of the tales and ancient wisdom of those around us. Elders were respected because of their insight into the human condition. When you needed guidance, you didn't turn to the internet for the newest content from the latest young blogger; you turned to your elder, who would tell you a story.

Today, pay attention to your relationship to new information and ancient wisdom. See if you can stop researching and instead grant more attentiveness to the deeper, repetitive practices and sacred tales that cultivate the wisdom we need for a suffering world.

You will love the circular, storied rhythm this change will bring to you.

### TODAY'S AFFIRMATION

I return to ancient wisdom.

### TODAY'S JOURNAL PROMPT

My typical practice of collecting new information vs. returning
to ancient wisdom is...

# DAY 45

## *Maybe you don't have a trust problem. Maybe they have a trustworthiness problem.*

Women who are hurt by others often describe themselves as the problem. She will say, "I have trust issues." This common complaint is a red flag for me. Firstly, it reveals that she has been hurt deeply in her relationships. Secondly, it reveals that when she is hurt by others, she blames herself.

You don't have trust issues. The people you trusted had trustworthiness issues. Not trusting was probably a very healthy response to what you went through. How does it feel to recognize that your reluctance to trust is actually the correct response to the situation you were in?

You can still have the goal of developing trust in trustworthy people. But remember, you don't have 'trust issues.'

Today, think about your thoughts and feelings about trusting. Think about your past relationships. Pay attention to whether or not the problem was that you had 'trust issues' or if they weren't able to provide a trustworthy space in which you could safely connect.

You will love the safe spaces of trusting this new practice can open up for you.

### TODAY'S AFFIRMATION

I am able to trust when I am in a safe relationship.

### TODAY'S JOURNAL PROMPT

My experiences with trusting others have been...Today, my thoughts
and feelings about trusting others are...

# DAY 46

## *We fear the stranger but are harmed by the familiar.*

We are so afraid. Our news storytellers make lots of money selling stories that shock and horrify you. Like a crash we can't look away from, we get sucked into these tales of danger and destruction, fearful that such an awful fate could befall us or our loved ones.

But the truth is that the unknown persons in our world are not as dangerous as we imagine. Stories of stranger danger have infected our souls with a sense of perpetual insecurity about outsiders harming, invading, or injuring us or the people we love.

I work as a therapist, and the truth is that we are harmed most by those closest to us. We are harmed by the people we trusted. And people who find themselves vulnerable and in need in strange environments overwhelmingly report the kindness of strangers in crises.

Where does this story of stranger danger come from? Do you find it in our most ancient tales? Or is this a modern story being used against you to monopolize your attention (and generate ad revenue for the self-serving storyteller)?

Today, pay attention to your own story. Who hurt you? Who hurt the people you love? Are you suspicious of the stranger? I am not saying that strangers never harm people. Of course that happens. But that is not the true story of how most of us are hurt.

You deserve the kindness of strangers this can bring you.

### TODAY'S AFFIRMATION
The world is safer than I have been told.

### TODAY'S JOURNAL PROMPT
My feelings about strangers and danger are…

# DAY 47

## *Your ego is a story.*

Who are you? How do you understand your ego identity? How has it changed over time? From Freud to Jung to mindfulness, we get a lot of different understandings of what our ego is.

I'd like to make the case that your ego identity is actually a collection of stories–a very plural narrative of (sometimes ephemeral) ever-changing stories of self, constantly being re-created in the imaginative space between the story of you and the story of your world (I am not arguing for a simple, linear narrative that neatly holds everything, but a plurality of changing stories that exist within you. Bits may contradict each other and very likely do).

The good news for you is that this is a dynamic process; you recognize that your story of self has already changed more dramatically than you could have ever foretold. Your job now is to remember that it will continue to do so.

What I want you to do is put more conscious intention into exploring, connecting, and imagining your ever-changing ego stories. Don't demand all the bits fit neatly together. Your job is to embrace your plurality as you stitch together all these disparate parts of yourself.

Things happened in your life, but your job is to remember that the story of you and of those events is still changing. You will continue to recover, remember, and revise your understanding of your earlier experiences. And you will continue to be changed by your encounters with experiences that are still ahead of you.

I hope you are looking forward to the rest of your stories.

### TODAY'S AFFIRMATION

I continue to imagine, create, and recreate my life story.

### TODAY'S JOURNAL PROMPT

A story that I've reflected on and changed my view on as I've aged is.

# DAY 48

## *Falling off your path is being on your path.*

As a young girl, you probably imagined a certain adult life for yourself. Your plan was likely very linear and neat and ended right where you wanted to land. Then, you started living an actual life, and things quickly got very confusing. You may have become depressed as the life you lived deviated farther and farther from your plans.

You believed that life for you was supposed to go in a certain way. Your partner was supposed to stay. Your kids were supposed to be happy and healthy. You were supposed to have enough money.

If we look at any ancient tale of journeying, sacred or secular, the pilgrims are always challenged by unexpected obstacles–one after another. Have you ever read a story that looked like the simple, linear, and happy tale you spun for yourself? They don't exist. Our real-life stories are filled with the twists, turns, and defeats we see in all ancient literature.

I wonder what it would be like if, as a young girl, you'd heard different stories about how life is 'supposed' to be.

Today, understand that, like every story ever told, the messy complexity of your life is how we all are doing it. Ignore fictional fantasies that don't exist in life or literature.

We aren't here to live perfectly scripted lives. Imagine how a different story may have prepared you for the life you've lived. Find peace with that truth. You deserve the comfort it can bring you.

## TODAY'S AFFIRMATION
There is no error in my life.

## TODAY'S JOURNAL PROMPT
My fantasies about how life 'should be' were…
These fantasies affected me in that…

# REST
# REVIEW
# REFLECT

## *You can tolerate their suffering.*

It is so difficult when the people we love are suffering. When our child, partner, or family member is not doing well, we feel the need to sideline our goals in order to help them get back to theirs.

There is nothing wrong with your desire to facilitate peace and comfort in the people you love. There is certainly nothing wrong with valuing your relationships and wanting to be of service. But it is wrong for you to sacrifice yourself in an effort to manifest something in someone else.

We are each on our own journey. People we care about deeply will persist in their struggles. Today, your job is to love and accept them exactly where they are. Your job is not to forfeit your agency in a misguided effort to help them establish their own.

Today, pay attention to how you are impacted by the needs and struggles of the people you love. Reflect on whether or not you feel comfortable with letting them walk their hard path as you walk your own. Tolerate the discomfort of letting them make their own decisions.

You will love the freedom this will bring you.

### TODAY'S AFFIRMATION

I let others walk their own path.

### TODAY'S JOURNAL PROMPT

I am most likely to feel the need to focus on others' needs when...

## *Ruminating is not processing.*

As you begin to reflect and feel your way through your life story, it is important to understand the distinction between productive and non-productive reflection.

For reasons we don't fully understand, at around age fourteen, many young girls develop a thinking and feeling pattern that correlates with increased rates of depression and anxiety–rumination. Rumination is when you get stuck in a repetitive story loop. You might replay a similar scene over and over in your head, usually accompanied by some negative thought about the world or yourself. This habit digs a rut of despair in our minds and is not a productive way to reflect on our past.

Processing is when you let yourself feel and imagine your way through your story. You might be intentionally changing some of your automatic and repetitive thoughts (e.g., "I was so stupid to do that!" changes to a more compassionate, "I was so young. How could I have known any different?" etc.). You bring in your healing imagination and her new perspectives. You expand the story with your older and wiser view. As you let your imagination open the story, you are no longer in a rigid, repetitive story loop but in a dynamic, feeling process that allows for healing change.

Today, pay attention to the different ways you reflect on past events. See if you notice that you are stuck in a repetitive, negative story loop (rumination) that is digging you deeper into despair. See if you can interrupt that rigid pattern by exploring your story in a more imaginative and creative way (painting, writing, etc.) that opens your story to new understandings.

Your story deserves more imagination and compassion.

## TODAY'S AFFIRMATION

I reflect on my stories with compassion and kindness for my younger self.

## TODAY'S JOURNAL PROMPT

The repetitive story loops I might struggle with are…

# DAY 52

## *Stop blaming anyone for anything. See what happens.*

Who are you mad at? Who is the target of your blame? All of us can come up with someone–from our personal to our political world. Today I want you to try something new. Today, I want you to stop blaming anyone for anything.

This exercise is not about them or whether or not they deserve blame. I am not asking you to forgive them or to understand their behavior. Today, I don't care about them. I care about you. This is an exercise to see how your blame/anger is functioning in your life. I'm curious what happens if we take it away.

We may discover that we like being angry at them. That our anger feels good. This could be because it validates us (when I focus on how awful he is, I feel better about myself). It might be because we like the feeling of self-righteousness. We might feel empowered by our anger (not always a bad thing, but a good thing to know!).

We might discover that we need the blame because, without it, we find we alone are responsible for our next steps. We may not be able to tolerate our shame about our own self-destructive patterns (we've all been there). It is so much easier if we can imagine the fault/responsibility lies with someone else.

This is not an exercise intended to shame you, as we are all capable of all of these things. This is an exercise to bring greater awareness, intentionality, and responsibility to your inner and outer world.

Today, you can't blame anyone. Your boss, your neighbor, your ex, those people, that politician. Anyone.

See what happens when you take that away.

Your self-discovery is worth it.

### TODAY'S AFFIRMATION
I don't blame anyone.

### TODAY'S JOURNAL PROMPT
If I stopped blaming them, I would...

## *Notice the stories you tell.*

Women are often self-conscious in therapy about repeating stories or telling stories that 'aren't important.' But, as a therapist, there is nothing I love more than when a client allows herself to tell the stories that are coming up, no matter how 'repetitive' or 'unimportant' they may seem to her.

Carl Jung taught us about complexes, but I like to use his concept to help me understand why a specific story is important. As an example, a woman in a group shared her fury that a person had stopped by her hobby farm to collect farm-fresh eggs but failed to pay her for their item. A similar event could happen to anyone, but this woman got ensnared in this story (this is where a Jungian might say a complex was activated). This woman was so angry that this person was taking advantage of her, didn't appreciate her work, or thought that they could take her items for free that she needed to process her experience in group. Do you have a clue of what this woman might need to explore in her own history?

None of us is immune to this. All of the things happen in all of our lives, but only some of the stories ensnare us. We retell these stories because they reveal something deeper about our own unexplored stories and wounds.

Today, notice if there is a theme in the stories you tell. See if you can tease out how the stories you are telling are actually revealing deeper truths to you about your own healing path.

You deserve the insight.

### TODAY'S AFFIRMATION

I notice the stories I tell.

### TODAY'S JOURNAL PROMPT

I tend to share stories about...this is probably because...

# DAY 54

## *Make good decisions on your bad days.*

We all have our bad days–those periods where we don't feel well and are most prone to indulging our worst instincts.

On those days, I want you to be compassionate with yourself. I am not asking you to engage in your best practices. But I am asking you not to totally self-destruct. If, when we don't feel well, we choose to quietly withdraw (rather than rage), binge on television (instead of food or substances), and wait (rather than act out), we are still staying with our best practices.

Remember, you will have bad days. This is the natural rhythm we are all living with. Don't use those as an excuse to engage in self-destructive patterns that you are trying to leave behind. You don't have to be your best self, but on your hard days, try to remain in at least a holding pattern of waiting until you can re-engage with your best practices.

Just as Demeter learned to wander and wait in the winter for her daughter Persephone to come back, you, too, can learn to wait until your sense of renewal returns.

When the darkness lifts, you will be very grateful that you did.

### TODAY'S AFFIRMATION

I am compassionate with myself on my bad days.

### TODAY'S JOURNAL PROMPT

When I am not feeling well, I tend to...
A better (not perfectionistic and still realistic) practice might be...

# DAY 55

## *Stop worrying about the future. You've been given enough in the present to keep you occupied.*

None of us can master present-moment awareness all the time. We all get lost in our small worlds and thoughts. The goal isn't to be perfect but to make an effort to do a bit more each day. Setting aside a few minutes for your practice means you are doing a good enough job.

It helps if you develop thoughts and habits that remind you to stay present. One that I like is remembering that you don't need to worry about the future because you have so much going on right now, in this moment.

It may not be the best exercise for building a deep mindfulness practice, but it is a good trick to have on hand when your thoughts are out of control–running too fast with realistic possibilities of terrifying situations.

For example, if you have a child struggling with a serious substance use disorder, it is easy to get terrified about what may happen. But, instead of letting your mind drift to those catastrophes, you can remind yourself that you have enough to worry about today, in this moment, such that you simply don't have the time to make up imaginary scenarios in the future.

Today, you can feel sad about your child (processing your present feelings). Today you can enjoy a conversation with your child (developing acceptance in your relationships). Today, you can set healthy boundaries with your child (cultivating healthy practices). But today, you cannot allow your mind to drift to imaginary and horrible possibilities; there isn't anything helpful to you about doing that. You already have enough important stuff to keep you busy today.

When you can't shut off your brain, and you are scaring yourself, see if you can use this exercise to bring yourself back to the present-moment tasks and goals that will help you along your path.

You will love the present-moment awareness this can bring you in your hardest moments.

### TODAY'S AFFIRMATION
I don't let myself worry about imaginary catastrophes.

### TODAY'S JOURNAL PROMPT
If I focused on actual–rather than imaginary–challenges, then...

# DAY 56

# REST
# REVIEW
# REFLECT

## *You are imposing a meaning upon the world that was imposed upon you.*

What are some of the things you believe are true about human nature? Relationships? The world? To explain today's meditation, I'm going to remind you of something you may have heard of–perceptual sets. This is that phenomenon where you decide, for example, to buy a new car, and you start seeing that (formerly never seen) car everywhere. Are these cars appearing more often, or have you changed your perspective?

This simple example about a car is intended to make a bigger point. You are walking around with much more *impactful* lenses that you *never* change. Stories you picked up on in your earliest years before you had the ability to reflect on your first interpretations. These are usually the things that you believe are absolutely true about people, relationships, and the world. With all of our early relational injuries, these unexamined perspectives are usually worth reexamining.

The good news is that you can expand your vision (you were able to see other cars, right?). Step one is *recognizing* that you are doing this–*you are not seeing the world as it is.*

Today, walk through the world with an awareness that you are wearing your lenses. Now, ask the world to show you something different. Keep an open mind and see what shows up. There is an entire world out there you haven't seen yet.

Enjoy. You deserve the delight.

### TODAY'S AFFIRMATION
Today I will see something I haven't seen before.

### TODAY'S JOURNAL PROMPT
My perspectives are probably impacted most by...

# DAY 58

## *Sometimes getting angry is your first step to getting better.*

So many older women come into my office declaring they have a new problem with anger. They want therapy to help them get rid of their problem so they can return to being the nice person they imagined they used to be. This can be a challenging intake session because I often have to question her stated goal for therapy.

When a woman shows up reporting problems with anger, I like to find out when it started (when your husband retired? When your adult child moved back home? When you realized you had to go back to work?). Sometimes it emerges after she starts some new self-care practice. As she is getting healthier, she is getting angrier about situations she used to tolerate. This is important stuff coming up. We don't want to use therapy to shut this down.

Anger is often (not always) bringing our attention to a (real or projected) injustice or boundary violation. It is usually trying to call our attention to something we should pay attention to. The fact is, when men get angry, they think they need to shake things up. When women get angry, they think they need to shut themselves down.

If you are feeling angry, the therapeutic goal is not to get rid of your anger. The goal is to find out why you are angry. If you are struggling with this, take the time to explore your answers to this question through journaling or free writing. You will likely learn a lot.

Maybe it is time for you to shake things up.

You deserve the change that anger can bring into your life.

### TODAY'S AFFIRMATION
I listen to my anger.

### TODAY'S JOURNAL PROMPT
I might be angry about…

# DAY 59

## *Healthier boundaries create happier relationships.*

Learning how to set up healthy boundaries seems to be a part of every woman's healing path. Most of us set our protective structures up in the wrong place and, after a series of relational failures, discover we have to tear down what we have and reconstruct something new much later in life.

Maybe you were deeply hurt and set up huge boundaries that won't let anyone in. Maybe you had an overbearing parent, and you set up few boundaries that let everyone and everything in. Wherever you are on this spectrum, it can be confusing and scary to figure out where your boundaries should be.

What I know is that you do know roughly where you are starting, as most women have a good gut feeling about this. Ask yourself these questions: Do I keep people out? Am I lonely (your boundaries are likely too big)? Or do I let too much in? Do I feel taken advantage of (your boundaries are likely too small)? It is possible you swing between these two extremes.

Take your answers to your questions and see where you can push yourself to make a small change. If your boundaries are too big, practice opening up (just a little) to a safe person and see how it feels. If your boundaries are too small, practice saying "no" when it feels hard to do so and see how that feels.

These small actions will start a larger momentum of moving you closer to where you want to be.

You deserve the relational comfort these healthier boundaries will bring you.

### TODAY'S AFFIRMATION
I can set healthy boundaries.

### TODAY'S JOURNAL PROMPT
When it comes to setting boundaries, I am probably…

# DAY 60

## *Become more protective of your imagination.*

People trying to make money off of your attention are experts at capturing your imagination. They exploit your innate feeling response to engage your imagination. If they are successful, you will read their story. You might have a feeling response in your body to their story. You might think about their story. You might even retell their story. Who is in charge of your creative imagination now?

If you are a person who follows the news or social media, I'd like for you to pay attention to their efforts. Read headlines and see if you can identify the emotion they are trying to elicit from you; it might be outrage, fear, horror, envy, or something else.

Once you start to notice this, you can't unsee it.

Now, before you decide to read more, you can make a conscious choice. Is this a story I need to include in my day? Or is someone using my feeling response to get control of my imagination? Paying attention to how they are trying to capture your attention gives you more control and more freedom to explore your own imagination.

Today, if you are engaged with any kind of consumer media, see if you can notice these patterns. Your healing desperately needs the creative freedom of your own imagination.

## TODAY'S AFFIRMATION

I am aware of their attempts to capture my imagination.

## TODAY'S JOURNAL PROMPT

I am probably most vulnerable to letting someone capture my attention when...

# DAY 61

## *All behavior is logical in some time and place.*

You may wonder why you can't stop an old, self-destructive behavior that doesn't make logical sense to you anymore. Or you may wonder why someone else does something that seems so self-defeating. As a therapist, I always know that this seemingly insane behavior made sense somewhere. My job is to find out where and to help her heal from that moment forward.

You know now that we all developed protective behaviors that worked in a certain time or place but might have become less helpful later in life. If you discover that trying to adopt new ways of being still eludes you, it is time to go deeper to untangle your riddle.

For example, a person who can't stop lying may discover that, earlier in her life, obfuscation was critical for psychological survival. If she can't stop, no matter how illogical it now seems to her, her job is to find the story. When she does, she can imagine and feel her way into that earlier story (or stories similar to hers) and explore different interpretations. She can creatively discover a new sense of safety that makes her old behaviors *feel* less necessary.

As we age, our job is to stop judging behavior and to start wondering where and why it made sense. Find the old story and ask yourself, is this story still true for me today?

Today, don't shame yourself or anyone else for their 'stupid' behavior. I promise you, it made perfect sense somewhere.

### TODAY'S AFFIRMATION

Everyone's behavior makes sense.

### TODAY'S JOURNAL PROMPT

Something I do that seems self-defeating is…I might do this because…

# DAY 62

## *Pay attention to where you seek your approval.*

Whose opinion matters to you? Is that person the right mentor for you and your goals? Have they achieved what you are seeking? Does this person even truly see you? Or do they see a version of you that you don't recognize?

Too often, we seek approval from the wrong people. Allowing yourself to continue to be shaped by their opinion is a self-defeating system for your personal and spiritual growth. Of course, your long-term goal is to accept yourself. But what are you supposed to do if you aren't there yet?

One method is to be intentional about mentors. Your mentor doesn't even have to be someone you have actual access to. My clients often use famous gurus and spiritual teachers they admire as a stand-in.

We find this wisdom in the teachings and sayings of various spiritual and secular traditions, both ancient and modern. Christians imagine, "What would Jesus do?" The twelve-step program advises the newly sober, "Stick with the winners."

Your job is to be more purposeful about who you are allowing to guide your development (even if in an imaginary relationship). You will grow in the spaces between you and them. Be intentional about who you use to frame your existence and identity.

Today, pay attention to whose opinion affects you. Be more mindful about who you want to imagine as your role model. Your personal and spiritual growth deserve these good guides.

## TODAY'S AFFIRMATION

I pay attention to the words and opinions of my most admired teachers.

## TODAY'S JOURNAL PROMPT

The person who has been or is critical of me that I might need to stop listening to is...The spiritual teacher I love would probably say to me...

# DAY 63

# REST
# REVIEW
# REFLECT

# DAY 64

## *Your only conflict is with yourself.*

Almost all of us have difficult people and difficult situations in our lives. We get into real trouble when we think that our problems are those difficult people and situations.

Because our problem is not with them, our problem is with ourselves. This may seem insulting, infuriating, or impossible, but this actually brings an incredible sense of autonomy and control into your life.

The irony is that when you completely let go of the need for someone or something to be in some way for your well-being, this letting go grants you a new kind of control. Another one of the paradoxes we discover as we age.

A person you have to live with may be annoying, irresponsible, or erratic. You can spend all day angry and hoping, wishing, trying to convince them to be different. Or, you can let them be annoying, irresponsible, and erratic, and instead, work on how you can still be okay in spite of them. It takes so much less time and actually works (as opposed to trying to change them, which doesn't!).

Today, pay attention to who or what situation you still let get to you. Reconceptualize that people 'problem' as a personal problem. Work your problem by focusing on how to either better protect yourself from them, be at peace in the storm, or both. See what happens.

You will love the peace and freedom this can bring you.

### TODAY'S AFFIRMATION

I am in charge of my inner peace.

### TODAY'S JOURNAL PROMPT

I focus on their problems instead of my inner peace because...

# DAY 65

## *Creative living requires more than common sense.*

Contemporary Western culture has a strong bias toward 'common sense' or a 'just the facts' level of understanding. This new way of knowing decimates your experience of finding meaning in your world. It is important to remember that this is a new (and terrible) concept. It used to be very different.

In the ancient Judeo-Christian tradition, readers of the sacred texts assumed many levels of meaning–so much so that they even outlined the four levels of meaning available in a text.

Scholars of scriptures knew that a story held a plain meaning, an allegorical meaning, a comparative/numeric meaning, and an esoteric or mysterious meaning.

How would your lived experience be different if your meanings of not just texts but everything in your world allowed for myriad meanings? How much more tolerant and creative could we be with ourselves and others as we find and make ourselves in this complicated world?

You don't need to become an expert in Biblical exegesis to understand this concept. My hope is that this helps you see that our simple, plainspoken understandings of ourselves and our world are a new story that is obliterating the richest parts of your lived experience.

Today, be open to more levels of meaning with every interaction. Remember this ancient truth, see beyond the facts, and look for deeper and different meanings. You deserve the richness this will bring into your life.

### TODAY'S AFFIRMATION
I am open to plural meanings.

### TODAY'S JOURNAL PROMPT
A story that I sense has more than one level of meaning is…

# DAY 66

## *Your triggers are your responsibility.*

I've heard it too often, "I do it because I have abandonment issues" or "That kind of thing is too triggering for me." These statements might be true on one level, but they are terribly wrong on another.

Because, too often, we imagine our triggers as stop signs. We think they rightfully assert an appropriate boundary between us and some uncomfortable experience. We mistakenly think our outsized response is appropriate because we are 'triggered.'

This is exactly wrong. When you say, "I am triggered," you are owning that your reaction to some present event is *inappropriate to the context.* You are acknowledging that because you have some unresolved trauma in your history, this present experience (that is presumably tolerable to others) is too hard for you.

The resolution? Work on your trauma. The world cannot adapt to accommodate all of our traumas. Our goal is not to avoid the story of our traumas. Your task is to get to a point where you are not triggered. Your goal is to get to a place where you can react appropriately to the present experience.

You are absolutely on the right track in learning to identify your triggers, but where we still get it wrong is in understanding what that awareness means for us and others.

Today, remember that you are responsible for your triggers. The world will not offer a safe space. Only you can create that.

### TODAY'S AFFIRMATION
I am responsible for my healing journey.

### TODAY'S JOURNAL PROMPT
Something I might be avoiding because it triggers me is...

# DAY 67

## *The story of the nuclear family is failing all of us.*

In listening to women's stories across the lifespan, there is one devastating story I see that hurts women in every decade–the story of the tiny nuclear family. This normative idea of a nuclear family was popularized in the 1920s in the United States. From the 1950s onward, it became the dominant family structure.

This story is killing us. The idea that we should function well, across the lifespan, in our isolated (often solitary) micro families is destructive to overwhelmed mothers, bored children, dependent adults, and our elderly.

Our history shows that as we gained the financial resources to live separately from our extended family, we chose to do so. This sociological shift resulted in increasing isolation for every demographic. You don't have to look far to see how cultures with intergenerational households function–the children are looked after by extended family, dependent adults, and the elderly are cared for at home. Yes, the strains of tolerating complicated family relationships add extreme challenges (we did choose to live separately when we could afford to do so).

But, the idea that we can and should live and function well outside of an extended family support network is not only causing financial hardship, loneliness, and child and eldercare crises, but it is stressing out the woman-led households who think this was 'supposed' to work. It isn't your fault. This doesn't work.

Today, if you are lonely or overwhelmed, explore how living with someone might ease the social or financial strains you are living with. Shared living works better. See if you can find someone to share your household with.

## TODAY'S AFFIRMATION

I wasn't supposed to be able to do this alone.

## TODAY'S JOURNAL PROMPT

My living situation is…It might be easier for me if…

# DAY 68

## *Don't let hurt feelings drive harmful actions.*

When we are learning to stand up for ourselves to defend ourselves and others, it can be confusing at first. What do you do when someone says or does something offensive to you (or a cause you care deeply about)? You feel a surge of anger. You are learning to pay attention to your anger. You are learning to set boundaries. And in your new angry glory, you torch them.

You were on the right track. As women, we do need to listen to our anger–it makes us aware of injustices that we shouldn't tolerate. We need to set healthy boundaries. But too often, when we feel humiliated or degraded, we let our unconscious take over. We might want the offender to feel what we are feeling. But following in the footsteps of our offenders by shaming, humiliating, or degrading them is not your healing path.

Every ancient and modern spiritual tradition teaches this–from Jesus telling followers to turn the other cheek to Ruiz's *Four Agreements* encouraging us to be impeccable in our speech.

When you feel that rage stirring within you, pause. Let it be there. Observe it. Notice what it is here to tell you. Then reflect thoughtfully on your goal in this interaction. Do you want to hurt this person (then don't say or do anything)? Do you want to teach this person (is that a realistic goal)? Do you want to let them sit in the gulf of silence and digest their own offensive words (this can be pretty powerful)? Do you want to set a healthy boundary?

I can't tell you how to respond to every infuriating thing, but I can ask you to not confuse feeling your anger with immediately acting out unconsciously in response to your surge of anger.

Today, notice where you feel anger. Let it be there. Observe it. Take action (or not) as you deem appropriate.

You will love the self-awareness and control this will bring you.

### TODAY'S AFFIRMATION
I can feel my anger without being controlled by my anger.

### TODAY'S JOURNAL PROMPT
When I get angry, I tend to…

# DAY 69

## *Sometimes we need to find the courage to quit things.*

The story of the protestant work ethic has us believing that we should stick with it, no matter what. Loyalty and perseverance are good qualities to have. Doing what we say we are going to do fosters trust in our relationships. But, like all good things, we need to approach these values with moderation.

The truth is, it takes courage to quit things–an unfulfilling project, a self-destructive pattern, an abusive relationship. There is a type of acceptance that is required to give up or quit.

If you are quitting everything you start, you may not need this guidance. But if you are trapped in the belief that you aren't able to revisit and revise your earlier commitments, pay attention to why you feel stuck with the decisions made by your younger self.

I'm not suggesting you make a rash change today, but I am asking you to explore these questions. If your commitment is killing you, ask yourself why you can't find the courage to quit.

You deserve the restart this freedom can bring you.

### TODAY'S AFFIRMATION

I have the courage to start things and the courage to quit things.

### TODAY'S JOURNAL PROMPT

Something I may be having a hard time letting go of is…

# REST
# REVIEW
# REFLECT

## *Find what feeds your soul.*
## *Do more of that.*

So many women show up in their work, with me feeling psychologically and emotionally dead. Popular self-help books telling her to pursue her dreams are useless because she doesn't have any dreams. She feels stuck and has no idea what she should do.

I'm going to tell you the work we do in therapy so that you can try this on your own. First, I listen to her. I pay attention to her body language. I notice when she tenses up, shifts in her chair, and especially when her face lights up. All of her body language communicates to me where she needs to go next.

If you are doing this on your own, I'd ask you to pay attention to what fantasy about yourself excites you (a gardener? A quilter? A world traveler? Being with your grandchildren?). Think about the things you search for on the internet. Think about the people you follow in the media. Who do you admire? What do the things you look for tell you about yourself? What do they represent? When do you feel movement in your physical body? When do you feel energy?

**Note:** Be careful of fantasies that have to do with external praise or acceptance. This is a look inward, not outward.

Once we find that (and it can be barely a glimmer), I ask my client to find a way to do more. And I ask her to pay attention to how she feels when she does. If she can't take any action, I ask her to fantasize about doing that thing and see how she feels. If we are on the right track, this will give her a boost of desperately needed energy and confirm for us that we are honing in on her path. It may still be very dark and confusing, but we are on our way.

Today, pay attention to what excites you—even if it is barely a glimmer! Notice what you feel in your body. Listen to those clues. Imagine doing more of that and seeing how you feel.

You will love the energy this brings you.

**Note:** When we are in a profound depression, we often can't see or feel glimmers. In those moments, one waits.

## TODAY'S AFFIRMATION
I pay attention to what feeds my soul.

## TODAY'S JOURNAL PROMPT
I feel most excited when…

# DAY 72

## *We've replaced a deep knowing of who we are with a shallow knowing of what we want.*

The story of wanting can derail our spiritual journey. Not only has it turned us into voracious consumers of disposable items, but it has fundamentally rewired our understanding of ourselves.

For most of the history of humanity, there was not an infinite supply of objects to desire. A gnawing sense of lack could not be filled with an endless supply of tempting items, experiences, or relationships. At some early point in life, one was forced to contend with oneself. That existential crisis inevitably brought one into a more reciprocal relationship with the sacred.

Today, most of us are not searching for the sacred in the first half (or more) of life. We are lulled into the story that the next acquisition or accomplishment is the missing keystone to our happiness. This model has been very profitable for companies but devastating to your inner journey.

Today, see if you can notice what you still want. Explore what happens if you try to let that go. Notice what happens when you are left with just yourself and nothing else to desire.

You deserve the present-moment peace this will bring you.

## TODAY'S AFFIRMATION
I am not distracted by desires.

## TODAY'S JOURNAL PROMPT
The "thing" that I still imagine will make me happy is...

## *You can hear and grow from them, too.*

You are learning to explore your feelings and set healthy boundaries in your relationships. But one thing we all need to be careful about is our natural tendency to center all this potential relational growth around our own inner (and outer) world.

As you start to pay attention to your feelings and work on the relationships that are still difficult, notice how you feel when you are the target of their constructive criticism. Are you able to hear and process the feelings and limits of others as well as you are able to feel and express your own? Are you open to the possibility that they are seeing blind spots that you are missing? With a safe person, this can be an extraordinary opportunity for personal growth (with an abusive person, it can be dangerous).

What is the criticism you hear from others that irritates you the most? Is there a part of it that you can, for a moment, imagine to be true? Even if it isn't true, try sitting in the space of their reality. This empathetic awareness is good for you, your relationships, and our collective growth.

### TODAY'S AFFIRMATION

I can hear their criticisms without reacting.

### TODAY'S JOURNAL PROMPT

A blind spot that other people might see better than me could be...

# DAY 74

## *What happened to their tragic hero? He became our villain.*

If you've studied literature or storytelling, you may have come across the classical text, *Poetics* by Aristotle. This is where we get the term "tragic hero" and the first recognition of how our empathetic responses to stories cultivate psychological healing.

In studying popular ancient plays, Aristotle recognized and wrote about the classic tragic hero. This tragic hero was always a moral man who suffered a cruel fate due to some mistake or character flaw. His suffering elicited intense emotional responses from the audience as they watched a presumably good-enough man suffer terribly because of his error. Aristotle identified the value of the cathartic response in the audience as they connected with and wept for the hero.

Our stories are different today. We no longer popularize stories of flawed, good men who are doomed because of their mistakes. Our heroes are much simpler. They are usually good. And they usually win.

You may think we abandoned their tragic hero, but, in truth, he lives on in our stories. You know where? The tragic hero of the ancient world has been recast as our villain–a person who deserves their terrible fate because of their error. Today, we try not to identify and empathize with this character. Instead, we separate and cast blame.

How different might your life be if you grew up on these ancient tales? How would you interpret the tragedies that every normal life includes? How might our naive and recent ideas of a just universe be complicated if we were filled with tales that told a different story?

I am not making a case for one being better or worse (or even exploring the concept of justice and divinity or the problem of evil here). What I am doing is asking you to notice how the way we tell our stories has changed. And that has changed the way you experience yourself and your world.

Their tragic hero became our villain. Where does that leave you?

## TODAY'S AFFIRMATION

I can connect and empathize with people who suffer because of their mistakes.

## TODAY'S JOURNAL PROMPT

When someone suffers a terrible fate due to their own error, I tend to feel...
When I suffer because of my error, I tend to feel...

# DAY 75

## *Caring about others is not codependence.*

Women show up in my office with a lot of negative labels to describe themselves. One I hear frequently is, "I'm just too codependent, don't you think?"

I don't want to minimize the reality of how real codependency can be a soul-destroying existence, but I do want to defend the experience of feminine interdependence–our tendency to care deeply about other people.

As a woman, you are very likely moved by suffering. When someone you care about is hurting, you might feel it physically.

This feminine, intuitive connectedness to others is not a bad thing. It can become harmful to you (and others) if your relationship is taking all of your emotional energy or feels one-sided. *But it isn't bad that you can empathetically connect with others.*

Today, pay attention to how you feel about how you are impacted by the people you love. See if you can honor a healthy balance of caring deeply about them but not being annihilated by their struggles or needs. Your care for others should be praised, not pathologized.

You deserve the honoring of your feminine way of knowing and caring.

### TODAY'S AFFIRMATION
My caring and compassion are good things.

### TODAY'S JOURNAL PROMPT
When I think about my experience of caring and codependence,
I tend to think I am...

# DAY 76

## *We forgot how to <u>grow</u> old.*

As we've moved from a culture guided by wise women storytellers to a culture dominated by young, for-profit storytellers, we've lost the entire story of *growing* old. This new narrative is so powerful that we can even say the word "grow" without hearing the word grow! How powerful is it that, only in this context, the word "growing" is no longer associated with growth?

Remember, you are *growing* old. And growth is a good thing.

Young people can't see your invisible world. When they are tasked with telling your story, they see what is visibly lost, but they are blind to what is gained. Many women in the latter decades of life know a different story. But we don't hear or tell this tale. Yes, parts of our mind and body do decay. But, in order to *grow* old, we learn to let go of the physical and material comforts of youth and grow into the wise women we are meant to be.

Today, reflect on your attitude toward the phrase 'growing old.' See if you can rediscover our lost story of *growing* into your old age.

You deserve a journey of continued growth.

### TODAY'S AFFIRMATION
I am growing into this new season of my life.

### TODAY'S JOURNAL PROMPT
When I think about 'growing' old, I think…

# DAY 77

# REST
# REVIEW
# REFLECT

# *You aren't longing for anything except for connection with the Divine.*

You know the restless discomfort–that nagging sense of emptiness searching for something to fill it. You've tried different things over the decades–relationships, vanity, substances, or maybe activities like shopping, sex, or gossiping. The prospect of these things was always enticing, but that restless emptiness always came back.

Here is what we know–humans are terrible at predicting what will bring them comfort. The things we seek don't work. They are superficial bandaids trying to mask a gaping wound.

Here is what else we know–people who have a well-developed spiritual practice are happier. *This thing that few people seek does actually work*. It doesn't matter what tradition you are working from–a well-developed spiritual practice of any faith cultivates a sense of the immanent and transcendent within, and without that brings incredible ease and peace into your life.

Today, even if you don't do anything else, engage for at least one minute in some aspect of your preferred spiritual practice; there is nothing else on your to-do list that is as important as this foundational work.

You will love the tranquility this will bring to you.

## TODAY'S AFFIRMATION

I am committed to my spiritual practice.

## TODAY'S JOURNAL PROMPT

The things I often do instead of my spiritual practices are.

## *Your relationships won't save you.*

You are exploring how your imagination can heal you, but I also want to remind you how our creative wanderings can lead us down dark alleys and into dead ends. A very popular story in the West is about being psychologically saved by love from another person. This is an intoxicating tale. It is wonderful to imagine that this new person is the long-sought answer to all of our psychological woes.

James Hollis, in his book, *The Eden Project: In Search of the Magical Other*, offers a beautiful explanation of the psychological dynamics that suck us into such a creative dead end. Hollis writes about how our longing for the elusive, perfect union allows us to easily project our psychological messes onto someone else, imagining that they are the resource that will finally save us (e.g., I will finally feel loved, valuable, etc.).

The problems arise when we inevitably discover we are in a relationship with another real and flawed human being–and not a magical cure (remember, we can project our mess onto any relationship–anywhere we think that other being is going to 'complete us'). Hollis' theory helps us to understand the intoxication of new love and the disappointment that ensues when we have to encounter another real human.

Your task is not to blame them for also being human but to take back your projected imaginings. Your harder task is to love and see them as they really are. You own what you are projecting, and instead of expressing disappointment in them, you recognize the unrealistic expectation from you.

Today, pay attention to what you imagine some relationship might do for you. Recognize that it is really a task for yourself.

## TODAY'S AFFIRMATION

I own my projections and inappropriate expectations.

## TODAY'S JOURNAL PROMPT

A love that I probably projected onto was…I learned then…I see now…

# DAY 80

## *You find and make yourself in a material and symbolic world.*

In our attempt to make sense of ourselves, we incorporate concepts from the world we see around us. Years ago, individuals imagined they were part of a family tree. After the industrial revolution, people protested, feeling like a cog in a machine. With the dawn of the computer age, people started thinking of their brains as a computer.

Your story of self is an ongoing imaginative and interactive relationship between you and your world. You may not have control over the fact that you find and make yourself in this world, but you do have some control over what you find and make yourself with. Instead of passively receiving these metaphors that shape your existence, you can be more intentional. This subtle act can have a profound impact on your psycho-spiritual-mythological self.

Notice the metaphors of self that fill your mind. Do you feel like a broken-down machine? An old computer with faulty software? Or an ancient tree with deep roots? Pay attention to how the different images impact you and your sense of self. Today, be intentional about the symbols of self you choose to bring into your story.

You will love the meaningful symbolic connection to your world and yourself this will bring you.

### TODAY'S AFFIRMATION

I am intentional about the metaphors I use to imagine myself.

### TODAY'S JOURNAL PROMPT

In relationship to my material culture, I have imagined myself as...
I prefer to imagine myself as...

# DAY 81

## *You are more than the story of your problems.*

The history and practice of Western psychology have us focused on the wrong things. Instead of learning how to be well, our mental health models have us exploring the various ways we are sick. With this approach, you end up with a story of self that usually includes a litany of personal problems that you should fix.

This "fix the problem with me" story is a modern invention born out of Freud's ideas and worsened by the self-help movement. You don't have to see yourself in this new, problematic paradigm. I'd like for you to try something different.

Today, stop imagining yourself as a woman who has problems–whether it is with self-worth, a traumatic past, or difficulty with relationships. Today, reimagine yourself as a woman who has aspirations. You are a woman who still wants to learn how to paint, who dreams of starting her first garden, or who wants to make a radical change to the status quo she is living in now.

Keep your mind from wandering toward their abbreviated story of you as a story of your problems. Direct your mind to wonder about your more expansive dreams. Try that for a few days and see what happens.

You are more than the story of your problems.

You will love the energy and enthusiasm this will bring you.

## TODAY'S AFFIRMATION
My story is unfolding ahead of me.

## TODAY'S JOURNAL PROMPT
The psychological/medical model tells a narrow, short story of me.
This story misses the fact that…

# DAY 82

## *Some relationships have to end.*

Many women I work with have the hope of repairing a relationship with a difficult family member. This can be a realistic goal as there are lots of things we can learn to do so we can be in relationship with fewer conflicts and misunderstandings. But it isn't a guarantee.

When you love someone who is blaming you and never taking personal responsibility, manufacturing conflict to meet their own emotional needs, or unable to ever truly understand your perspective, the goal of getting to a functional, egalitarian relationship may need to be dialed back.

When you realize you don't have the power to change their behavior, you may have to face the grief that this relationship won't be what you wished it would be. You can still be in a relationship, just with better boundaries and more realistic expectations (e.g., she is going to blame me; I won't take that on or react to it). Or you may choose to end the relationship. There is no right answer. Sometimes you don't have options. Either choice is okay.

The important point is to remember that you don't have the power to make all relationships heal.

Today, pay attention to the relationships that work best for you and the relationships that you might be working too hard for. Invest in (or find new) relationships that work and set better boundaries with the ones that do not.

You will love the peace this will bring into your life.

### TODAY'S AFFIRMATION
It is not my job to change them.

### TODAY'S JOURNAL PROMPT
The person I feel most frustrated with is...I could probably
set better boundaries and expectations by...

## *No, it isn't fair.*
## *Your job is to learn how to cope.*

As children, we start out with a black-and-white view of our world. We know certain things are right and other things are wrong. We expect the just to be rewarded and the unjust to be punished.

As we age, we recognize this isn't the case. We face the reality that 'good' people are hurt and 'bad' people still win.

Wrestling with this uncomfortable truth shows up in every spiritual and philosophical tradition. From the 'problem of evil' in theology to the existential crisis in philosophy, how do we make sense of the fact that life isn't fair?

We can waste a lot of time protesting and grieving this truth, but that is a waste of your precious time. We aren't the first generation of women to have to face this reality. Your mother learned it; your grandmother learned it; and every one of your ancestors before.

Your job is to stop expecting the world to be fair. You are too old and wise for that. Your job is to learn to cope with the world as we all find it.

You will love the peace this will bring you.

### TODAY'S AFFIRMATION
I can be in this world as it is.

### TODAY'S JOURNAL PROMPT
When I encounter painful injustices, I tend to…

# DAY 84

# REST
# REVIEW
# REFLECT

# *You can handle your life.*

Every woman struggles with finding the time to take a quiet moment for herself–at first. Then she gets hooked on her centering practice, recognizing that her entire well-being is completely dependent upon finding those few minutes. It is a choice you make every day. And one for which we are each completely responsible.

A woman said to me recently, "I am so tired of feeling like everything is always on the precipice of failure. I wish I could be more optimistic about my future, like you." That made me laugh as I replied, "I also know that everything in my life is on the precipice of failure. The only difference is that it doesn't bother me."

This is the difference that taking that five to forty-five minutes each day can make for you. It doesn't turn you into a naive optimist about life. It turns you into a realistic optimist about *your ability to handle your life*. No matter how busy, overwhelmed, or overtired you are, there is no excuse for not finding that five minutes.

Today, make sure you are committing to your practice, whatever it may be.

You will love the deep stillness this discipline will bring you.

## TODAY'S AFFIRMATION
I take the time each day to find my peace.

## TODAY'S JOURNAL PROMPT
If I engaged in my spiritual practice for one to five minutes each day, I...

# DAY 86

## *You are hurt in relationship. You are healed in relationship. Stay connected.*

Traditional models of mental health prioritize independence and autonomy, but therapists who study women find that we grow toward and with connection. Traditional models of mental health prioritize logic and better thinking, but therapists who study women find that we grow through deeper feelings and the cultivation of empathy and intuition.

This is why traditional therapy may not have worked for you. You were hurt in relationship, and in therapy, you should have had the opportunity to heal in relationship. In that therapeutic connection, you should have the opportunity to cultivate your sense of intuition and empathy in relationship with a safe person.

But you don't have to have a therapist to do this work. You can do this in any healthy, healing, and respectful relationship or group (it is harder to do with another person, who may have their own agenda, but this is absolutely possible. You may also choose to start your healing in relationship with your spiritual source or nature).

Today, pay attention to where you feel you may have shut down your desire for connections due to being hurt. Make a commitment to open your feeling and empathic self up again to a (safe) person, group, or, if that is too much right now, to your spiritual or nature practice.

You deserve the reconnection and empathetic growth this will bring you.

### TODAY'S AFFIRMATION
I reconnect in safe places to heal.

### TODAY'S JOURNAL PROMPT
The idea of healing in relationship with others feels…

# DAY 87

## *Stop clinging to that sinking ship.*
## *Your job is to learn to swim.*

When things bring us comfort, we are slow to let them go. You've seen this with children–a comforting blanket or stuffed toy that they can't be without. You've seen this with young adults–staying in jobs or relationships because they are afraid to move on. You've seen this in older women–unresolved grief because they can't metabolize their loss.

The problem is not the situation. The problem is our idea about the situation. We believe we can't be okay without that thing, so we cling to the lost object. This can cause long-term suffering.

When we change our idea about the situation, we can change our suffering. We let go of the idea that we must have this person, ability, health, or situation in order to be comforted. We accept the idea that we must learn to process our feelings and grow in order to feel comforted.

You are old enough to know that many precious things have come and gone. Your job is to honor their presence and to keep growing after their absence.

Today, pay attention to what you think you may still be clinging to that is no longer here. See if you can reframe your perspective from that of being in a deficit to that of being in a challenge to let go and keep growing.

You will love the peace and acceptance this will bring you.

### TODAY'S AFFIRMATION
I can continue to grow after loss.

### TODAY'S JOURNAL PROMPT
The thing/person/ability that I am without that still haunts me is...
If I accepted this/them as being gone, then...

# DAY 88

## *Practice trusting people.*

We tend to have a black-and-white view of trust. We imagine we are able to trust or are not able to trust. We imagine that people are trustworthy or not trustworthy. This extreme spectrum makes it challenging to rebuild your ability to trust in new relationships. How are you supposed to learn to trust again when it feels so enormous?

At this stage, it is important to remember that your task is not to immediately jump into the deep end of the pool. After your experiences, you cannot demand that you open up completely with someone else. Just as you would gently guide a tentative child into the shallow end, your job is to make small steps toward opening up to someone who feels like they might be safe.

Remember, you are not learning how to blindly trust everyone. You are learning what a safe person looks like. You are learning how to open up to safe people.

A safe person is someone who can hold the hard parts of your story and never (and I mean ever) use it against you. A safe person can both give and receive feedback. A safe person takes responsibility for their behavior. A safe person doesn't blame you or others for their emotions.

When you find someone you believe might fit this criteria, your job is to test. Try opening up just a little bit. Try sharing a part of yourself that feels less vulnerable. Then wait. See how it goes with this person. Over time, you will learn if this person passes the test or fails. Over time you will relearn how to read the signals of safe and unsafe people so that you can be increasingly vulnerable with people who have *earned* your trust.

Today, pay attention to how well you recognize the signs of safety in a person. Imagine being open to someone who is worthy of your trust.

You deserve the connection this brings you.

### TODAY'S AFFIRMATION
I can practice trusting more.

### TODAY'S JOURNAL PROMPT
When I think about trusting people, I realize I tend to…

# DAY 89

## *If you believe that God is a disapproving parent, you will always remain an ashamed child.*

Seekers in the East are often fascinated by the West. Seekers in the West are often fascinated by the East. Our own spiritual traditions are so laden with cultural baggage that we often find it easier to seek new spiritual direction in places that feel strange.

Because as you developed ideas about the divine in your youth, you probably reduced the ineffable mystery into something simple that you could understand. Maybe a father (God). Maybe a mother (Mary). As you grew into an adult, your limited and childlike conception may have started to feel oppressive and not nourishing.

Remember, the problem isn't with the divine. The problem is with your childlike ideas about the divine. If you feel stuck with your spiritual growth, explore your ideas about divinity. Go back to your earlier stories. See what you discover that you actually believed. See if what you find in your own stories looks like a divine mystery or more like the construct of a child.

As you grow into an old woman, your job is to remember your own stories, explore our most ancient ones, and connect to the larger mysterious divine that is beyond all of our conceptions.

You deserve the spiritual growth this will bring you.

### TODAY'S AFFIRMATION
The mystery/divine is a love beyond my understanding.

### TODAY'S JOURNAL PROMPT
What I've believed about God and spirituality is...

# DAY 90

## *Free yourself from the stimulus/response way of being.*

It is good for you to be connected to your world, but it is important to notice if that feels like a cooperative rhythm or a passive enslavement. We can get so unconscious in our responses to the outside world that we forget to pay attention to how much we are controlled by it. You smell good food, and you want to eat. You see a pretty place, and you want to go there. You hear nostalgic music, and you long to see your old friends.

None of these responses are necessarily bad, but it is important to pay attention to how much you are engaged in a cooperative exchange with your world and how much you are just being driven, unconsciously, by powerful external stimuli.

When you step out of your unconscious stimulus/response mode, you take back more control. You are more present. You notice your world, and you notice what comes up from within. You choose to respond or not respond.

Today, see if you can pay attention to how the world around you is eliciting responses from you. See if you can bring more consciousness to the actions you choose to have in response.

You will love the energy, calm, and focus this will bring to your life.

### TODAY'S AFFIRMATION

I am not driven unconsciously by external stimuli.

### TODAY'S JOURNAL PROMPT

When I reflect on my awareness of external and internal stimuli, I notice…

# REST
# REVIEW
# REFLECT

## *Your Season of Responsibility.*

You are learning about the four seasons of a woman's life, *Receptivity, Responsibility, Reflection,* and *Return.* Most of *OMM 365* is focused on the last two seasons of our lives, but as part of understanding your journey, I'd like to bring your attention back to an earlier developmental stage, your season of *Responsibility* (the original root of this word is the Latin word, "respondere" which means "to respond").

Whether your home was a constructive or totally chaotic place, you were eventually thrown into the world as a young woman who had to figure out how to live. Some women may have gotten married and had children, others started a career, many of us struggled with being functional, developed addictions, or ended up incarcerated.

It doesn't matter what happened. The point to remember about this season of your life is that you were a young woman flailing about in a world with very little inner wisdom. Whether you were working at a bank or serving time, the developmental status was one of responding to your outer world and having very little awareness of your inner world.

Today, remember this young woman. Hold her with compassion. She was arriving in the world with very little wisdom, trying to figure things out.

Your younger self deserves the compassion.

### TODAY'S AFFIRMATION

I hold my younger, naive self with more compassion.

### TODAY'S JOURNAL PROMPT

When I reflect on my *Responsible* years (of mothering, working, etc.), I think/feel...

## *Being present is not a way to avoid pain. It's a way to be with pain so that you can let it go.*

Westerners are always caught up in the latest self-help fads. Mindfulness and being present, which are powerful methods for soothing our soul, are in their heyday. The problem isn't with these practices but that we misunderstand how they work. So many women are looking for a self-help trick to quickly make them feel better. Being present doesn't necessarily do that, so she may have tried it and given up on it when it "didn't work."

Learning to be present isn't a quick fix like taking a drug. In fact, it can be exactly the opposite. Unlike the deadening effects of mood-altering substances, being present is about being with your joy, anger, or grief. It honors the holistic human experience, pleasurable or painful. The beauty of this practice is that it protects us from getting stuck on a painful feeling by avoiding it.

If you are sad about something, stay present with that feeling until it begins to ebb away on its own (unlike repetitive thoughts, feelings are dynamic. If you are allowing them to come up, they are guaranteed to change).

Today, remember that being present is about being with whatever is in front of you (remember, we are not seeking perpetual happiness!). That may be grief, joy, anger, delight, or something else. The emotions may be hard to sit with, but in the long run, being with them is much less painful than avoiding them.

You deserve the comfort this practice can bring you.

### TODAY'S AFFIRMATION
I am present with what is.

### TODAY'S JOURNAL PROMPT
When I imagine being present with my pain, I feel…

# DAY 94

## *You are not what you can do.*

As you move into your wisdom years, you are moving from a focus on linear time to an increasing awareness of our more ancient and circular time. From a world of Logos and doing to a world of Eros and being.

Gaining and losing are part of a long, circular process. As babies, we couldn't do much. We grew stronger and eventually could do a lot (we experienced life as progressive and linear). We grew old and could do less again (we open up to circular or spiral time).

Paying attention to this circular process teaches us something important about who we are. What we can do is very dynamic. It changes by the decade. But who we are does not. We are still the same being in the midst of the gain, growth, and loss of these abilities.

If we don't understand this, we get bitter about our losses. We think we need to hold on to everything we've ever been to maintain our sense of self. Your journey now is exactly the opposite. Your journey is to know yourself as something more than what you used to be able to do. Your journey is to connect with your being, not your doing.

When you do that, you can't lose yourself.

Today, reflect on how much you identify with the straight progress of linear time and the measurements of what you are able to do. See if you can reconsider your identity outside of that narrow paradigm. Meditating on or in nature can help with this (e.g., what can the flower do? What can the grass do? What do the seasons do?). See if you can let go of the measurement of doing and sink into the spiritual spiral of return.

You will love the peace this will bring you.

### TODAY'S AFFIRMATION
I am living in circular time.

### TODAY'S JOURNAL PROMPT
When I reflect on my sense of myself and my relationship to progress and loss,
I notice…

# DAY 95

## *You aren't procrastinating.*
## *Go deeper to discover what blocks you.*

So frequently, my clients will report that they aren't doing some creative project because they are 'just procrastinating.' I've worked with women long enough to know that this is not the case. It isn't procrastination but something so much more powerful that blocks you.

When you are 'procrastinating,' some part of you is trying to protect yourself from something. Your job is to stop calling it procrastination and figure out what it really is. We can ask ourselves, "What am I gaining or avoiding by not taking the action that I say I want to take?"

We might discover we can't tolerate failure and are frozen in our perfectionism. We might realize we fear success. We might discover that we are waiting until we feel ready, not recognizing we have to rely on courage instead of waiting for comfort to come. We might discover that we actually don't want to change and have reasons to keep things the way they are. There are infinite options, so I can't tell you what your reason is. What I can tell you is that you can (and should) find it.

When you understand more about the internal dynamics that are blocking you, you have the opportunity to work with them. Stop saying that you are just procrastinating, and allow yourself to explore the deeper, meaningful movements within you.

Today, pay attention to what you are persistently postponing. Saying you are 'just lazy' is lazy. Have the courage to honestly explore why you are choosing to avoid it.

You deserve the insight and productivity this can bring.

## TODAY'S AFFIRMATION

I have the courage to explore the deeper meaning behind my inaction.

## TODAY'S JOURNAL PROMPT

How is not moving forward on this project serving me?
I am afraid to take action on this because…

## *Use the music.*

As you reflect on and reimagine your stories, I'd like to offer up another trick that might help you. You probably have already experienced this method, but I'd like for you to be more intentional about using it.

Because, oftentimes, we want to explore our earlier stories but struggle because we simply cannot remember. One way our body can remember old feelings is with music. And I don't mean just the music you have on hand. I want you to go online (e.g., YouTube) and search for playlists from the years or decades you feel curious about. You will find things you have forgotten.

Our memories usually won't bring up what an online archive can. Pop through the songs until you hit one that evokes a strong feeling. It is okay if you can't pull up the memory. Your body is still feeling its way through your stories. Music is uniquely powerful (and accessible), but you can play in this space with other explorations, like, "popular kid toys in the 1950s."

Don't push too hard if you feel an aversion. But play in this space if you feel curious and drawn to it. We are trying to elicit feelings in you. If the music is doing that, you are doing your work.

### TODAY'S AFFIRMATION

I use music to connect to my unremembered stories.

### TODAY'S JOURNAL PROMPT

A decade I could probably play with music is…

## *Choosing kindness is not waiting to feel kind.*

Many of us lament the lack of civility or kindness in our current world. Women express frustration with others but also with themselves. They struggle, wishing to feel more compassion toward people they don't like. "But I just don't feel any kindness or compassion. I feel hate!" she will declare. This statement is an example of where we have a fundamental misunderstanding about practicing kindness.

Women mistakenly believe that there is something wrong with them because they don't feel kind. She doesn't want to feel anger or frustration with this difficult person. I want to remind you that there is nothing wrong with you if you aren't feeling kind. In fact, that is the norm.

Remember, if our goal is to be kind because we feel kind, then we are simply indulging our own whims. *The challenge and discipline is to choose to be kind in the face of frustration or irritation.* That is how we grow in our compassion.

In a world with so much suffering, we choose to be kind.

Today, notice how you are acting with those around you. Continue to notice how you feel, but choose to act in kindness.

This will bring so much peace to your inner world.

### TODAY'S AFFIRMATION
I choose to be kind.

### TODAY'S JOURNAL PROMPT
When I imagine being kind to people that irritate me, I...

# REST
# REVIEW
# REFLECT

# *Imagine coping.*

We often hear that we need to develop our coping skills, but we don't get enough guidance on how to do so. I'd like to share another method for using your own stories and imagination to improve your ability to cope with your current and future challenges.

When you feel like you can't deal with something, your first step is to find the underlying belief that is undermining your confidence. This is usually a general story that you have, like, "I am weak," or "Bad things always happen to me," or "I can't trust."

Once you've found the negative story, write out the opposite (e.g., "I am strong," or "Good things happen to me," or "I can trust," whatever feels like the right opposite to your story).

Now, reflect on your previous experiences. Can you remember an experience where you felt this opposite truth? This is an exercise. Try hard to find something.

When you've got it, use your imagination to return to that experience where you felt the opposite of your negative story. Notice how you feel as you revisit that story. Notice what you think. Imagine moving those feelings and thoughts into yourself as you face this new challenge.

If you can't find an experience in your own story (this is actually quite common), there is another exercise to do. Try to imagine a mentor or a symbolic or spiritual reference that cultivates a feeling of competence and capability with regard to your task. Use your imagination to have a conversation or spiritual engagement with whatever you come up with.

When you are faced with something that feels like it is too much for you, remember to use your own story and your own imagination to find that extra bit of courage you need.

## TODAY'S AFFIRMATION

I allow myself to remember and imagine new stories about myself.

## TODAY'S JOURNAL PROMPT

The challenge I could use this exercise with might be…

# DAY 100

## *You are co-creating meaning with everything.*

Do you remember in high school when you had to find 'the meaning' of a story? It may have seemed like there was a 'right' answer you were supposed to find. This exercise is close to what you need to do, but it is not exactly right. Because whatever meaning you find–no matter how different from everyone else's–is *always exactly the right meaning.*

You're discovering that your interpretation of everyone and everything is your co-creation between you and your world. All of us are always projecting our unconscious imaginings into our world–onto stories, onto people, onto experiences. This merger is where we open ourselves up to a trans-rational reality that creates and heals. If you are open and imagining, you are in the process of constant co-creation.

Today, I want you to remember that you are not just creatively reimagining yourself in relationships with actual stories but in relation to everything and everyone you encounter. You are changed, not by them, but by your imaginative space in between you and them. A good story or relationship offers that space in between. It is a space where you creatively reimagine yourself and your world. The co-creation gives you back something new. It changes you.

We heal in these empty spaces in between. Your subjective meaning is true. And it will change. It is the sacred, playful, creative, and imaginative space where you heal.

Today, pay attention to the empty spaces and to your imaginings that fill them up. See if you can find that invisible and magical world in between.

### TODAY'S AFFIRMATION

I am open and imagining.

### TODAY'S JOURNAL PROMPT

When I imagine what I might be projecting into the world, others, and into stories, I notice...

# DAY 101

## *Practice when life is easy so you have the skills when life gets hard.*

Most of us have grown strong in the storms. When things are difficult, we turn to the soulful practices that develop our depth of spirit. We can expand our resilience and our awareness of our ability to endure hard things.

When things get easier, we can be grateful, but we often lose our focus on these spiritual tasks. Needing them less to get through each day, we fall off the practices that carried us through our darkest moments.

This is the opposite of what we should be doing. We don't have to learn how to handle the storm in the midst of the storm. With a disciplined commitment, we can continue to grow in times of calm so that we may increase our ease in times of crisis.

Today, pay attention to your commitment to the practices you know build your spirit and strength. See if you are able to prioritize them even when you aren't desperate for the comfort they can bring.

You will love the future ease this will bring to moments of difficulty.

### TODAY'S AFFIRMATION
I am committed to my spiritual practices.

### TODAY'S JOURNAL PROMPT
When things are going well, I tend to...

# DAY 102

## *You are not responsible for how they hurt you. You are responsible for how you heal yourself.*

I know you have been hurt. I know walking this path has sometimes been unbearably hard for you.

You are not responsible for what has happened to you. But you are responsible for what you do next. Those people or experiences may have left you broken, but the truth is, no one is going to pick up the pieces except you. Don't lose any more decades in resentment or grief.

I work with women who have experienced the worst wounds, from wealthy women who feel completely trapped in an oppressive, observing community to homeless teen girls who have been violently trafficked by sociopaths. I have heard the worst stories. And I have seen the difference between those who heal and those who get stuck.

What I know is that there is no relationship between the severity of the wounds and the potential for healing. There is a direct relationship between the commitment to the healing journey and the potential for healing.

Today, notice where you are still stuck in anger, grief, or blame. Tell yourself that you will take responsibility for your healing from this point forward. Whatever happened to you, the ball is in your hands now. Get up and do your work.

There is hope on the other side if you are willing.

You are worth it.

## TODAY'S AFFIRMATION

I have the courage to do my healing work.

## TODAY'S JOURNAL PROMPT

I might still be blaming (who?) …If I stopped focusing on their actions and started focusing on my healing I…

## *You don't owe anyone an explanation.*

In my work with women, we are often trying to figure out why she feels stuck. We can all get stuck in so many different ways, but one that is often working very destructively in the background is the mistaken idea that you need to be able to defend your choices to some real or imaginary figure. You aren't taking the risks you need to take because you know what 'they' will say.

I'm not suggesting that criticisms aren't hard to hear. I'm not even suggesting that we don't think they might be true (I've heard some repeatedly that I know are true about me)! What I am suggesting is that you stop allowing these outside insults to shape your life.

Maybe I do quit a lot of things. Maybe the idea is unrealistic. Maybe we have messed up quite a few times. So what. I don't owe them an explanation, and neither do you. Your job is to not let these negative statements from others keep you from moving forward toward your dreams and plans.

Because most of us have to get it wrong a lot of times before we find our way. If we allow these criticisms to stop that healthy process, we are allowing them to keep us stuck.

Today, pay attention to what you are afraid to do because you fear having to defend yourself. Remember that you don't owe anyone an explanation. Push yourself to take some action on that goal today in honor of your commitment to keep walking your own tangled and confusing path.

You deserve it.

### TODAY'S AFFIRMATION
I don't have to defend my choices.

### TODAY'S JOURNAL PROMPT
I probably fear criticism from…
This impacts my ability to move forward in that…

# DAY 104

## *Practice coping.*

As we grow old, we all have to be careful with our tendency to retreat from a world that can still hurt us. If we don't challenge our overprotective instincts, our world will get smaller and smaller as we allow ourselves to feel increasingly frightened by an increasing number of people and places.

But the goal to push yourself into areas that feel risky can be too daunting, so I'd like to suggest a more tolerable method. Instead of thinking that we need to push ourselves into fearful exercises, I'd like for you to imagine that your current task is merely to *practice your ability to cope.* This significantly lowers the bar. Today, you don't need to do anything radical, just do a tiny bit more than you have been doing.

When you take action (or imagine doing so), notice the hard feelings that surge up. *Practice tolerating those feelings.* Recognize that you can be with them and survive. Now you are building a psychological muscle slowly. This new practice builds your self-confidence and resilience as you recognize you are able to tolerate increasing levels of psychological challenges.

Today, think about where you may have retreated in order to protect yourself from further injury. Reflect on whether or not this habit is aligned with your longer-term goals for personal and psychological growth. Explore places you can push yourself just a bit, and practice tolerating your feeling response today.

You will love the freedom this new practice will bring you.

### TODAY'S AFFIRMATION
I practice my ability to cope.

### TODAY'S JOURNAL PROMPT
Something I am afraid to do is…
a tiny task I could do to practice is…

REST
REVIEW
REFLECT

# *Stop repeating the mean things they said to you. It is making you sick.*

If I could make you do one thing in an attempt to quickly fix some of your problems, this is what it would be. I know this is a problem you might have because almost every client I see has it. The fix is really simple. And the research proves consistently that the treatment truly works. Ready for this miracle cure?

Stop saying mean things to yourself.

This is not self-help fluff. Peer-reviewed research studies prove it works. For all the suffering in the world, this is one of the easiest and cheapest problems to fix. No, this isn't going to heal your deepest injuries, but it is going to help you.

What happens to us is that, even if we get away from an abusive person, we often incorporate some part of them into ourselves. They might be gone, but we pick up where they left off, often by saying the horrible things to ourselves that they said to us (we all do this; you are not uniquely awful for having done so).

You don't need hours of therapy to learn this. This is one of the rare circumstances where you just do it.

Will you try this for me? See if, for at least one minute, you can say nice things to yourself. Say them over and over again. Notice how you feel (you may cry at first; that means you are tearing down the old stuff, keep going!).

This change will have a profound impact on your physical and mental health. Please do this.

You deserve the comfort it will bring you.

## TODAY'S AFFIRMATION
I am kind to myself.

## TODAY'S JOURNAL PROMPT
Some of the things I might need to stop saying to myself are...

# DAY 107

## *Use whatever feelings are present as your gateway to your deeper healing.*

So often, we are looking for the formula for how to get to a more comfortable space. We read books, go to church, or hope to find a teacher who can show us the way. These are all great methods for getting started, but the problem is that eventually, you have to forge off their trail and follow your own unique path inward.

Fortunately, there are many doors to your deeper self. One way is through your feelings. If your emotions are overwhelming you, instead of trying to get rid of them, use them as a gateway to go deeper. There are a number of ways to do this–writing, painting, or asking for dreams to offer you more information.

It's okay that it feels confusing–it is supposed to. You aren't supposed to understand anything; you are supposed to be with and experience what is coming up. Allow it to affect you without the demand of completely understanding it.

Paint a picture that explores your feelings. Expand on your rage by turning it into a creative piece of fiction. Feel these experiences and emotions without judgment or too much logic. Nonsensical work is really useful here.

When you allow the experience to seep into your consciousness without the oppressive logic of understanding, you are moving into that deeper space. Be with this creative, feeling experience–in all its pain and confusion, until something changes. It will.

You deserve the deep healing this will bring you.

### TODAY'S AFFIRMATION

I use my most intense feelings as a gateway to my deeper self.

### TODAY'S JOURNAL PROMPT

The feeling that I deal with most frequently is…
I could explore it more deeply by…

# DAY 108

## *Slow down.*
## *Take one thing at a time.*

We are a multitasking society. We talk on the phone while cooking meals, watch TV while we eat, even read on our phones while in the bathroom. We've lost the incredibly basic but deeply centering practice of doing one thing at a time.

This practice sounds so silly, but it can powerfully impact how you move through your day. When we focus on one task at a time, we are less anxious, less forgetful, we are more appreciative, and, most importantly, we develop the discipline of staying present with the place or process we are actually in. Over time, this discipline of focus heals our wandering, anxious minds. I've yet to meet a person who wouldn't benefit from that.

Today, see if you can incorporate this practice into your daily tasks. When you are cooking, just cook. When you are eating, just eat. When you are listening, just listen. Pay attention to how often you are engaging in multiple tasks at once (tablets and phones are often a problem here). Pay attention to how you feel when you limit yourself to staying focused on just one task at a time.

You will love the centering (and better memory!) this will bring you.

### TODAY'S AFFIRMATION
I am focused on the task in front of me.

### TODAY'S JOURNAL PROMPT
How often do I stay focused on one task?
How often am I trying to do more than one task?

# DAY 109

## *Your happiness is not the measure of your health.*

In our happiness-obsessed culture, we learn to feel bad about feeling bad. In this narrow view of life, we pathologize healthy processes like grief, anger, or guilt.

Instead of walking through the long pain of loss, women think they should solve their grief problem and get back to 'normal' happiness. Instead of listening to the messages of injustice or boundary violations that anger is communicating, women try to 'get over' their anger. Instead of recognizing the ethical guidance of sincerely felt guilt, women feel bad about the feeling instead of listening to its call to make a change.

Being unhappy is sometimes the healthiest space for you to be. Your happiness is not your measure of your health.

Today, pay attention to whether or not you have bought into this view that happiness is the 'correct' way of being. Explore whether or not you have feelings about your feelings when you need to process hard things. See if you can give yourself more permission to be with the feelings that come with the experiences you are having.

You will love the fullness this will bring into your experiences.

### TODAY'S AFFIRMATION

My happiness is not the measure of my health.

### TODAY'S JOURNAL PROMPT

When it comes to being with appropriate unhappiness, I tend to...

# DAY 110

*Ancient wisdom resonates for you because it is already within you.*

When you hear or read things that 'ring true' for you, it is important to remember the distinction between learning something new (like a foreign language) and recognizing something you seem to already know (like ancient wisdom).

You know what I am talking about—you hear or read something, and instead of an experience of thinking or trying to learn, you have an experience of deep recognition that this is true. This is you intuitively connecting to your deepest self and the wisdom we find in all of our sacred traditions.

Your thinking brain can help you think and learn, but your intuitive wisdom is your best guide for knowing what to do.

Today, pay attention to whether or not you are taking the time to tune into this kind of intuitive knowing. See if you can listen to yourself more.

You will love the intuitive growth this will bring you.

## TODAY'S AFFIRMATION
I listen to my intuition.

## TODAY'S JOURNAL PROMPT
I tend to rely more on my (thoughts/intuition)…

# DAY 111

## *Imagine yourself courageous.*

Have you been practicing your courage with small tasks? I hope you have been learning to tolerate the fear and develop your courage with smaller challenges.

But mustering up your courage for a bigger task is still intimidating, so I am going to walk you through a helpful exercise that is less daunting. When imagining a bigger task that frightens you, instead of taking action, I'd like for you to just imagine taking action. Imagine yourself being more courageous. This imagining is a productive task on many fronts.

First, when you allow yourself to imagine yourself doing the thing you wish you could do, it immediately reveals all of the obstacles that are blocking you. These will show up as the immediate thoughts that tell you to stop. Revealing these often secret but powerful thoughts give you something new to work with. Pay attention to what obstacles come up. Write them down. Make a conscious effort to explore them.

Imagining yourself as courageous is also a positive visualization. This relaxes your body and lets you creatively imagine radically different stories for yourself.

Remember, as you explore your obstacles, there is no 'right answer." Sometimes we discover that now is not the moment to take a big risk or explore a big dream (in our interdependence, sometimes we really have to put our immediate dreams aside as we cope with our obligations). But I am encouraging you to use your imagination to more consciously explore why you are making the decisions you are making.

You have the courage to do this.

### TODAY'S AFFIRMATION
I imagine myself courageous.

### TODAY'S JOURNAL PROMPT

The secret thing I really wish I could do is…The thoughts or obligations that stop me are… (re-read what you wrote and explore, challenge, and think creatively about what came up).

# DAY 112

# REST
# REVIEW
# REFLECT

*Aging is not a disease.*

As I attempt to make the case that your aging can be a positive developmental process for you, I recognize I am up against a number of dominant narratives working against me. One more that I would like to warn you about is your relationship to your medical care. I am not at all opposed to you seeking any specific type of care, but I am asking you to be mindful of how medical professionals (often younger than you!) tell the story of your aging body.

As an example, a woman came in, distressed to discover that her worsening neck pain and stiffness had been diagnosed as degenerative disc disease. She was, of course, very upset to be diagnosed with a degenerative disease!

But what is the real story? The changes in her neck and spine were actually part of the normal aging process. By the age of sixty, almost 90% of us have some disc degeneration.

I am not minimizing the reality that some of us get illnesses that others don't get. I am not suggesting that the physical challenges of aging aren't real. What I am trying to bring your attention to is how the medical establishment can tell a story of degeneration and disease that scares women who are actually in a normal process of aging.

Whether you are measuring mobility, memory, or something else, it is all less than it was before for most of us. Today, remember that this is our normal story of aging. This is not our disease.

### TODAY'S AFFIRMATION
Normal aging is not a disease.

### TODAY'S JOURNAL PROMPT
When I think about my feelings about my diagnoses, I notice I...

# DAY 114

## *Embrace your power to choose.*

Lots of smart philosophers over the centuries have brought us many great insights about how to live in the world with more comfort. One philosophical approach that can be helpful in your most difficult moments comes from the existentialists. Often criticized as a particularly despairing life philosophy, it can be just what we need when we are suffering and feeling torn between our thoughts and feelings.

The existentialists embraced a tragic fate. It is a highly rationalistic philosophy that allows you to be miserable and not be in error. But what it demands from you is great. The existentialists believed in your power to logically choose your path in the face of overwhelming pain or contradictory feelings.

This can bring a strange comfort in your hardest times–when you feel torn between thoughts and feelings, but you know you need to follow your thinking (e.g., with addictions, unhealthy avoidance, or caretaking a family member, etc.). You might be afraid to go outside, but you are not letting your feelings decide; you might want to eat that dessert, but you choose to adhere to your blood sugar goals. You might want to abandon your dependent loved one, but you stay. You are aware of your feelings, but they aren't running the show. You are embracing your power to choose.

I am not arguing that our logic is always the right path; often, we need our feelings and intuition to help us find our way. But in our most challenging moments, when we feel torn between what we want and what we know we need to do, this existentialist approach can help you find a method and even *meaning*.

Today, notice where you feel a discrepancy between your thoughts and feelings. Notice if this is a circumstance where your logical thinking is your right path.

There are so many ways of knowing. You deserve the positive outcomes that your meaningful choices will bring you.

### TODAY'S AFFIRMATION

I make use of my power to choose the actions I feel good about.

### TODAY'S JOURNAL PROMPT

Discrepancies between thoughts and feelings in my life
are probably most present with...

# DAY 115

## *The things you worried about never happened. The things that happened you never worried about. Worrying isn't working.*

When we are trying to lessen our anxiety, we usually need to engage our body and mind across multiple fronts. We use spiritual practices to ground us in the present-moment. We engage our physiological processes through deep breathing and fitness. We use cognitive exercises to change our automatic thoughts.

But we can also trick ourselves into stopping our catastrophizing by realizing how bad we are at it.

One day, it finally occurred to me that most of the things I worried about never happened. And the catastrophes that befell me I never saw coming. This recognition of my poor prognostic skills gave me pause. The realization that I was so bad at predicting what bad things might happen helped to free me from my chronic habit of letting my mind wander into these future catastrophes.

Today, reflect on your own history. Pay attention to the wasted time you've spent worrying about things that never happened. Remember the hardest hits you've taken that you never saw coming. See if you can use this recognition to help break your habit of worrying about the future.

You deserve the present-moment peace this will bring you.

### TODAY'S AFFIRMATION

I am very disciplined in what I allow myself to wonder about.

### TODAY'S JOURNAL PROMPT

When I reflect on what I've worried about happening vs. what has happened,
I notice...

# DAY 116

## *It is better for you to get lost than to stay stuck.*

It's scary when you know you need to do something different, but you don't have any idea what that something different is. You might be waiting for some clarity or insight into what the correct path is for yourself.

This waiting is a trap. As we age, we can forget that our job is not to walk our path with certainty or deep knowing. Our job is to continue to walk our path, trusting the process of not-knowing. At every stage of development, including old age, we have to flail around a bit. Fail at several things. Try lots of things and realize they don't work for you. This is the way we all do it.

Yes, it is scary to move from your place of known routines into a place of unknown outcomes. But this is the only way you can grow into your next stage of development. Your job right now is to tolerate that fear and keep going.

Today, pay attention to whether or not you are holding yourself back because you are afraid of getting lost. Remember that this demand to know is working against your goal of growth. See if you can tolerate feeling lost and walking into something new.

You will love the growth this will bring you.

### TODAY'S AFFIRMATION
I can tolerate feeling lost.

### TODAY'S JOURNAL PROMPT
When I imagine moving into a new stage of growth and development in late life, I feel...

# DAY 117

## *Choose your brainwashing.*

Have you ever gotten a song stuck in your head? Or an advertising jingle? It's something we joke about, but the effect is actually something that should give us serious pause. People trying to sell you things know something that most people don't–how to enslave your attention with their stories. When you are singing their songs in your head unconsciously, it is a huge win for them. They have literally taken over your mind.

Since our body and mind are like sponges that soak up whatever we immerse them in, why don't you be more intentional about using this to your advantage? Who are some teachers and/or thinkers that you like? What are some psychological, intellectual, or spiritual texts that inspire you?

Find these texts–preferably in audio format. When you wake up in the morning, before your mind gets going on social media or the news, turn on your audiobooks. Give yourself at least ten minutes of listening (or more). Do this every single day. It takes no effort (and it is totally fine if you aren't grasping or paying enough attention to it! You are still getting it at a deeper level).

You won't notice the slightest difference at first. It will seem like a waste of time. But, after a month or more, you will notice the words start to rise up in you–just like that jingle. The texts that you choose to brainwash yourself with are in your body and mind.

Today, see if you can find the audiobook that inspires you. It can be a sacred text, self-help, prayer, poetry, or something else. Just make sure it is something you really want to absorb deeply.

You will love the new stories this will bring to you.

### TODAY'S AFFIRMATION
I control what goes into my mind.

### TODAY'S JOURNAL PROMPT
The people and books that inspire me most are…

# DAY 118

## *Be receptive to your remembering.*

As you start to explore your stories–past, present, and future–I'd like to remind you to be gentle; remember how to flow with your natural rhythms. Sometimes, our 'protestant work ethic' story can push us into aggressive and ambitious excavations into our own history to 'clean out' all the dark corners.

Many trauma therapists work this way. I do not. I believe you can wait until the story surfaces in its own time. If you are working on your spiritual practices (e.g., not constantly distracting yourself), you can sit in that receptive space and know that, in its own time, your memories and injuries will surface. They will not come in order. They will still be confusing as you encounter these little bits of yourself trying to become a part of you.

Whatever you are receiving in dreams, synchronicities, current conflicts that remind you of old wounds, or actual memories coming up is where you are supposed to be exploring, remembering, and integrating.

Don't be too ambitious and go on a blast-mining effort to open up every dark corner. Have faith that your body, soul, and spirit will gently lift into your consciousness the next bit of your tale you need to know, remember, and process.

## TODAY'S AFFIRMATION

I have the patience to let my story return in its own rhythm.

## TODAY'S JOURNAL PROMPT

When it comes to my story,
I tend to avoid/dig/wait for the next bit to surface…

REST
REVIEW
REFLECT

# *Worrying about their behavior is a distraction.*

I hear a lot of women talk about their life journeys. It is a bumpy and windy road for all of us. Sometimes it feels like we are going backward instead of forward, and it can be difficult to get used to the natural rhythms of life that sometimes feel like failure.

There aren't many things we can do wrong in our healing journey, but there are things that can slow us down. One that I see too often is a fixation on other people's behavior. This is a hidden addiction we use to avoid focusing on our own work. It is easier for me to talk about how my adult child won't make better decisions, or how my sister keeps going back to that bad relationship, or how my spouse refuses to take better care of himself.

All of these things might be true, but they aren't your problem to solve. It is okay to love people and want for them to do well, but it is not okay for us to spend too much of our emotional energy on their life stories.

Today, pay attention to who or what you get fixated on. Notice if you are using their life story as a distraction from engaging more deeply with your own. Pay attention to why it feels easier to think about them instead of yourself. Today, see if you can.

You will love the (sometimes painful!) growth this will bring you.

## TODAY'S AFFIRMATION
I am the subject of my own story.

## TODAY'S JOURNAL PROMPT
The person or thing I might be using to distract myself
from my own work is…

# DAY 121

## *Remember, you should feel that way.*

There are a few phrases that I wish I could strike from our collective communication. One of them, frequently declared, is, "Oh, but you shouldn't feel that way!"

This is often said out of kindness (e.g., you shouldn't feel guilty), but it is invariably a total silencing of the speaker trying to share her inner world. She *does* feel that way. Can we allow her feelings to be the case for a moment?

We often hear this negation when the listener is uncomfortable. She is switching to her need for this to stop and not remaining open to shared discomfort. The problem is that it stops the needed exploration. One person opened a door by expressing this, and the other person was trying to close it.

Whatever the feeling, I am here to tell you, "Yes, you should feel that way." Now, maybe as we explore more, we will discover that you are inappropriately projecting your anger, or that you are blaming others and not taking responsibility for your journey, or that you are struggling with perfectionism that is bringing up negative feelings about yourself.

Whatever the underlying story, right now, in this moment, *you do feel that way.* Our job is never to say, "You shouldn't feel that way." Our job is to say, "Tell me more? Where is this coming from?"

Whether to ourselves or to others, let's stop saying, "You shouldn't feel that way." Let's make a collective effort to let all of our ways of feeling our world be present.

Our world could use the feelings.

### TODAY'S AFFIRMATION
I let all feelings in me, and others be present.

### TODAY'S JOURNAL PROMPT
When I hear, "You shouldn't feel that way..." I feel...

## *Facing my truth today is easier than fearing my truth forever.*

So many women arrive at their work with complaints of fatigue and brain fog. When I hear how much their mind is going, it makes sense to me that they are worn out in both mind and body. Our unconscious efforts to avoid our pain exhaust us.

Are you tired? It may be that you are expending a lot of energy avoiding the stories that are trying to surface. Because the truth is, it is actually freeing and energizing when you face a hard truth.

There is no question that getting into your deep work is intimidating. None of us likes the encounter with the wounded or ugly sides of our experiences and ourselves. Many of us can spend decades avoiding going into this dark room.

But the avoidance isn't bringing you the ease that you imagine. You feel that avoiding this exploration is providing you with respite, but the reality is that you are locking yourself out of the room that is the locus of discovering yourself.

Yes, it is scary. Yes, it requires all of your courage. But the reality is that going into that scary space is much easier than spending years avoiding it. It is like the old junk drawer that annoyed you, that you refused to clear out, but that took less effort than you imagined and brought more comfort than you hoped when you finally dove into the task.

Today, pay attention to what you are avoiding and not engaging in. Remind yourself that you are using your precious energy to avoid the exploration that will ultimately enliven you. See if you can begin to imagine opening that door.

You will love the freedom and energy facing your own truth will bring you.

### TODAY'S AFFIRMATION

I have the courage to explore the parts that I've been avoiding.

### TODAY'S JOURNAL PROMPT

I might be avoiding...If I explored this, then...

# DAY 123

## *Grab the reins.*

In the oldest texts of Hindu scripture, there is a story that is probably one of our earliest metaphors for how we can take spiritual and psychological control of our being in the world–the chariot metaphor.

In this ancient story, you are conceptualized as a woman in a chariot. The horses are your senses, the reins are your mind, your driver is your intellect, and your self is the passenger. We can go deep into this ancient metaphor, but today I want to explore one aspect of it–taking control of your mind.

Are you in control of your thoughts? Or has your driver dropped the reins, letting your senses (the horses) drag you wherever they want to go? Not only are most of us being controlled by this out-of-control thinking but even worse, most of us aren't even making an effort to tell our driver to grab the reins. When you do, it is life-changing.

Instead of being dragged about by wild horses all day and night (sounds exhausting, right?), our intellect can take hold of the reins and direct our thoughts where we want them to go.

To get started, try to keep your mind focused on the task at hand. Don't let your mind wander to other thoughts. If you find this difficult, you might <u>practice silently narrating to yourself what you are currently doing</u> (this may sound ridiculous, but I promise, it is less ridiculous than what else would be going on in your mind).

As you begin this practice, you might be shocked to learn how quickly your mind wanders and returns to the same objects of hope and angst that are dragging you to exhaustion.

The more you do this, the more calm you will bring to the constant chaos and static of your thinking. You will feel more focused, less forgetful, and more energized.

You deserve the energy and focused attention this will bring you.

### TODAY'S AFFIRMATION
My intellect is in control of my thinking.

### TODAY'S JOURNAL PROMPT
When I think about my wandering mind, I notice…

# DAY 124

## *You are in relationship with everything.*

When asked about our most important relationships, we tend to think of the significant people in our lives. But, as you move into the latter decades of your life, it can be useful to explore your lifelong relationships with the cultural and institutional structures that have been on this path with you. If you are like most women, you've probably not given these formative relationships much thought.

What were the major institutional influences in your life? Religious institutions? School? Employers? What were your relationships with them like, and how did they change over the decades? How did your sense of yourself in the context of cultural views of gender, religion, race, or income impact your sense of self? You can explore different examples than the ones I've given, but please take a moment to explore.

Maybe you conformed and then rebelled against some structures. Maybe you rejected beliefs and then came back around. Or maybe you felt rejected and incorporated negative beliefs about yourself from the institutions or cultural norms that came into your life.

However you responded, it is important to remember that it wasn't just the people you interacted with that shaped your stories of self and agency in the world. We often explore the immediate personal relationships of our past but remain blind to the impacts of these larger structures.

Today, pay attention to your lifelong relationships with the big structures across the decades of your life. What did you learn about yourself in these relationships? How did that change over time? Were they healthy? Harmful? Something else?

You were shaped by more than just the people in your life.

You deserve the insight into your development this can bring you.

### TODAY'S AFFIRMATION

I pay attention to my relationships with everything.

### TODAY'S JOURNAL PROMPT

The institutional and cultural norms that have been present across my life are...
My relationships with them could be described as...

# DAY 125

## *Intention and disciplined practice are required.*

As we've lost the tradition of elder storytellers guiding our path into the wisdom years, we've lost touch with the intentional, practiced discipline necessary for the transition into this stage of life. Indigenous cultures had prescribed rituals for moving forward into the different seasons of a woman's life.

We, on the other hand, have advertisements for retrogressive age-defying makeup and pharmaceuticals. Instead of approaching our thresholds with the discipline and sanctity of old, we are promised quick fixes and easy cures. This lazy story is killing you.

The truth is that growing into your wisdom years requires intentionality and discipline. As you transform from a young woman into an older woman, you are forced to look at yourself more honestly. As the artifices of youth fall away, you are faced with your naked, true self.

Many women choose to escape this hard journey through distraction and addiction. If we do accept our life tasks, we are forced to reckon with our dark side, the mistakes we've made, the repressed parts of ourselves, the people we've hurt. This is the beginning of a hard journey that ends with a deeper sense of self-compassion and a much greater love for others.

This doesn't happen unless you make a valiant effort. Today, notice where you still have deep healing work to do. Promise yourself that you won't abandon your path in this season of life. Growing into old age requires discipline and practice. Do the work you were always meant to do.

You deserve the wisdom and contentment this will bring you.

### TODAY'S AFFIRMATION
I am disciplined and committed to my practices.

### TODAY'S JOURNAL PROMPT
When I think about my psychological and spiritual growth,
I imagine I need to...

# REST
# REVIEW
# REFLECT

## *No, you don't know.*

We have so many invisible blocks that keep us from moving into a different, healing space. One I see too often is when a woman will say something like, "I know too much about reality," in response to her experience with something difficult. Whether it is relationships with men or experiences with aging, illness, and dying, she believes that the conclusion she drew in some earlier moment is the final truth and entire story of that situation.

This woman is trapped in a static story. She lost connection with her healing, imaginative capacity in this area. It isn't the world but her failure to imagine any alternative that has become an obstacle to her opening up to different experiences, interpretations, and conclusions.

Today, notice where you hold rigid thoughts about something in life, love, or loss. I see this failed imaginative response most often with regard to illness and aging. Ask yourself if you know everything or if you might still have more to learn.

You deserve the growth.

### TODAY'S AFFIRMATION

I am open to imagining new possibilities.

### TODAY'S JOURNAL PROMPT

A static story I might still be holding onto might be.

# DAY 128

## *You are still discovering yourself.*

We have this weird developmental myth in our culture. A story that we should spend our young adult years 'finding ourselves' and our older years in some known-self state. In this mistaken myth, self-discovery is only a project of youth. Because of this, older women who show up in my office on a path of self-discovery feel foolish, saying to me, "Shouldn't I know myself by now?"

The truth is you are on a constant, dynamic journey of psychological and spiritual development. You never arrive at a static place of 'knowing yourself" but, instead, continue to walk a path of growing, gaining, and losing in your self-discovery.

When you forget this, your normal and healthy process of feeling lost feels like a failure. This misunderstanding not only causes unnecessary suffering but aborts the openness to the necessary growth into old age that awaits you.

You are discovering yourself as an older woman. You are still losing things and gaining things. You feel confused about things. You want to change things.

Today, pay attention to whether or not you think you 'should' know more about yourself and your path. See if you can let go of this mistaken story of static identity and embrace a more dynamic and developmental view of your journey.

You will love the openness and continued growth this will bring you.

### TODAY'S AFFIRMATION
It is good that I am still discovering myself.

### TODAY'S JOURNAL PROMPT
When I think about still 'discovering myself,'
I tend to think/feel...

## *Your growth is not linear.*

Our Western world is steeped in the masculine mindset of constant progress and growth. We live in a forward-looking, solution-seeking culture.

The problem is that this Western myth of perpetual progress doesn't match any of our lived experiences. We all know that we have setbacks and long periods of feeling like we've moved backward. All of our most ancient tales reflect this more complicated journey. A simple study of your natural world will tell you a story of growth, retreat, and growth again.

This more feminine spiral or circular journey is how we actually experience our life. This newer story of linear, progressive growth makes our natural way of feeling feel like an error.

Today, pay attention to how you feel about your own fallow periods–when your life feels more like the tide going out, the falling leaves, or our barren, wintry earth. Notice if you impose this myth of perpetual progress on yourself. Look outside at the natural world and see if you can embrace the more feminine, circular understanding of your own journey.

You will love the patience and flexibility this will bring you.

### TODAY'S AFFIRMATION

Like the tides going in and out,
I embrace the natural rhythms of my life.

### TODAY'S JOURNAL PROMPT

When I find myself in a fallow period, I tend to feel/think...

## *Start asking why you do it.*

Clients squander a lot of precious time in therapy sessions. One thing I wish I could magically make my clients stop doing is wasting time judging themselves for their behavior. This is completely nonproductive. As the therapist, my task is to get you out of that loop by moving you from judgment to curiosity. To better understand the unhelpful loop, I'll describe how it works:

1. You feel bad.

2. You engage in some undesirable behavior to get relief from feeling bad.

3. You judge yourself as bad because of your undesirable behavior.

4. You feel bad (return to the top).

See how this is a repetitive and unhelpful loop?

What I want you to do instead is to stop judging and get curious. Insert the very disruptive 'why' question into this cycle. You can add it anywhere:

1. Why do I feel bad?

2. Why do I engage in this undesirable behavior?

3. Why do I judge myself so harshly?

Keep inserting the disruptive 'why' question in response to your answers (for example., I feel bad because I think I was a bad mother; Why? Because I was drunk all the time, abusive, and my kids don't talk to me. Why? Because I didn't have the coping skills I needed; Why…?).

This exploration may seem painful at first, but bringing light to what is unconsciously driving you can ultimately bring you so much relief and self-compassion.

Today, pay attention to where you are judging yourself harshly. Recognize that this is a waste of your precious time. See if you can introduce the disruptive 'why' to break that cycle.

You deserve the insight and peace this will bring you.

### TODAY'S AFFIRMATION

I ask myself why I do things instead of judging myself.

### TODAY'S JOURNAL PROMPT

The patterns that bother me the most are…If I explored why…

## *You were meant to be a creator of beauty and desire, not an object of beauty and desire.*

The problem of women as 'objects' can feel like an old and confusing feminist rant. Many of us had a hard time understanding what that statement even meant. Or why it was a problem. What is wrong with wanting to be wanted? Isn't it okay to want to be desirable?

There is nothing wrong with wanting to be loved, but there is a problem when your goal is to construct yourself into a particular and superficial mold in order to win the prize of being desired by someone else. Instead of a wondrous inner journey of creative self-discovery, women end up in a desperate external search to discover what someone else thinks is valuable.

That journey leaves you empty. It also makes it hard to age, as our faces and bodies no longer look like that 'object' of desire. When we've conflated our values with the values of someone else, we eventually end up feeling worthless.

Today, pay attention to how much you are still steeped in the myth of women as objects (e.g., thinking you should be something that someone else values or wants). Imagine yourself letting go of those external traps and returning to the deeper voyage into your creative self.

You will love the inner world this will bring alive for you.

### TODAY'S AFFIRMATION
I am a creator, not an object.

### TODAY'S JOURNAL PROMPT
When I think about being loved by someone else,
I imagine I need to be…

*Healing doesn't move you back into what you were before. Healing moves you forward into what you must become.*

So often, when we have been terribly hurt or experienced an unbearable loss, our grief is laden with the despair that things will never be the same again. We can't believe we can ever heal because we know we can't put the broken pieces back the way they were.

This is a huge misunderstanding about healing. Healing is not a cure. You won't be restored by regressing into your former self. Healing allows you to grow into something new, something that includes the hardships and challenges you have lived through.

You might not like the story you are walking today, but you can only walk forward with what has happened so far. Don't dream of going backward.

Today, notice how you conceptualize your own healing and growth. Pay attention to whether or not you imagine yourself regressing to an earlier, known self or remaining open to moving into a new and unknown one.

You will love the healing and growth this can bring you.

## TODAY'S AFFIRMATION

My healed self is not my old self.

## TODAY'S JOURNAL PROMPT

When I think about moving forward into who I will become…

# DAY 133

# REST
# REVIEW
# REFLECT

## *Young women seek romance.*
## *Wise women seek transcendence.*

As a younger woman, the stories you read and saw probably matched up with the challenges you were facing. Maybe you wanted a romantic partner, professional success, a happy family, or all of the above. You could turn on the TV or walk into a bookstore and find lots of popular narratives for sale that mirrored your journey.

You probably had less interest in ancient literature with its confusing parables and myths. In these narratives that sustained humanity for millennia, stories are filled with complicated old women–the crone, the hag, the fairy godmother. These enigmatic old women are the wisdom keepers, holding onto something magical and/or threatening. She isn't seeking a prince but appears to be a threshold character pointing to someplace beyond.

These wisdom women are often embedded with nature–talking with fairies, meeting with witches and goblins. She is a boundary transgressor with one step in this world and one step out. As an old woman, she is no longer interested in the tasks of the young woman.

These lost stories are telling your tales. Your job now is to go deeper. To let go of the pursuits of a younger woman. To take the brokenness and use it to connect to the transcendent relationship that will fulfill you in a way that no superficial gain of your youth ever could.

Today, pay attention to how you have grown from the young woman who wanted a house, a job, and a partner. Notice the internal shifts that long for something more. Reach into the sacred and secular literature and reconnect with these lost, wise old women.

You will find your story and retell the ancient story of all of us. You've earned it.

### TODAY'S AFFIRMATION
I walk the ancient and sacred path of growing old.

### TODAY'S JOURNAL PROMPT
When I think of these old women in fairytales and what they represent to me…

# DAY 135

## *Vulnerability cultivates compassion.*
## *Be vulnerable.*

We hear so much about how we should be more compassionate with others and with ourselves. But we so rarely talk about the companion to compassion, vulnerability.

If you've ever felt a pang of unexpected compassion for someone, odds are you unexpectedly witnessed their vulnerability. We can be exploited this way with commercials that include puppy dogs and babies, but we can also use our awareness of vulnerability to cultivate compassion in ourselves and others.

If you've ever had to caretake for someone who wasn't kind, you may have experienced that rare and unexpected moment of feeling compassion for someone who hasn't always been very nice. When you really see them in their total vulnerability, your resentments and rage can ebb away as compassion sneaks in. When you are struggling to feel compassion for someone, it can help us to try to see their vulnerability.

We can also build compassion by showing our vulnerability. I know you have probably needed to stay strong to endure your challenges, but I'd like to remind you that revealing your own vulnerability can open up that reciprocal connection with someone else.

Today, notice your relationship with vulnerability–in others and in yourself. See if you can make space for it to be more present and open us all up to a more compassionate world.

You deserve the compassion.

### TODAY'S AFFIRMATION
Our vulnerability opens up our compassion.

### TODAY'S JOURNAL PROMPT
My experience with feeling unexpected compassion was when...

# DAY 136

## *You can't have a better past. You can have a better present. Stay in this moment.*

What happened to you then is not happening to you now. Maybe you weren't safe then; you are safer now. Maybe you weren't protected then; you can protect yourself now. Maybe you weren't validated then; you can learn to validate yourself now.

If you are like most women in the latter decades of their lives, hard things have happened to you. It is very normal to wish that they did not. And to grieve that they did.

But you cannot change the suffering that you experienced in the past or how you reacted to it. You can change how you experience your present-moment, no matter what choices you made then.

Today (unless you are reprocessing events in an intentionally therapeutic way), don't let your mind float back into non-productive ruminations. Stay present with what you feel today. Stay present with what you know today. Stay present with what is happening today.

Whether you find the present-moment pleasant or unpleasant, it is always easier than being stuck in a difficult past one.

You deserve the present-moment peace this will bring you.

**Note:** If you are not able to stay present, your old stories are surfacing, and it might be time to consider processing those old experiences in an intentionally therapeutic way.

### TODAY'S AFFIRMATION
I am not stuck in the past; I am centered in the present.

### TODAY'S JOURNAL PROMPT
Some of the old stories/experiences that still hang around for me are...

# DAY 137

## *It's easier to admire greatness in others than to risk finding that greatness in yourself.*

When you think of things you suppress, you probably think first about things that hurt you or that you feel ashamed of. But, as a therapist, I see a much more pervasive problem with the things we push down. Women suppress their gifts and their dreams.

Jungian Analyst Marie-Louise von Franz warns us that when women don't live out their potential, they become increasingly miserable and difficult. She explains that this suppressed creative energy floats around and attaches to the wrong things (e.g., romance, professional conflict, etc.). With this misplaced energy, she will get worked up over minutia and meaningless events. Does this sound familiar?

As a therapist, I also see that my clients prefer to admire someone else rather than recognize their own gifts. It's easier to project these admirable qualities onto another, but hard to believe they are possible for ourselves.

Today, pay attention to who you admire. Ask yourself, "What is it in me that connects with her? What parts of her are actually within me?" Imagine living out what you see in her. Remember, this is a fantasy exercise. Don't be practical. Be bold. Be wild.

Meditate on that fantasy. Journal about it. See what happens.

You deserve the connection with self this will bring you.

### TODAY'S AFFIRMATION
The things I admire in others are within me.

### TODAY'S JOURNAL PROMPT
The people I admire most are…
I connect with them because…

# DAY 138

## *Self-care isn't indulging in superficial distractions. Learn how to truly care for yourself.*

I hear it so often from women, "I drank too much because I felt like I deserved a reward," or "I did some retail therapy and felt better," or "I just scrolled on my phone to give myself a break."

Yes, these things might make you feel better temporarily, but they aren't the same as self-care. Self-care is a critical practice to implement when we are dealing with big challenges. In fact, when you are overwhelmed with life's demands, the only way to survive is to effectively practice self-care.

So, what does real self-care look like? Self-care is something that cultivates and nurtures your deepest self. It might be engaging in a creative project, like getting the sewing machine back out and working on that quilt. It might be studying a new topic that excites you. It might be taking a nature walk when you have twenty minutes to spare. It might be finding time to meditate or pray.

Creative and constructive activities will restore you in ways that drinking, shopping, or browsing online will not. When you come back to the challenges of your daily life after these indulgences, you haven't been restored. You have merely distracted yourself for a wasted precious moment.

When you engage in real self-care, you build up a sustainable practice for getting through hard times. When we are in the midst of our hardest challenges, these nurturing practices are non-negotiable.

Today, pay attention to whether or not you are indulging in superficial distractions or practicing real self-care.

You deserve the resilience that better self-care practices will bring you.

## TODAY'S AFFIRMATION

Today, I will engage in truly restorative self-care.

## TODAY'S JOURNAL PROMPT

What I tend to do when I need a break is...
A better practice might be...

# DAY 139

## *Are some feelings good?*
## *Are some feelings bad?*

You remember that our goal is not to get rid of difficult feelings. Intense feelings come with our intense experiences. You know your goal is to allow yourself to feel everything, to stay emotionally engaged in your life, and not be driven to act out by intense emotions.

What I'd like for you to notice now is whether or not you are still categorizing some emotions as 'good' emotions (generosity, compassion) and other emotions as 'bad' emotions (selfishness, envy). What if you imagined that they have no inherent value but that all are equally okay?

When we allow ourselves to notice that we feel selfish, envious, or vengeful, we open the first door to our more complicated inner stories. "I feel envious that her kids are doing so well" is a much more productive exploration than trying to pretend that this is not present for us. We learn to observe our feeling state with curiosity and compassion. We pause, reflect, feel, and take responsibility for our choices and behavior.

Today, notice your feelings about your feelings. Pay attention to whether or not you consider some 'good' and others 'bad.' See if you can expand your acceptance of all the ways we emotionally respond to our experiences and our world.

You will love how feeling your way through your life will enrich all of your experiences.

### TODAY'S AFFIRMATION
I accept all of my feelings without negative judgments.

### TODAY'S JOURNAL PROMPT
The emotions that I have the hardest time with are…
This is probably because…

# REST
# REVIEW
# REFLECT

# *She deserves more compassion.*

Are you having a hard time being kind to yourself? Or showing compassion for the younger you that made so many mistakes in her naivete and overwhelm? I am going to teach you a therapeutic trick to help you.

You've heard that writing or journaling can help you process, but I am going to tweak that just a bit. Instead of writing in the first person (that means writing with "I"), try writing about yourself in the third person (that means writing yourself as "she").

I know this sounds like something out of satire, but the research shows this is actually an unexpectedly powerful tool. When you write in the first person, you are harder on yourself. When you write in the third person, you move into a space of observing self and invariably find more insight and compassion for your subject.

Please try this. Today, if you have some aspect of your life or history that you are still struggling with, try writing in your journal about this experience in the third person (using the subject "she" instead of "I). Notice how this changes your engagement with your own story.

You deserve the wisdom and compassion.

## TODAY'S AFFIRMATION

I can approach my story from many perspectives
to gain insight and compassion.

## TODAY'S JOURNAL PROMPT

A story I might want to explore in the third person would probably be...

# DAY 142

## *Know the difference between chronic pain and unnecessary suffering.*

Getting older includes an increasing variety of aches and pains for most of us. As pain becomes our new companion, it is important for us to remember the difference between the pain that we can't stop and the extra suffering that we can.

In their book, *You Are Not Your Pain*, authors Vidyamala Burch and Danny Penman share their own stories of dealing with chronic pain. They provide eight weeks of mindfulness training that has proven to be as effective as prescription painkillers for dealing with chronic pain.

I can't summarize their eight weeks of exercises here, but I can share one of their key premises about coping with pain. Burch and Penman remind us that there is a difference between the immediate pain we feel and the extreme suffering we cause ourselves. Basically, this is the difference between the immediate physical event and the story we tell ourselves about that event.

This involves our neurobiology, and I've seen it countless times in my clients. Something painful happens, and her brain suddenly wakes up a huge series of catastrophic memories. Often these are embodied memories, not actually things she can say or remember.

What I see is her whole body in alarm as she lights up all these old pathways associated with pain, danger, and suffering. Then she starts to tell herself a story to fit this physical response, which amps up her anxiety and feeling that she can't tolerate this.

Mindfulness doesn't stop the original pain, but it stops this entire mess that follows. What I see in my practice is that most of the suffering comes from the latter.

Today, pay attention to the space between pain and suffering. We usually can't see or feel our body light up, but mindfulness will grow this capacity.

You deserve the respite.

### TODAY'S AFFIRMATION

I know and feel the difference between immediate pain
and amplified suffering.

### TODAY'S JOURNAL PROMPT

I do/do not have fears associated with being in pain.
If I practice mindfulness, I might…

# DAY 143

## *Shame isn't always a bad thing.*

Training for therapists often includes discussions about the problem of shame in our clients. I remember sitting in some trainings and thinking, "Yes, but this is not exactly right."

Shame has been redefined over the last few decades. In the beautiful panoply of feelings we can have over the course of our lifetimes, this one has been relegated to the heap of 'bad' feelings that we need to get rid of.

The problem is not with shame; the problem is with our redefinition of shame. Shame has been described as a negative interpretation of our self-worth. Of course, a negative interpretation of our self-worth is a 'bad' thing, but we are losing something important when we redefine the (sometimes transient) feeling of shame.

For those of us who lived selfishly and unconsciously in ways that hurt other people, being able to feel our shame about our hurtful behavior is part of our healing response.

When I am selfish or mean, it is my feeling of shame that is communicating that I am out of line, that I care about how I impact other people. When I feel authentic shame, I wonder if I need to apologize for being selfish or uncaring to someone else.

So, feeling like we are an inherently shameful person (poor self-esteem) is a good thing to overcome. But shame, like all of our feelings, is a necessary part of our complicated repertoire of knowing ourselves and loving others.

Today, pay attention to where you fall on this spectrum of shame. When shame rises up, pay attention to what she might be trying to communicate. Is it a feeling of total unworthiness? This is not helpful. Is it a feeling that my behavior needs correction? Then listen to your shame. Remember, we are not trying to shut up the painful parts of ourselves we don't like. We are learning to listen to our whole story.

You deserve the wise guidance that comes from engaging with all of your feeling responses.

### TODAY'S AFFIRMATION

I listen to all of my feelings.

### TODAY'S JOURNAL PROMPT

My belief about shame is…

# DAY 144

## *Let them have their reality.*

As a therapist, I see women walk through so many different types of hard things. But for all the challenges we face that are different, most of the coping skills we need to develop are the same.

A frequent one that comes up is the challenge a woman faces when she is viewed negatively by people she cares about. It may be her children, her partner, or even public opinion. She comes into session fretting about how to deal with this 'impossible' situation of being seen as the 'bad' woman.

This is a big opportunity for growth as nothing will force you to get real with yourself as an attack like this from the outside. In these moments, we are forced to accept that others think we are awful or weird. We are forced to learn how to be okay with ourselves in the face of brutal and aggressive critique. We are forced to learn self-forgiveness when others won't afford us that compassion.

Today, pay attention to how you feel when someone thinks or speaks poorly of you. Notice if you panic and/or scramble to change them or defend yourself. See if you can learn to settle into yourself instead, letting them have their reality and remaining comfortable in your own skin.

You will love the centered peace this will bring you.

### TODAY'S AFFIRMATION

I accept myself, even when others do not.

### TODAY'S JOURNAL PROMPT

When I am criticized, I...

# DAY 145

## *Pretend that what you see is a symbolic message. Play with meaning.*

We all get stuck in our rigid stories and interpretations of our world, so I'd like to offer you a fun, playful experiment.

Today, pretend like your experiences in the world are symbolic communications (if you are struggling with psychosis or keeping a grip on our shared reality, maybe you don't need this exercise).

I am not making the claim that these are symbolic messages. I am not making the claim that we are correctly interpreting potential symbolic messages. What I am doing is attempting to break apart our sometimes rigid ways of making sense of our world. I want to randomly open up some doors to see if we can get you feeling and thinking about yourself and your world in new ways. We are trying to get into relationship with your imagination.

Today, play with this. Have fun. See what you can find when you step into a magical and symbolic way of knowing.

You deserve new ways of knowing.

### TODAY'S AFFIRMATION

I am open to more ways of knowing than just logical meanings.

### TODAY'S JOURNAL PROMPT

Imagining multiple meanings to everything feels...

## *Don't confuse not having expectations with not having healthy boundaries.*

Words sometimes fail us. Words are also misused to manipulate and abuse. One that I've seen too frequently is a client coming in saying a new partner believes she should move into a more intimate relationship with (a presumably spiritual-sounding goal) of 'no expectations.'

The fact that I've heard this more than a few times is alarming but not entirely surprising (when forgiveness was a hot topic, the language of forgiveness was also used to excuse unhealthy behavior).

This is a misuse of a spiritual concept. Here is how to understand the difference:

When you set the spiritual goal of not having expectations, you do your work in the world without an unhealthy attachment to outcomes. For example, you write a book, but you aren't attached to how well it is received.

But this spiritual goal doesn't really translate into newly forming intimate relationships. When you are making choices about increasing psychological intimacy, you must assess feelings of safety in that relationship. That requires a comparison of what you are seeking in relationship with what is happening–a healthy expectation.

When we choose to set a goal of no expectations in a relationship, this usually means we are accepting a difficult person as they are. This can be necessary in long-term committed relationships where we aren't going to make a change (in this case, you are accepting what is and not attempting to get something from that relationship that you already know you can't get).

If someone is suggesting this as a goal at the beginning of a relationship, keep the conversation going to better understand what potential limit (or 'expectation') is scaring them.

You have a right to expect safe and intimate relationships.

### TODAY'S AFFIRMATION

I understand the difference between relationships in which I expect safety and intimacy and relationships where I have no expectations.

### TODAY'S JOURNAL PROMPT

My understanding of 'no expectations' is…

# DAY 147

# REST
# REVIEW
# REFLECT

*You are not shaped by what happened to you.*
*You are shaped by the story you tell yourself*
*about what happened to you.*

If you've made it to the last decades of your life, you've seen a lot. You've survived a lot. As a therapist, I've sat with hard stories and witnessed the amazing healing that can occur when we process them together.

One of the biggest changes I see when a woman experiences healing is how she tells the story of her life. Instead of feeling trapped and hopeless in a chaotic and frightening surge of emotions (or shut down), she is able to reflect on events with a manageable distance. Instead of being overwhelmed by them in the present, she recognizes they are in the past. She says things like, "It's still a sad story, but it is over now, and I survived it."

When we process the hard things that happen to us, we feel and tell a different story. It isn't that we erase the past. It isn't always that we are okay with the past. It is that we can now live with our past in *peace.*

Today, remember that the way you feel about the hardest parts of your story can still change. You won't change what happened, but you will change how you feel in the present-moment about what happened in your past.

You deserve the present-moment peace.

### TODAY'S AFFIRMATION
My way of telling my story will change as I heal.

### TODAY'S JOURNAL PROMPT
When I think about my life story, I feel...

# DAY 149

## *Don't wait for permission. It isn't coming.*

There are so many reasons we don't do the things we dream of doing. But one unconscious one that can impede our progress often slips by unnoticed. On some level, you might be stuck because you imagine that someone or something outside of you needs to tell you you can do it. This isn't something you would usually be explicitly aware of; it typically is blocking you without you even knowing it.

Your imaginary block might be from a specific person–your child or your spouse. It might even be a deceased person–a parent or grandparent. It might be your church, local community, or some other institutional club. Whatever it is, your job is to bring to consciousness who or what you are imagining holds the keys for you to move forward.

We are so embedded in our relationships that it makes sense we have this expectation that someone else is going to tell us when it is time to open our door. The problem is that they aren't going to.

Like every girl in every fairytale who has to find the key and unlock the secret room, this is a task that only you can do.

Today, think about the things you still dream of doing. Ask yourself if you are still imagining that someone or something else needs to give you the push. Realize that this permission slip won't come from them but from you.

You will love the empowerment this will bring you.

### TODAY'S AFFIRMATION
I give myself permission.

### TODAY'S JOURNAL PROMPT
The individuals or institutions that I might be imagining don't approve of my dreams are…

# DAY 150

## *You were never responsible for what they did to you.*

As a women's therapist, I sometimes think that every woman has the same secret. And every woman thinks she is the only one with this secret. I'm going to tell you what I believe this 'universal secret' is.

Something awful happened to you—a terrible violation. But you secretly believe you are at least partly responsible. Maybe you think this because you sought out the relationship when you were too young to understand what was going on. Maybe you think you are responsible because you were intoxicated. Maybe you blame yourself because you wanted attention and got into a dangerous situation. Maybe you think you were responsible for some other reason.

What you need to know: This false sense of responsibility is a normal response to trauma. When something terrorizing happens to us, we re-conceptualize the experience in a way that makes us have some responsibility. This gives an illusion of having some control over this awful experience. Believing we have some bit of control is psychologically soothing.

It can take a long time in therapy for a woman to admit her belief. She will often offer up evidence or examples to prove to me that she was partly responsible for what happened to her. I have to walk her through the experience, imagining it happening to another girl or woman she cares about. I ask her, "Even if she did all those things, would you think she was responsible for what happened to her?"

If you do relate to this universal secret and a false sense of responsibility, walk yourself through that exercise. Imagine how you would feel if the story involved your daughter, niece, or another girl or woman you know. See if you can find some of the protective compassion you easily can have for her, for yourself.

You deserve the healing this realization can bring to you.

## TODAY'S AFFIRMATION

I am not responsible for the actions of others who hurt me.

## TODAY'S JOURNAL PROMPT

With regard to my wounds, I feel responsible for…

# DAY 151

## *Your projects are valuable because you find them valuable.*

At some point in your long life, the materialist and celebrity stories of the West probably left you feeling very confused. When you come of age in a culture that publishes annual lists of the richest and most beautiful people, it's understandable that you might equate finding your value with achieving these kinds of external goals.

But a person with true self-worth is actually less likely to make these lists because she is not so interested in acquisition or accolades. This woman is probably not going to show up anywhere on your media radar because she is likely living a very ordinary, simple, and meaningful life.

The truth is, the projects that make these big lists are often driven by the powerful energy of being afraid–a driving fear of our failures and our flaws.

I am not saying you must forfeit any kind of success to prove you find your own value. It is okay to pursue the dreams and goals that excite you. It is okay to enjoy sharing your projects and products with your community and having success with them. Just don't confuse the pleasure of sharing your work with the mistaken idea that *their evaluation of your work is the necessary ingredient for your self-worth* (remember, work here can mean any activity–cooking, caretaking, painting, singing, etc.).

Today, pay attention to whether you are able to enjoy your activities and creations because of your own sense of value coming from them or if you mistakenly think the external acknowledgment of your project needs to get you there.

You will love the simplicity and creative energy this brings you.

### TODAY'S AFFIRMATION

My creations and contributions are valuable because
I find them valuable.

### TODAY'S JOURNAL PROMPT

When I think about my projects, I feel…

## *Eros is healing you.*

You've been exploring your stories and how you can heal in the creative spaces in between. Today I'd like for you to reflect on your source of internal creative healing.

The most popular healing modalities in the West are built upon cognitive behavioral therapies (CBT)–the basic premise of CBT is that if you can change your thoughts, you can change your feelings. CBT practices are part of all of our healing journeys. Most of us have to change some of our repetitive thoughts. But working on our cognitions is the logos-centered, masculine dimension of your healing practice. I'd like to make a case for the transrational healing power of your feminine aspect–eros.

Eros is the root word for erotic. Sadly denigrated in our world as superficial sexual desire, eros is actually the entire embodied, creative, and affective energies that flow through you. It's the transrational feeling you feel when you hold your grandchild. It's the creative flow you feel when writing poetry. It's your gut feeling that has no rational basis. Eros is what makes your body want to sing or move when you hear music.

Eros is also the creative, desiring force that fills in the spaces between–between you and our stories, between you and others, and between you and your world. What is elicited from you, creatively, when you are called into a relationship with a story, person, or our world goes beyond reason–this is eros at work. She is not subject to logic and reason. She is her own force, creatively telling and retelling your stories.

Today, pay attention to your relationship to this healing resource–your affective, trans-rational desirous energies. You deserve the healing she is bringing you.

### TODAY'S AFFIRMATION
Healing eros flows through me.

### TODAY'S JOURNAL PROMPT
When I imagine eros energy flowing through me, I...

# DAY 153

## *Keep trying. There is dignity and meaning in refusing to give up.*

Do you know what philosophers understand about the meaning of life? That meaning is the meaning of life. Your job is to find your meaning. When life (or suffering) feels meaningless, we can want to give up. But when we experience our burdens in the context of a larger purpose, we can endure almost anything.

Meaning is a keystone to your resilience.

When life gets really hard for you, you won't be able to see a point in the suffering. But, when you are trapped in that experience, see if you can find meaning in the assertion that you aren't going to be a quitter. See if you can find meaning in the fact that you feel good about your choices (to caretake, provide, endure, etc.), despite finding the challenges of your day-to-day existence almost unbearable.

We often talk about the purpose of suffering after the fact. But we need to know how to endure suffering when it is our day-to-day life. Today, pay attention to what you believe about suffering. Pay attention to your larger context of meaning. See if you can find a space in which those two intersect.

You need the resilience this will bring to you.

### TODAY'S AFFIRMATION

I can find meaning in…, despite the difficulty.

### TODAY'S JOURNAL PROMPT

My belief about suffering is…
My belief about living with suffering is…

# REST
# REVIEW
# REFLECT

# *Find a safe space.*
# *Imagine going there every day.*

Do you have a favorite place? A space where you feel most connected to your self or Spirit? Maybe this is a place you haven't been to in years or decades. Maybe it is a place that no longer exists (or never existed).

When I am doing trauma work with a woman, our first step is to find a place where she feels safe and comfortable. The place can be real or imaginary. Over the course of our work together, we will return to this place (in her imagination) to bring her more comfort. The impact is real. Using this imagined space, a woman can pull herself out of trauma memories and return to this safe and peaceful place. She feels comforted and calm.

Most women can't literally go to the place that feels safe, so I encourage you to find this place in your imagination (remember, the location can be real or imaginary).

Your exercise is to think of a place where you feel more peace and comfort. Describe that place using all your senses (I'd encourage you to say it aloud, as hearing your voice describe the space deepens the experience). What do you see? Hear? Smell? Sense (temperature, etc.)? After you've reflected on all that sensory data, pay attention to what you feel in your body physically (e.g., calmer, more peaceful, etc.), and describe that as well.

Enjoy that space for one minute each day. Or whenever you are feeling stressed or overwhelmed.

I encourage you to try this. It will bring you the peace and comfort you deserve.

**Note:** For women with trauma, it is very normal for a safe space to become "contaminated" with something that ruins the place. If that happens, start over with a totally new place that has some protection from whatever negative imagery that came in.

## TODAY'S AFFIRMATION
I can always go to my peaceful and safe space.

## TODAY'S JOURNAL PROMPT
If I imagined a place where I felt completely peaceful and safe,
it would be...

*Dangerous people taught you to
ignore intuitions about dangerous people.
Remember how to listen to yourself.*

Women often lament that they end up in the same types of relationships. She may be frustrated that so many people in her life seem to take advantage of her. She wonders if any of her friends really care about her despite all she has done for them.

I see this way too often. She may (or may not) have a lot of acquaintances, but she doesn't have one safe, intimate relationship where she feels safe and connected.

As is typical, this woman usually blames herself, saying, "Well, I must be the problem, right?"

What I explain to this woman is that we learn how to be in a relationship in our earliest relationships. When those were too hurtful or toxic, you learned how to shut down your warning flags.

You couldn't live with a warning flag about a primary caregiver upon whom you were totally dependent. So you learn, bit by bit, to ignore your intuition about violating or hurtful behavior. Having effectively silenced this protective inner voice, you were easily lured into later relationships that are similarly hurtful.

Today, pay attention to the patterns in your relationships that aren't working for you. Reflect back on your earlier experiences and see if you can connect your current patterns with those from before. Bring more awareness to what you learned to shut down as a child as you make an effort to bring it back to life.

You will love the healthy, intuitive boundaries this can bring you.

## TODAY'S AFFIRMATION
I pay attention to my inner voice.

## TODAY'S JOURNAL PROMPT
I may have stopped hearing myself because…

*How you breathe is how you live.*
*Breathe Deeply.*

How are you breathing right now? Deep? Shallow? You've heard the expression before, "Take a deep breath,' but I wonder if you know that there is new science to support this old advice.

So many of us are living in a constant state of low-grade anxiety. Whether it is caused by real-life stressors or media-induced fears, being in this mildly anxious state raises your heart rate, your adrenaline, and your cortisol. These are physical responses to mental stressors that are taking a real toll on your mind and your body.

The good news is that you already have a free and easy way to overcome this response. Breathing deeply.

Taking deep breaths actually shuts down this physiological stress response. It has a measurable impact on heart rate, adrenaline, and cortisol. It inhibits inflammation and improves your short-term memory.

You can actually practice breathing as a preventative measure, so don't wait until you are stressed out. Today, try to find one or two minutes to take some deep breaths. Notice how you feel afterward. Do this daily.

You deserve the physical and mental comfort this will bring you.

### TODAY'S AFFIRMATION
I breathe deeply.

### TODAY'S JOURNAL PROMPT
When I notice my breath, I notice that...

# DAY 158

*A young woman discovers how to be the best.
A wise woman discovers there is no such thing.*

Young women want to do everything well. Remember that girl? You see these young women who haven't yet fallen down to that space where they get back up, different. She is still focused on winning. She lives in a world of better and worse, and she knows where she wants to land.

You, on the other hand, have lived long enough to see the envied girl face tragedy and the outcast girl gain success. As you grew old, you discovered that the things you feared never happened. The things that happened, you never feared. It all becomes ironic and funny at some point, bringing to mind our contented, laughing Buddha.

There is a natural relinquishment of control and expectations that comes with walking through these hard and humbling experiences.

We all have the goal of growing into our wisdom years, but today I want you to pay attention to how much progress you have already made.

You are no longer caught by all the superficial projects and frenetic pace of that young girl. You are growing old.

You've earned this peace, wise woman.

## TODAY'S AFFIRMATION
I see how much I have grown.

## TODAY'S JOURNAL PROMPT
I am different from my younger self in that now I can…
(reflect on growth, not regrets)

# DAY 159

## *Let it all come crashing down. You will be okay. They will be okay.*

We can get so obsessed with our tasks that we stress ourselves out and make ourselves sick. Lost in the minutia of our world, we start to believe that we must keep up with our to-do list or there will be some catastrophe.

This delusion of our importance is our narcissism at work. I am not suggesting you be irresponsible with your obligations. I am suggesting you lighten up on yourself and the belief that you have to get everything done or else. Let go of the false urgency and self-criticism. You can pay a bill late. You can leave the house a mess. You can forget to water the plants.

The truth is, as we age, we simply get to a point where we can't keep up. So, this letting go will happen for all of us, intentionally or not.

Today, take a bigger picture view of the obligations that are stressing you out. See if you can take a gentler perspective and give yourself a bit of respite from the stress and pressure.

You will love the peace of mind this will bring you.

### TODAY'S AFFIRMATION
I don't need to keep up with everything.

### TODAY'S JOURNAL PROMPT
When I imagine allowing things to fall apart or not get done, I feel...

# DAY 160

## *You can't change the world. You can change the way you experience the world.*

When life gets really hard, we can wonder, "How can I ever be content when these things are going on?"

"My only child hates me."

"I'm caring for my younger sister with Alzheimer's."

"I've just been hurt too much in the past to ever trust the future."

You can't change the world. But you can change how you experience the world. I'm not making this up. Research proves it. You do this by changing what you are thinking about the situation. This is Cognitive Behavioral Therapy (CBT). When you change what you think, you can change how you feel.

Here is how to do it:

Your first step is to identify the thought that is causing the feeling. Any time you are feeling uncomfortable, angry, hurt, or any negative emotion, try to identify the thought that preceded your feeling.

For example, "I can't endure this anymore!" or "My child should be nicer to me."

Now, construct an opposite statement, even if it seems impossible. For example, "I have endured this, and I can endure this," or "I can be okay even if my child is cruel toward me."

Force yourself to digest that (impossible!) thought. Pay attention to how you feel when you say it to yourself. Pay attention to how you feel when you imagine it to be true.

You've just gotten an insight into how to walk through a suffering world with greater peace.

Keep practicing. You deserve it.

### TODAY'S AFFIRMATION
I can change the stories I tell myself.

### TODAY'S JOURNAL PROMPT
I probably need to change my imagining about…

REST
REVIEW
REFLECT

## *You are not trying to improve yourself.*

Women in the West are always working to improve themselves. It sounds like a good thing, right? What feels like such a normal way of being for you is actually a very new phenomenon. The first self-help book was published in the nineteenth century (aptly titled, *Self-Help*), but the explosion of the genre from a small niche to mainstream has been in the last fifty years–basically, your entire adult life.

This growing interest in how to improve our (presumably deficient) selves parallels the growth of for-profit storytelling. We've lost our wise woman storytellers and their folk wisdom that comforted us.

I'd like for you to push back against the stories of this for-profit, youth-celebrating marketing blitz. Imagine the wise elder of an ancient tribe. Isn't it ridiculous to imagine her seeking some popular text on how to improve herself? It is just as ridiculous for you. You are learning to know your deepest self. That you are absolutely okay. There is nothing about you that needs improvement.

You can read about spirituality, nutrition, or exercise as they nourish you, but for today, I'd like for you to remember that your biggest goal is to know that you are exactly correct as you are in this moment. You don't need any self-help book to tell you how to do that.

You are doing a great job.

### TODAY'S AFFIRMATION

I don't need to improve myself.

### TODAY'S JOURNAL PROMPT

When I think about self-help or improvement
and my spiritual beliefs, I...

# DAY 163

## *Talk with your inner critic.*

Is it hard to be kind to yourself? Have you tried to shut that mean voice up without success? Maybe it isn't the mean voice that is the problem, but our method of dealing with it so far.

Let's try a new approach. Instead of trying to get your mean voice to be quiet, try a kinder approach. Let's listen to what she might want to say.

Ask yourself, "Why can't I be kinder to myself?" Use some creative methods for exploring your answer (writing, painting, etc.). Allow yourself to listen to the part of yourself that is struggling with being nice to you. Be kind to this critical voice. Listen to her. See where she is coming from and if she can go beyond the constant, superficial critiques and tell you more about why she is doing this. See if this process allows you more progress than the unproductive battle of trying to get her to just shut up.

You might discover she is trying to protect you because she has learned that risk or relationships are dangerous. You might discover she fears success. You might find an old voice that is envious or in competition with you. You might find something else. Your task is to listen and learn.

Remember, the goal of these OMMs is to bring you into a relationship with yourself, not to silence the parts you don't like. The conversation with this critical part of yourself might be challenging, but I know the process of listening rather than avoiding it will bring you more insight.

You deserve the self-compassion these hard conversations can bring to you.

### TODAY'S AFFIRMATION

I can be in a relationship with my whole self,
even the parts of myself that I don't like.

### TODAY'S JOURNAL PROMPT

If I were to engage in a relationship with this critical voice,
to go beyond the superficial criticisms, I might discover…

# DAY 164

## *Virginia Woolf's Angel.*

In 1931, writer Virginia Woolf gave a speech titled "Professions for Women" to the National Society for Women's Service (it wasn't published until after her death). In this essay, Woolf describes how she was tormented by the presence of and eventually had to kill off this pious, self-sacrificing construct.

*I discovered that if I were going to review books I should need to do battle with a certain phantom…It was she who bothered me and wasted my time and so tormented me that at last I killed her…She was intensely sympathetic. She was immensely charming. She was utterly unselfish. She excelled in the difficult arts of family life. She sacrificed herself daily. If there was chicken, she took the leg; if there was a draught she sat in it—in short she was so constituted that she never had a mind or a wish of her own, but preferred to sympathize always with the minds and wishes of others. Above all—I need not say it—she was pure… And when I came to write I encountered her with the very first words. The shadow of her wings fell on my page; I heard the rustling of her skirts in the room…She slipped behind me and whispered: "My dear, you are a young woman. You are writing about a book that has been written by a man. Be sympathetic; be tender; flatter; deceive; use all the arts and wiles of our sex. Never let anybody guess that you have a mind of your own. Above all, be pure.*

Meeting, knowing, and letting go of this false angel was part of finding her voice and vocation as a writer. Woolf suggested that the younger generation might not understand what she means, but I believe you do.

Today, remember how hard Woolf had to work to meet, know and say goodbye to this angel to become who she needed to be. Is there something in your psyche that needs to leave so that another part of you can speak?

### TODAY'S AFFIRMATION

I let parts of me go so that other parts can grow.

### TODAY'S JOURNAL PROMPT

A phantom I might need to do battle with would be…

## *"Good" girls have a harder time.*

As young women, we work so hard to discover what the world wants of us. Because of this, we are heavily impacted by the personality and psychology of the people who raised us and/or the persons we partnered with. That may have gone well or poorly for you, but in the last half of your life, those outside voices don't matter anymore.

Because, in the latter seasons of life, we all have the same task. Whether we were praised or blamed before, we all have to stop paying attention to what the outside world thinks of us.

This path is hard for both women, but I will tell you, it is sometimes easier for the woman who was scapegoated because she had to learn how to get okay with herself in a world that wouldn't validate her. The woman who might struggle more here is the woman who always did everything right because disappointing the people she loves is something she hasn't had enough practice with.

Today, reflect on your history of being the good girl or the bad girl. Notice how your history is impacting your ability to cultivate the courage you need to have today.

You will love the relationship with self this will bring you.

### TODAY'S AFFIRMATION
I am still okay if they disapprove.

### TODAY'S JOURNAL PROMPT
I was accepted/rejected by others...
This impacted me in that...Now I must...

*Maybe women don't need assertiveness training.*
*Maybe the world needs more cooperativeness training.*

Have you ever been told that you are too passive? Too codependent? That you fear success or competition? Or that you need to learn how to put your foot down?

The truth is, you've come of age in a culture that idealizes masculine models of development. This isn't a radical feminist argument, but the accidental reality of us being heir to the theories of smart men who studied and wrote about their experience of healthy men. These original theorists recognized that healthy men valued justice, conquest, rules, and autonomy and assumed these male models of health were universal.

When women entered the academic discourse, they noticed how the differences in women were often conceptualized as disease. These new female theorists recognize that, in general, women value mercy over justice, cooperation over conquest, relationships over rules, and community over autonomy.

These later theories are less popular, so you are still probably being measured against a masculine yardstick of good mental health (if any of the opening phrases feel familiar, then you definitely are).

We can explore how our world might be different if feminine values of mercy, cooperation, relationship, and community were the highest standard, but today, I want you to at least explore for yourself.

Today, pay attention to where you land within these value systems. See if you have adopted the cultural idea that your way of being is deficient rather than just different. See if you can reconceptualize and celebrate what your feminine way of being actually brings to our community.

You will love the self-acceptance this can bring you.

## TODAY'S AFFIRMATION

I embrace my values, even when they are different from the norm.

## TODAY'S JOURNAL PROMPT

As I think about my conceptualization of myself over the decades, I see/don't see how the dominant masculine values have impacted my sense of self…

## *We are wise enough to forgive the young for not being wise enough.*

A woman in one of my groups expressed exasperation that a young woman in her family was making such bad decisions. Another woman replied, "She is too young to know better, just like we were when we made those same bad decisions." A collective response of recognition and laughter ran through the group as these older women recounted bad marriages, bad habits, and other youthful decisions that impacted them for decades.

This woman, in her jest, reminded us all that we, too, can forget. We often talk about how older women can become invisible, but we, too, can fail to see these worlds that are now so far away from our own. Young people can't see your invisible world, and we can sometimes forget theirs.

Reflect on how your present wisdom is so different from those years of naivete, chaos, and responsibility. Pay attention to your desire for young women to be the reflective, older women they can't yet be. Remember that this was simply beyond all of our capacities, then.

You are wise enough to forgive her for not being wise.

### TODAY'S AFFIRMATION
I can remember and see her world.

### TODAY'S JOURNAL PROMPT
When I think about myself or other younger women
and their decisions, I feel…

REST
REVIEW
REFLECT

## *What you believe is what you become.*

We range from believing that we have complete control to feeling like we have absolutely none. Where do you fall on this spectrum? Can you embrace the paradox of both? Recent studies show our imaginings can have a significant impact.

Much of this research relates to the placebo effect–the healing impact of fake treatments in medical and mental health studies. Scientists don't know how it works, but the results prove that people have real and measurable neurobiological reactions to fake treatments.

Your mind is a powerful healing tool, so how can we bring this into our daily practices? I'd like for you to try an experiment that will show you how.

Today, take five minutes to engage in meditation or contemplative prayer. Follow this centering activity with a five-minute positive visualization. I encourage you to use music that you know may amplify the positive emotional effect of the visualization (you can search YouTube for guided meditations and inspirational music if you need some).

After the ten-minute experiment, notice how you feel. Reflect on whether or not this is a practice you would find useful to incorporate into each day.

Remember, we can't visualize ourselves out of our fate and certainly not our death, but see how this practice can improve your experience of being here.

You will love the comfort and healing this can bring you.

### TODAY'S AFFIRMATION

I am open to the possibilities of positive visualization.

### TODAY'S JOURNAL PROMPT

When I think about imagining something positive,
my reaction is…

# DAY 170

## *Your insomnia is a message from Spirit to get up and meditate.*

Are you up at night? Or awake way too early? A surprising number of older women struggle with interrupted sleep patterns. It is torturous when you are trying to go to sleep (or stay asleep), but your mind won't wind down.

I am going to teach you a trick that will help you. Stop trying to sleep. Instead, change your belief about your not-sleeping. Tell yourself that you are not sleeping because you are supposed to get up and meditate, pray, or engage in some spiritual practice.

I know this sounds crazy, but it works. Get up. Meditate (or pray; any kind of centering spiritual practice will work). Now you aren't wasting time. Now you are calming down your mind. You might meditate/pray for an hour or all night. It doesn't matter. You weren't going to sleep anyway! And this practice is good for you.

Insomnia is so hard to deal with. Being awake at night can amplify your anxiety and worsen the problem. But you can transform that stress into a spiritual practice.

You deserve the mindful peace this will bring you.

### TODAY'S AFFIRMATION
I use all situations for my spiritual practice.

### TODAY'S JOURNAL PROMPT
My experience with relaxation and sleep is…

# DAY 171

## *If you want to be heard, learn how to listen.*

Our cultural obsession with individualism and independence robbed us of the understanding that we grow and heal not as autonomous agents but in relationship. If you pick up any self-help book, it is likely trying to teach you how to get what you need. Whether it is through manifesting positive outcomes, better time management, or effective goal setting, the end is always the same, "How can I get what I want?"

The irony is that we might have more success if, instead of focusing on what we want, we tried offering back the thing we believed we needed most. It is true that so many women are wounded from not being seen or heard. As a result, we've ended up with an epidemic of women clamoring to find or assert their voice in a sea of unheard people.

So what if we approached this differently? What if instead of believing we need to be heard, we start believing we need to listen? When you listen deeply to someone–anyone– you profoundly interrupt this frantic dynamic. You use your own stillness to let her be heard.

Next time you are with someone, see if you can practice deep listening. Pay attention to the story the person is telling you, remember your reflective stillness, no matter what it is or how you are reacting to it. See if you can reflect back on their thoughts or feelings. Like, "It sounds like that makes you angry!" or "You really wish things could have turned out differently, huh?" Don't offer any advice–just listen. Repeat what she says. Let that person have the experience of being heard.

You will be astounded by how this soothes the person you are with. When you learn how to listen, you are teaching others to learn how to listen, too. In a sea of unheard people, this healing act can start a ripple effect of healing in all of your relationships.

I'm not asking you to be a doormat–you need to be heard, too. But try this exercise for a bit and see how it impacts your life and relationships.

You will love the calm this deep listening will bring to your relationships and yourself.

### TODAY'S AFFIRMATION
I can listen deeply without reacting or giving advice.

### TODAY'S JOURNAL PROMPT
My experience with feeling seen (or not seen)
and heard (or not heard) is…

# DAY 172

## *Give to yourself what they couldn't give you.*

You, like most women, were probably raised by people who were too young or too wounded to provide you with what you needed emotionally. You may wish that you had a more secure foundation upon which you could have built a more fulfilling life.

But this story of not enough is the story of almost everyone. For whatever reason, it seems to be the path we all walk. Your task is to figure out what to do next.

Where I see women get stuck is with the story that they still need a particular person to do something in order to grow or repair a wound. This fantasy of healing is rarely how it works. The outside world did not and will not provide your healing. Your task is to provide for yourself what was not given to you.

If you never felt validated, then your job is to learn self-validation. If you were harmed by an abuser, then your job is to heal on your own therapeutic journey. If you have experienced unbearable loss, then your job is to fall apart and grieve until you come back together.

Today, notice where you believe you still need someone else to do some task in order for you to move forward in your healing. Recognize that this is keeping you stuck. Reflect on how you can take control of your journey through your own healing practices.

You deserve the comfort this can bring you.

### TODAY'S AFFIRMATION

I am on a healing journey.

### TODAY'S JOURNAL PROMPT

I need to heal from…I am still expecting someone else to…

# DAY 173

## *Write your way to health.*

Our culture has no sense of the tragic. Take a look at the self-help best-seller list, and you will see our frantic attempts to sanitize the dark spaces out of our lives (these self-help authors are usually in the first half of life).

There is a place for their positive affirmations; they do help. But we also need to find space for grief, pain, loss, and our own hard stories.

The work of psychologist James Pennebaker proves that engaging with, rather than avoiding, our most painful experiences actually improves our mental and physical health. Patients with chronic autoimmune disease who wrote about their most stressful experiences for twenty minutes a day on three consecutive days saw improvements in both their mental and physical health.

There is a catch–the writing must include both thinking and feeling. If you are ruminating over the painful experience in a repetitive way without processing (e.g., without changing, developing insights, etc.), you may feel worse. Keep writing until you gain a deeper sense of meaning about your experiences.

When that cloud of misery has descended upon us, we can always try to shoo her away with positive affirmations. If that doesn't work, go deeper. Sit with your dark spaces in writing and processing until you understand the story. Then she will start to move.

You are worth it.

### TODAY'S AFFIRMATION
My writing brings me healing and new insights.

### TODAY'S JOURNAL PROMPT
When I think about writing out my difficult experiences,
I think and feel...

# DAY 174

## *Believe that everything is purposeful.*
## *See what happens.*

You know by now that so much of what causes our suffering is not only what happens in our life but the stories we tell ourselves about what happens in our life. You've experienced this when you recognized the value of some experience that you never would have asked for (for example, finding meaning in a vocation when you were forced to go back to work; or developing deep connections with a new community when you gave birth to a child with special needs).

You've already had the experience of realizing things are purposeful after the fact, so let's see if you can use this insight to alleviate the challenges that are still coming your way. Hard things will happen. I am not trying to minimize the difficulty of what you are enduring, but trying to teach you a trick for feeling better.

When you are faced with something you can't stand, try to tell yourself that this experience/event is totally purposeful in your life. Experience the event as 'correct' and here for something meaningful that you might not understand yet. Explore this further by imagining what this experience might be bringing into your life.

See what comes up in your mind when you approach all of your most difficult experiences this way.

You deserve the small respite this can bring to your hardest moments.

### TODAY'S AFFIRMATION

Everything is purposeful, even if I don't understand why yet.

### TODAY'S JOURNAL PROMPT

My belief about hard experiences is…

# DAY 175

REST
REVIEW
REFLECT

# You don't need freedom from responsibility to be free.

We can get so tired of working so hard that we become obsessed with fantasies of total freedom from our responsibilities. We imagine if we could just do what we wanted each day, we would be happy. It sounds like a good recipe, but unfortunately, it doesn't work.

When we allow ourselves to grow lazy with no responsibility, we become increasingly impacted by the ephemeral and temporal events around us. We sleep later, eat what is advertised to us, and attend to whatever social media is offering up today. Instead of taking charge of your own life, you end up totally dependent upon the manipulative whims of what is occurring around you. That isn't the freedom and comfort you are seeking.

When we stop believing we need freedom from responsibility and instead embrace the responsibilities required for true freedom, we can let go of elusive and destructive fantasies of total freedom that have no place in our world (it is okay and good to explore why you are having such a fantasy, just don't mistakenly think this is your solution).

You will move from dependence upon the whims of the outside world to a new focus on your intentions and your inner world. This is the freedom and comfort you are seeking.

Today, pay attention to how you feel about freedom and responsibility. Notice if you are allowing yourself to drift into lazy practices in an effort to find comfort. Remind yourself that it won't work.

You will love the freedom and comfort your self-discipline will bring you.

## TODAY'S AFFIRMATION

I find freedom with responsibility.

## TODAY'S JOURNAL PROMPT

My belief about the relationship between freedom
and responsibility is...

# DAY 177

## *Be wary of their imagination violations.*

When you are feeling enlivened by or drawn to a story, be careful about letting others, who are probably trying to help you, 'interpret' the meaning of your connection to this story.

Many smart people prioritize the sacred value of the myth or the story. Many believe that our ancient stories hold apocryphal keys that we can unlock with enough amplification or interpretation. This search for other people's meanings is exactly the opposite of what you need to do.

If you've ever felt that deadening response when someone enthusiastically explains to you what your symbol, dream, or connection to a myth 'means,' then you know the danger of this abortive imaginative move.

Remember, the story is not the source of wisdom–something coming up within you in response to this story is the source of wisdom. The story is a tool–a complicated paradigm calling you into a healing relationship. Stories that have held on for millennia are stories that do a good job of eliciting this response from us. They are stories that can hold our breadth of meanings across our lifespan–from the literal in early life to the transcendent in late life.

Your meaning might be close to the meanings that others have found; that is why and when their interpretations might feel useful to you. But don't confuse the fact that others have found meaning in a story with your meaning in that story.

We are looking for your spaces in between. Remember to listen to what comes up from within, not without.

### TODAY'S AFFIRMATION
I listen to and honor my own interpretations.

### TODAY'S JOURNAL PROMPT
A story that is really meaningful to me is…I love it because…

## *Choose what you see.*

The information age has changed our relationship with our world. For the entire history of humanity, up until less than about one hundred years ago, most of us would have started our day surrounded by the sounds of nature and our world. We would have had very limited access to information about everyone else. As recently as twenty years ago, your information likely came once or twice a day in the form of a daily newspaper or evening television news program.

Today, your days are filled with competing news and social media fighting to capture your attention. In this information age, you aren't just getting access to information. *You are being attacked by information.*

If you want to get control of your mind, you must be intentional about what you allow yourself to see.

Today, pay attention to whether or not you are a passive recipient of aggressive media or if you are being intentional about the information coming into your day. Notice your habits. Notice how the information makes you feel. Going forward, be more intentional about what you choose to see.

You deserve the natural peace this practice will bring you.

### TODAY'S AFFIRMATION

I am intentional about the information I feed my mind and body.

### TODAY'S JOURNAL PROMPT

When I cut off the constant input of news and social media, I feel...

# DAY 179

## *Your wise woman can help your wounded girl.*

As you reflect on some of your hardest stories, whether they are stories of you being hurt or stories of you hurting others, I'd like to offer you a way to approach these painful memories with more compassion.

Whatever happened to you–or whatever you did–was experienced by a younger woman who didn't know as much as you know now. Your job is to use your imagination to connect with your own inner wise woman. Let this (growing) aspect of you be the witness to this story.

Pay attention to how the memory feels different went approached by your old, inner wise woman. Does she have more patience? Compassion? Resilience? Notice how you can imagine her response to be different than your default response.

The younger you was too overwhelmed to cope with this, but the older you can. Imagine your way to your inner wise woman and guide her to help your wounded, younger self.

You deserve her compassionate guidance.

## TODAY'S AFFIRMATION

I can connect with my inner wise woman.

## TODAY'S JOURNAL PROMPT

My inner wise woman is different from my more conscious ego story in that she...
She could help me by...

# DAY 180

## *Surrender is not passive compliance. It is active acceptance.*

Surrender is a real trigger word for women. It can bring up memories of abusive relationships with individuals or institutions that tried to negate your individuality, truth, or dignity. The word has been used as a cover to oppress or control disenfranchised persons for centuries.

I'd like to rescue this word, surrender, because, in its truest and most spiritual sense, it is none of those abusive, self-negating things.

Surrender is about taking action on the things that are meaningful to you but being completely open to outcomes. Surrender is about accepting what you can't change. Surrender is about letting go of your desire for control and having faith in a loving, transcendent reality that is co-creating your life with you.

Today, pay attention to your feeling responses to the word surrender. See if your associations have been contaminated by past experiences where the word was used to manipulate, abuse, or control you or the people you love. Reflect on the true, spiritual meaning of surrender and see where you can incorporate this practice into your life.

You will enjoy the contentment this will bring you.

## TODAY'S AFFIRMATION
Spiritual surrender brings peace.

## TODAY'S JOURNAL PROMPT
To me, surrender means…

# DAY 181

## *We misunderstand love and how it heals us.*

Most of us have heard that love is our greatest healer. Sadly, most of us have a naive and/or passive view of how love can help us heal and grow.

The greatest mystics of every faith tradition speak of love as an effort we make. From Jesus' instruction to love our enemies to the Eastern practice of loving-kindness meditation, we can see how love is something we are called upon to bring forth.

But too often, people in the West believe that love is supposed to show up (or failed to show up) for them in the correct and non-injurious way. People in the West often believe they are wounded because they weren't loved correctly. They misunderstand how love heals.

The story of passively waiting for some other human to arrive and love you into wellness does not appear in any sacred teaching. This false story only shows up in our superficial romance novels and films.

When you dive deep into any faith tradition, you will discover again and again that love is an effort that you make. You work to love your neighbor (or your enemy). You learn to love yourself by discovering the kingdom or divinity within. You practice loving-kindness meditation toward others.

You aren't hurting because you weren't loved correctly. You are hurting because you weren't taught correctly about how making an effort to love can still heal you.

Today, see if you can make an effort to bring forth more love through praying for your enemies or practicing loving kindness toward all.

You deserve the love this will bring into your life.

## TODAY'S AFFIRMATION

I bring love into the world.

## TODAY'S JOURNAL PROMPT

My belief about love and healing is…

# DAY 182

# REST
# REVIEW
# REFLECT

# Your Season of Reflection.

As a woman entering the season of *Reflection*, you move into a new developmental phase–into an invisible world. The big questions of your mid-life challenges opened you up to bigger explorations. A woman in this season might fear that she is becoming selfish, uncaring, or angry. Welcome the feelings that often accompany this paradigmatic shift.'

This is when you start to tune into the deepest rhythms of a different story. It might rise up in creative projects, disruptive nightmares or dreams, or frustration with the status quo. However it shows up for you, your task is to develop a more cooperative relationship with your deepest self.

Being in your season of *Reflection* doesn't mean you are no longer receptive to change or no longer laden with responsibilities. You are still receiving and changing as your stories continue. You might have responsibilities of grandchildren, caretaking, or financially supporting others. The earlier seasons still live on in you, but the point is that now you are adding in something new.

Many of us are forced into this reflective look inward as suffering brings us to our knees (it can start in any decade of life). With reflection, your unconscious, reactive way of being in a world that you think you understand is over. It can be the shock of your life, and you might think it is more than you can endure.

This is your underworld journey. When you feel overwhelmed with your developmental tasks, turn to our most ancient tales. Remember the underworld journeys that exist in every tradition, East and West.

It is hard. It will be dark, but like our ancient heroines, you will return, transformed.

You deserve the rebirth.

## TODAY'S AFFIRMATION

I read the ancient tales of underworld journeys as I embark on my own.

## TODAY'S JOURNAL PROMPT

My understanding of these ancient underworld journeys is...

# DAY 184

## *Sometimes it is not a problem you need to solve but an experience you need to walk through.*

We live in a culture that celebrates doing. We value people who take action, people who change things, and people who get things done. This isn't a bad thing; your call to action has probably served you well in a crisis.

But this isn't *always* the best approach to hard things. Because, sometimes, you can't fix it. And when you can't, you can waste a lot of precious energy on a problem that has no solution. This is an especially important lesson as we age and encounter more and more challenges that we won't ever 'fix.'

What if we imagined this experience differently? What if we stopped imagining that we need to fix this, or change this, or be better after this? What if we imagined that this is simply an experience I need to have? Can we let our experiences just be things that happened? That we had the opportunity to have this experience (even and especially when it is a terrible experience)?

Please know I am not trying to minimize the pain. I am trying to change the way you imagine your terrible experience. When we do this, it can alleviate some of our sufferings. And you deserve that.

You will love the respite this change in perspective can give you in the middle of hard things.

### TODAY'S AFFIRMATION

I can simply be with my hardest experiences.

### TODAY'S JOURNAL PROMPT

Imagining that this is simply an experience I need to have (and not something I need to fix, change, or learn from) makes me think/feel...

# DAY 185

## *I am responsible for cultivating peace across all of my senses.*

Sometimes we don't know why we don't feel well. We may be able to come up with a few reasons, but we also know there is a pervasive discomfort that persists. We can't put our finger on what the problem is.

There are a lot of reasons this can be the case, but I'd like to highlight one that you might be missing. What are you taking in? In every sense? What are you hearing? Seeing? Smelling? Feeling physically? Therapists can focus a lot on our thoughts and feelings, but everything else that is going into your senses is also affecting you–physically and mentally.

Are you looking at a messy house? Are you listening to the buzz of electronics or television? Are you reading distressing news? Are you taking shallow breaths? Are you holding your body tense? The most recent research proves that all of these things impact our physiology and psychology.

Today, notice if you are making an effort to bring peace and comfort across <u>all of your senses.</u> Notice what you are bringing into your mind and body. See if you can improve in one or more areas. The more you do this, the better you will feel.

Please don't be perfectionistic in trying to master comfort across every domain. Most of us are living with challenges, messes, and pains, so improve where you discover you have room to do so.

You deserve the comfort this will bring you.

### TODAY'S AFFIRMATION
I cultivate simplicity and peace across all of my senses.

### TODAY'S JOURNAL PROMPT
When I notice the input across all of my senses, I notice...

# DAY 186

## *It wasn't supposed to be easy.*

Women are not only consumed with their suffering. They are confused about their suffering. Because most women still operate under the mistaken story that life should be easier–for themselves and for everyone else. This is a story that is making us sick. When we believe this, all of the inevitable challenges, losses, and pain make no sense. It is just a very big, very painful "Why?"

Real life causes real pain. But most *psychological* suffering is fed by the mistaken belief that life is not as it should be. The belief is that there is something about life that is incorrect. When you are fighting against reality with beliefs like this, you amplify your suffering. This is not a new-age idea. Look to the ancient wisdom advising us to accept the world as it is in statements like, "Don't push the river" or "Let go of your expectations."

When you accept what is the case, you are no longer fighting against the current. You have more peace and more energy (note: this is not a call to total passivity; it is a call to stop the psychological torture of fighting reality. You may still choose to fight for personal and social justice. In fact, you will likely have more energy and be more effective in doing so).

Explore where you believe that life should be easier. Identify the thing or circumstance that you believe should be different. Say to yourself, "It is exactly as it is supposed to be because it is."

Accept what is the case and find the peace and energy that you need.

### TODAY'S AFFIRMATION

I accept what is.

### TODAY'S JOURNAL PROMPT

I might have a hard time accepting what is the case because…
If I did accept it, then…

## *Be uncomfortable in the natural world.*

You are probably reading this message indoors, under the protection of walls, a roof, and the comforts of climate control. As we've gained the resources to build more comfortable living accommodations, we've worked to eliminate the aspects of the natural world we think cause discomfort. The protections and comforts should make you feel better, right?

But what if I told you that being in nature, even when it makes us *uncomfortable,* improves your memory and your mood? That is exactly what psychology researcher Marc Berman discovered. Participants consistently showed improvements in memory and attention spans after spending an hour interacting with nature–even in bad weather and when participants reported that they didn't like it! A later study with persons diagnosed with major depression also showed significant improvements in memory and mood.

Don't have access to a natural environment? Amazingly, the research showed similar gains when looking at nature photographs.

Interacting with nature is as good as a daily meditation practice. There is no money to be made in this practice, so no one is selling you this story.

Today, pay attention to whether or not you avoid the discomforts of the natural world. See if you can remember that being uncomfortable in nature is good for your memory and mood.

You deserve the comfort this will bring you.

## TODAY'S AFFIRMATION

I can be in nature, even when it feels physically uncomfortable.

## TODAY'S JOURNAL PROMPT

My thoughts and feelings about being in nature when
it is uncomfortable (cold, rainy, etc.) are...

# DAY 188

## *Connect your story to the story of all women.*

There is no question that the challenges that come our way make our life more difficult. It was easier when we were healthier or not in pain. It would be easier if we weren't struggling financially. Life wouldn't be such a challenge if the people we loved weren't hurting so much.

These experiences in life may cause suffering, but our cultural stories about life are what make us really sick.

We can grieve that our son is in rehab again. We can resent that our partner died when we see other couples sharing their lives with each other.

But we need to remember that women throughout the centuries have suffered. Our most ancient tales, both sacred and secular, make this very clear to us. But our recent move from our ancient sacred stories to our superficial, for-profit stories has disconnected us from our lineage of feminine suffering, strength, and storytelling.

Today, pay attention to what is true in the story of your life. Reflect on the history of women who have walked hard paths. Find their stories. Notice the thing you are grateful for and the things you grieve. All of these parts are part of all of our stories.

You deserve the connection this will bring you.

### TODAY'S AFFIRMATION

I am part of a long lineage of women who have struggled and survived.

### TODAY'S JOURNAL PROMPT

When I consider my story in the larger context of this history of women's stories, I feel...

REST
REVIEW
REFLECT

# DAY 190

## *Your Spirit messages are only in the present-moment.*

We've touched upon the goal of staying present, but I'd like to underscore one of the reasons why we practice present-moment awareness. My goal with these meditations is to get you to connect more deeply with your spiritual self. Learning to stay present is a healing practice because the non-rational synchronicities and meaningful moments of the spiritual world only occur in the present-moment.

When you are lost in thought in the past or the future, you don't see the butterfly dancing around your head, trying to draw your attention. You don't notice your mother's birthday pop up on the odometer as you pass her favorite garden. When you stay present, the world becomes more magical; this nourishes and restores you. There is nothing magical to be found in your overthinking brain; it only depletes and exhausts you.

Today, commit to a few very specific moments of staying present. Tell yourself that you will notice the present-moment when you walk to your car or coffee pot. If the practice is confusing to you, just remember to tune into your sensory data. For that brief second or two, pay attention to what you see, hear, feel, and smell. Remember, your senses always bring you to the present-moment.

These tiny moments of present awareness will bring so much magic and nourishment into your life. Keep doing this, and you *will* keep doing this.

You deserve the comfort it will bring you.

### TODAY'S AFFIRMATION

I am present for the magic of the present-moment.

### TODAY'S JOURNAL PROMPT

When I am in the present-moment, I notice...
When I am thinking about the past or future, I notice...

# DAY 191

## *When you allow yourself to engage in toxic conversations or thoughts, you are feeding yourself toxic energy.*

It can feel so harmless–gossiping about a mutual acquaintance to a friend or raging about a politician you loathe. It is addictive to engage in these kinds of thoughts or conversations as they serve our shallowest sense of separate and superior self-ness.

The problem is that it isn't harmless to you. Every spiritual practice warns about these kinds of actions. From the most conservative faiths to New Age teachings, you find warnings not to do this.

We are mistaken if we understand these spiritual warnings as merely moral (e.g., 'be good') truths. Every spiritual tradition warns about these actions because they know they are spiritually harmful to you (and others).

Don't believe me? The best way to test whether or not this is true for you is to try it. For one day, don't allow yourself to indulge in any negative thoughts or conversations about others. Pay attention to how you feel.

Once you discover how much impact this has on you, the self-discipline to not engage will be easy.

You deserve the positive, energizing time this will bring you.

## TODAY'S AFFIRMATION

I am intentional in my thoughts and speech.

## TODAY'S JOURNAL PROMPT

I tend to allow myself to indulge in this most often with...
I probably do it because...

# DAY 192

## *You don't have to do your practice well.*
## *You just have to do your practice.*

It can be frustrating when you are trying to start a new spiritual practice. I often hear, "I tried, but I just couldn't do it," from my clients when they talk about starting a meditative or contemplative habit. They feel justified in their abandonment with complaints of, "My mind was just all over the place," or "I just can't sit still that long!"

This is a perfect example of East meets West. The practices are here to teach you *how to slow down,* but you quit because you can't master them *fast enough* (we Westerners are used to quick-fix solutions!).

Remember–you are learning to slow down. It is going to take a while. Right now, you aren't supposed to meditate like a Zen master or pray like a saint. You are supposed to meditate or pray like a beginner. It will be frustrating, not fulfilling, at first. You will probably spend twenty minutes with your mind wandering and body shifting as you deal with the psychological and physical discomforts of trying to sit still. Stay with it.

Reflect on the words and images of our medieval women mystics or ancient teachers. They complained of the tortures and discomforts. You can tolerate this process, too.

Today, your job is just to show up. Today, see if you can practice tolerating doing your spiritual practice poorly. With lots and lots of practice, over time, it will change.

You deserve the centering peace this will eventually bring you.

## TODAY'S AFFIRMATION

I have the courage and discipline to stick with a practice I can't do well yet.

## TODAY'S JOURNAL PROMPT

My expectations of my spiritual practice are...
These expectations may be interfering with my practice in that...

# DAY 193

## *It is not your fault.*

We have so many descriptors of our guilt–a mother's guilt, a Catholic guilt, or living out the guilt we picked up from our parents.

I'd like to bring your attention to a key contributor to your feelings of guilt that you might not be recognizing–your delusional omnipotence–or a mistaken belief in your power. Your guilt is dependent upon a logical premise, "If I had done something different, the outcome would be better." But is this really true? You know, the bad mom that got the amazing, successful child. You know the good mom whose child struggled terribly. Do you really think you have that much power?

Yes, we all half-screwed up in ways that live on in our children (as your parents did with you and as your children will do with their offspring). But excessive guilt is dependent upon this false story that you had a lot more power than you ever actually had. That, somehow, you could have forced the story to go differently for yourself or someone else.

Today, reflect on the sometimes arbitrary outcomes of people who did 'better' or 'worse' than you on these things. Notice that we all seem to have a lot less power (and therefore less culpability or guilt) than we imagine.

You deserve the self-compassion this can bring you.

### TODAY'S AFFIRMATION

I am not as in control of outcomes as I imagine.

### TODAY'S JOURNAL PROMPT

One thing I still imagine I should have done differently is...
As an older woman, I realize...

## *Learn to do things badly.*

If there is one thing I could wish for you, it isn't that you could become the best at something, but instead that you could enjoy doing the things you do terribly.

We have a terrible bias toward excellence in our culture—where only those who are talented are recognized. This external orientation is missing the whole point. We do things because of the joy (eros) they bring into our lives, not because of the awe they inspire in others.

Maybe you love hiking, but you can't make it very far. Maybe you love painting but know your work isn't meant for an art gallery. Maybe writing brings you comfort, even if you don't want to share it.

When we tolerate doing things terribly, we open up whole new worlds. What are the things you are terrible at? Do any of them sound fun? Reflect on how you can bring in accommodations that still allow you to participate or create in ways that inspire you.

Tolerate doing things badly. And love the process.

You deserve the fun this brings into your life.

### TODAY'S AFFIRMATION

I can engage in things that I can't do well.

### TODAY'S JOURNAL PROMPT

The thing I don't do because I don't do it well enough is...
If I allowed myself to do things badly, I might...

# DAY 195

## *What did they want you to be? What do you want to be? Pay attention to the difference.*

As young women, we paid a lot of attention to what other people wanted from us. It isn't wrong that you did this–in the earlier stages of your development, this was required for your emotional and psychological survival.

But as you age, your developmental task changes. Instead of paying attention to what others want from you, your job is to learn what you want from yourself. This is far more challenging than it sounds. Many women are lost in a purgatory of having no idea what they want.

So, here is an exercise for you. Write out a list of what you believe other people want you to be. Review that list. Write out another list of what you want to be. See how these two stories of you compare. See what is different. See what is the same.

Have compassion for the young woman trying to find her balance in the midst of this tension. Look at the discrepancies and see if you can imagine what you want to let go of and what you want to move toward.

You will love the clarity and development this will bring you.

### TODAY'S AFFIRMATION

I am aware of the difference between what others want from me
and what I want for myself.

### TODAY'S JOURNAL PROMPT

Other people wanted me to be…I wanted to be…

# REST
# REVIEW
# REFLECT

# *Ask your future wise woman, 'What is the purpose of this present action?'*

What do you visualize when you imagine your future self and her psychological and/or spiritual well-being? Who is that woman? What is she like? What does she do each day? How does she behave? Let's use this woman to help with our current challenges.

How does that imagined self match up with your current way of behaving? What you might notice here is a common discrepancy. In our day-to-day life, we are constantly striving (consciously or unconsciously) for things that are not even aligned with our own goals. Maybe you are still seeking approval. Maybe you want to be rescued from your own anxiety. Maybe you are worried your views will be offensive to someone, so you choose to keep quiet.

Whatever it is, your first job is to just notice it. With each action and interaction, pay attention to what you are seeking in that act or word (note: you might like what you see! I just want you to be conscious of what it is).

After you start to notice, move back into the visualization of your best spiritual self. Imagine what she might say to you. Imagine what she wants for and from you. Put these two parts of yourself (present and future self) in conversation. See if you can listen to her guidance and make your present actions and your words in alignment with your own highest values.

You will love the inner peace this can bring you.

## TODAY'S AFFIRMATION

My future wise woman lives within me and guides me.

## TODAY'S JOURNAL PROMPT

My older self might say to me…

# DAY 198

## *Accept the world as it is, and you receive its gifts.*

How often are you stuck in the habit of wishing something or someone was different than they are? This could be a person, your messy desk, your yard, or anything. This is a habit we get into, often with good intentions of improving ourselves, others, or the world. The problem is that you do this at an enormous cost to yourself. You can't focus on all things. And you've developed a habit of focusing on things you don't like or that aren't even there (like a clean desk or a beautifully landscaped yard).

I'm not making this up. Professor Nancy Fagley studied how this habit impacted our life satisfaction. She measured appreciation, defined in her study as "acknowledging the value and meaning of something–an event, a behavior, an object–and feeling a positive emotional connection to it." She discovered that appreciation was *twice as significant* as gratitude in correlating with life satisfaction.

I'm not suggesting you do this because you should be a nicer person. I'm trying to prove to you, in a very practical way, that this will dramatically improve your experience of living.

This requires that you stop thinking, "I need to pull those weeds overgrown in my yard," and instead notice something like, "Look at those pretty birds sitting up on the electrical wire." When you do this, you stop focusing on a world that doesn't even exist. You stop focusing on what you don't like. You start to see what is. You start to notice what is beautiful and present.

You receive the present-moment gifts from others and the world.

Try this today. You deserve the joy it will bring you.

## TODAY'S AFFIRMATION
I can see what is present and beautiful.

## TODAY'S JOURNAL PROMPT
If I focused on what is present and beautiful, then…

# DAY 199

## *It is your responsibility to cultivate your self-compassion.*

We tend to misunderstand the practice of self-compassion. No matter how much we read or study, most of us still think of it as an indulgence. It is tragic that the habit of being nice to ourselves seems so luxurious.

The truth is exactly the opposite. It is not an indulgence–you have a responsibility to cultivate your self-compassion. Because the way you see yourself shapes the way you see everyone else. And that has an impact on how they see themselves. When you are cruel to yourself, you have less compassion for a world that desperately needs more of it. When you learn to love yourself, with all of your quirks and failings, you are better able to love a world with all of its quirks and failings. You are teaching others how to love themselves.

Today, reflect on how you feel about the practice of self-compassion. Notice if you consider it an indulgent luxury. See if you can reframe it as a responsibility you have to a world that needs more kindness.

You will love the peace and tranquility the self-compassion will bring you.

### TODAY'S AFFIRMATION
I have a responsibility to be kind to myself.

### TODAY'S JOURNAL PROMPT
With regard to my compassion for myself and others,
I am probably...

# DAY 200

## *Practice being okay when things are not.*

Despite our best efforts, we can all drift into our own depression. These are the moments when life just hurts and when we might start to feel like we are experiencing pointless suffering. Every woman knows this space.

When you are in those moments, you might not be able to connect to any spiritual practice that will bring you comfort, so I want to tell you about one that might.

In that low point of extreme suffering, whether physical pain, shocking grief, or unrelenting mental illness, we can use a cognitive technique to ease our burden.

In your crushing despair, tell yourself that you are practicing being 'okay' no matter what life deals you. Conceptualize it like a challenge. You might even connect with your anger, in defiance, like, "I'm not giving up! No matter what you throw at me! I won't quit!"

This subtle shift moves us from feeling overpowered by our extreme suffering to empowered by our inherent dignity and ability to keep going in the face of crushing circumstances. You are moving from the immediacy of the suffering to a higher level of observing and responding to your suffering.

Today, notice where you feel defeated. See if you can connect with this practice to re-engage with your journey.

You deserve the empowerment and endurance this will bring.

### TODAY'S AFFIRMATION

I rise to the challenge of staying committed to my spiritual practices,
even in my dark nights of the soul.

### TODAY'S JOURNAL PROMPT

When I feel defeated, I usually…

## *Beyond conformity, beyond rebellion, you find yourself.*

Starting out in your original family unit, you received stories about what your family valued or disdained. Whether your home was comfortable or chaotic, you drew conclusions about yourself and about how you should be in the world.

As you tried to forge an independent identity in your early years, you may have rebelled against your original paradigm. If they were 'this,' you were going to be 'that.' This is a very good start. You are in motion. You are thinking about your world and who and how you want to be. But we need to realize this reaction against another is not the final step.

Because when we construct an identity in rebellion against something, we are still defining ourselves in reaction to that thing. Your job is to go beyond that. The breakaway can feel good, but you still need to connect with something deeper inside of yourself that is the source of who you are still becoming.

As you move along the spectrum of conformity with and rebellion against, pay attention to where you also feel more connected with something that feels true to you.

When you find this space, you can find the people or texts that feel closer to who you are becoming.

Learn to co-create a sense of self in a relationship with your world rather than in reaction against it. You will love the deep knowing this will bring you.

### TODAY'S AFFIRMATION

I am in a relationship with myself, not in a reaction against others.

### TODAY'S JOURNAL PROMPT

I probably rejected the ideas about (or ways of being that)...
I find myself to be more...

# DAY 202

## *Memorize your sacred texts.*

In our culture of constant entertainment and distraction, we've lost so many ancient and useful practices. As a child, you probably remember the assignment to memorize poetry or scripture. Today, I want you to remember this forgotten practice but with more wisdom and intentionality about what works for you.

What poetry or prose speaks to your soul? Who is telling the tale of life and spirituality in a way that connects you to your deepest self? These are the texts you need to cultivate a deeper connection with.

Because when you find prose or poetry that speaks to your soul, you can more deeply incorporate the meaning and values they connect you with by memorizing them.

What you will notice is that, in your more challenging moments, the sacred poetry and prose you chose to study will rise up within you. It will be there for you in your hardest moments.

This is not a spirituality imposed upon you, but you finding your relationship with your own spiritual truths.

Today, see if you can identify the sacred or secular poetry or prose that speaks to your soul. Find the passages that are most resonant for you. Commit yourself to memorize one tiny bit of that text. See if you can recite it.

Bring these healing stories into your body and soul.

You will love how this will bring your spirituality into your body and life.

### TODAY'S AFFIRMATION
I memorize the texts that connect me with my deepest self.

### TODAY'S JOURNAL PROMPT
The texts I connect with most are…

# DAY 203

# REST
# REVIEW
# REFLECT

## *Find safety with people like you.*
## *Find growth with people unlike you.*

For your mental health, it is healing to connect with people who understand you. I've seen this in the power of groups. When women share private challenges with anxiety, depression, struggling children, or chronic illness and pain, it eases their burden as they laugh, cry, and learn to cope in a community that understands the experience.

So, while finding spaces where we feel truly connected can be healing, it is important not to totally cocoon yourself in a space where you don't have to hear things you disagree with. I'm not talking about unblocking the annoying relative with his constant sharing of religious, social, or political cartoons that irritate you, but about engaging in a substantive and meaningful way with ideas that are different from your own.

When we stop conceptualizing each other as caricatures and attempt to truly hear the beliefs and concerns that underlie an opposing view, we open ourselves up to deeper levels of connection and understanding in them and in ourselves.

Today, pay attention to where you might be simplifying or caricaturing the views of people who hold different views from you. See if you can cultivate more empathy by hearing what they are truly concerned about.

It is easy to rest on our lazy belief that we've got the answers and that someone else is just not understanding as clearly as we are. But, if we want to push ourselves to grow, we have to demand more from ourselves than that. When we do this, we are cultivating a sense of community in the midst of difference. This is a task for all of us. No matter what we believe.

When it comes to safe spaces for healing, similarities are good. When it comes to challenging places for cultivating compassion and connection, embrace and grow with those differences.

You will love the deeper connections this can bring into your life.

### TODAY'S AFFIRMATION

I try to deeply hear the concerns of people who are different from me.

### TODAY'S JOURNAL PROMPT

The ideas, persons, or groups that irritate me the most are...
If I were to listen to their views more deeply, I might...

# DAY 205

## *We've lost ourselves in our individuality.*

We all have the habit of thinking that the way we are is the natural way to be, forgetting that we find and create ourselves in the context of our time and place. An important example is the Western idea of individualism. If you were raised in Western culture, you probably value individualistic practices and values–goal setting, independence, and self-discovery. Being unique is good, and being dependent is bad.

If you were raised in the East, Latin America, or Africa, you probably value collective practices and values–family focus, the greater good, and responsibility to others. Being self-sacrificing is good, and being too focused on selfish goals is bad.

We see the differences in how each culture takes care of their elderly (more likely in the family unit in collectivist; more likely outsourced in the individualistic) or pursues their dreams (more often sacrificed in collectivist; more likely realized in the individualistic).

We have to be careful about idealizing one over the other, but it is important to pay attention to which one we got a bigger dose of and to reflect on whether or not our ingrained cultural influences are truly in line with our deepest values.

Today, notice where your practices fall on the spectrum of collectivism vs. individualism. Pay attention to where you think this works for you and your society and where it falls short. Think about ways you can incorporate more of the other and find a balance that feels in line with your deepest values.

You will love the balance of autonomy and connection this can bring you.

## TODAY'S AFFIRMATION

I reflect on my cultural influences and make conscious choices
about how to be in the world.

## TODAY'S JOURNAL PROMPT

When I think of the collectivist vs. individualist values,
I probably am…

# DAY 206

## *Who is too hormonal?*

Have you ever described yourself or another woman as 'hormonal?" What does this mean? From teenagers to middle-aged women, you know of women who've been told they need to pharmaceutically manage their hormones to better regulate their weepy or raging moods.

I am not here to critique the use of pharmaceutical interventions that may provide relief, but I do want to ask why this is such a gendered critique of hormones and moods. Have you ever heard of a man being told he needed to better regulate his hormones? To maybe take some pills to lower his testosterone?

In a culture that struggles with rape and rage from men, doesn't it seem strange that no one ever would dare suggest we regulate men's hormones?

I am not against men. I am not suggesting we lower men's testosterone. I just want to bring awareness to this story of women being defective and needing regulation with regard to the impact their hormones have on their moods. Is it possible that we are all plagued with the physiological impacts of our hormones? Why can't men be included in this story?

Today, reflect on how you have imagined women and the problem of their hormones. Notice if this 'problem' has been a gendered critique. See if you can be open to a bigger story about all of us coping with our bodies.

### TODAY'S AFFIRMATION

My body impacts me, just as everyone's body impacts them.

### TODAY'S JOURNAL PROMPT

When I reflect on my relationship with my body and whether or not
I imagine it as uniquely problematic, I notice...

# DAY 207

## *You aren't going to "arrive" anywhere in this life. Enjoy the journey.*

One of the things that keep us from staying in the present-moment is the fact we are always working toward something–a personal goal, relief from some present burden, even spiritual enlightenment. We become addicted to this shallow intoxicant of living in an imaginary future. The problem is that this way of being actually works against what we really wish to accomplish–peace in our present-moment.

Imagine being on the trip of a lifetime where, upon your return, you realize you spent the entire journey missing the cultural sights and sounds because you were wondering how you were going to arrive at your next destination. Many of us live our lives this way.

When we stop focusing on arriving at some future moment but instead remember we are here to experience our long journey of life, we can learn to stay present. Instead of wondering what is next, we learn to be with what is right in front of us. That future moment is not the key. This one is.

Today, take a few moments to stop and pay attention to where you are right now. Make a commitment to notice the sights, sounds, and interactions of this moment.

You deserve the peace in the present that this can bring you.

### TODAY'S AFFIRMATION
I am with my present-moment.

### TODAY'S JOURNAL PROMPT
I might be distracting myself from the present with thoughts about…

# DAY 208

## *Forgiveness is not your first step.*

So many women believe that there is something wrong with them because they 'can't forgive' the person who hurt them. She might believe that she is 'stuck' because she can't achieve this seemingly elusive, healing goal.

In my work with women, forgiveness isn't ever a therapeutic goal. In fact, I'm often suspicious when it shows up. When the goal or topic of forgiveness arrives, I often find something far less benign hiding beneath its seemingly good façade.

It might show up as a demand from a perpetually abusive family member who uses 'forgiveness' to avoid responsibility. It might be a way that a client is trying to avoid facing the horror of her experiences by jumping to the claim that she has 'already forgiven' the perpetrator.

I am not saying forgiveness doesn't exist. It does. I've experienced it and witnessed it. What I am saying is that forgiveness happens to you after you do the hard work. It isn't something you can mandate or order up.

Your job is to feel your pain, tell your story, and honor your truth. As you grow in wisdom and compassion for yourself and others, forgiveness, in a guise you never expected, will come to you.

Today, pay attention to your relationship with forgiveness. Are you demanding it from someone else? Are you setting it as a goal for yourself? See if you can let go of your wish to control the long process of forgiveness. She will come in her own time.

You will love the deep work this can bring into your life.

## TODAY'S AFFIRMATION
It's okay that I don't forgive them yet.

## TODAY'S JOURNAL PROMPT
My experiences and belief about the role of forgiveness
in my journey are...

# DAY 209

## *What breaks us apart is what binds us together.*

The things that happened that we can't forget. The things we did that we can't undo. We all have these hard parts in our life stories. These are the experiences that break us.

But, as a therapist, I see the miraculous paradox of this breaking.

Have you ever met a person (usually young) who hasn't been through anything hard yet? You may notice you can't connect with her in a meaningful or authentic way. She is essentially isolated from everyone. Have you ever known an old woman who has been through everything? Who has reflected and healed her broken spirit? There is a softness to her soul. She is humble and open. She is, essentially, connected to everyone.

This is the huge irony about these experiences that 'break us.' We need the breaking. I am not suggesting that any of us celebrate our terrible experiences, but I am saying that your breakdown is actually the breaking open that ultimately allows you to connect in a deeper way with others.

Today, reflect on the women you've admired. Reflect on the adversities you know they've overcome. Reflect on yourself. Reflect on the adversities you have (or still need to) overcome.

You don't ever have to welcome the terrible events, but you can love the way they will call you into deeper communion with yourself, with others, and with the divine.

### TODAY'S AFFIRMATION

My hardest experiences can open me up to connect with others.

### TODAY'S JOURNAL PROMPT

When I think about people who haven't been through hard things,
I notice…

# REST
# REVIEW
# REFLECT

## *Your loneliness is a healthy impulse.*
## *Listen to it.*

Women tell me, "I'm so lonely," speaking of themselves as if they are sick. I usually respond, "Good!" Because feeling lonely is a good thing–it is a sign that some living part of yourself is seeking a life-sustaining connection.

When you are in total, deadening despair, you probably don't feel lonely because you probably don't feel anything. As you start to get healthier, your appetite for relationships comes back to life. This is like being hungry after recovering from an illness–it is a life-affirming impulse.

Of course, feeling lonely doesn't feel good, so I understand the complaint. But, like being hungry or sleepy, your job is not to pathologize the need but to listen to it and respond. Maybe your current relationships aren't working. Maybe you are too disconnected from others. Your job is to get creative and think about how you can still bring more connection into your life.

Your loneliness is a healthy impulse. Listen to it and find ways to feed your need for more connection.

You deserve the connections.

### TODAY'S AFFIRMATION
Loneliness is a healthy impulse that guides me
to make more connections.

### TODAY'S JOURNAL PROMPT
I feel more lonely when...
I feel least lonely when...

# DAY 212

## *Your life is a beautiful kaleidoscopic tapestry.*

The metaphors we use to conceptualize our life are a powerful force in determining what experiences we believe are good and/or bad. When we are trapped in the progressive model of a straight line up (meaning things should always improve), we use this narrow paradigm to evaluate our experiences–things that improve our lives are 'good,' and things that make our life harder are 'bad.'

But what if you changed the metaphor? What if, instead of an upward model of progress, you imagined your life as an expanding, kaleidoscopic tapestry?

Bring the image of a huge, complicated kaleidoscope to mind. Imagine a variety of colors and patterns that arise and disappear in this dynamic image. See the movement of the dark and light patterns–they all belong. When you imagine your varied experiences in this paradigm, the way you evaluate your experiences changes. Ease and hardship are part of the whole. Delight and loss are all perfectly present.

Your life, like an ever-expanding and changing kaleidoscope, is getting larger and more varied in color and pattern. It takes on a beauty and shape that no one could have predicted or expected.

Your life is your complicated, ever-growing, creative creation, not a singular path of upward (or downward) progress. Keep up your good work.

You deserve the holistic acceptance of all of your experiences that this can bring.

## TODAY'S AFFIRMATION

My life is my creation. I am here to experience all things.

## TODAY'S JOURNAL PROMPT

The metaphor I probably use to understand my life is…If I think of my life as a creation or a complicated tapestry, that should include all things…

# DAY 213

## *You will feel isolated until you remember the total interconnection of all things.*

Much of our isolation lives in our heads. Feeling lonely is a healthy drive to connect with others, but feeling isolated is often a false construct in our imagination.

Isolation is when you imagine you are 'the only one.' The only mother struggling with an addicted or incarcerated child. The only sister left to care for a homeless sibling. The only wife caretaking an ailing spouse. You are overwhelmed by the solitary burden and feel isolated, amplifying your pain.

If you feel isolated, your job here is to connect with the stories of women like you–ancient and contemporary. Read and remember the stories of the mothers, sisters, and spouses who also walked these difficult trials alone. As you do, your isolation will ebb away.

If you are feeling lonely, it means it's time to find ways to reconnect with others. If you are feeling isolated, remember that your story is interwoven with the stories of all the women who are walking the hard path before, with, and after you.

Remember their stories and weave them into your own.

You will love the interconnection this will bring you.

### TODAY'S AFFIRMATION
I know the difference between loneliness and isolation.

### TODAY'S JOURNAL PROMPT
I am most likely to feel isolated when...

## *Wisdom Sits in Places.*

As you reflect on your stories and the stories that have helped shape your sense of yourself and your world, I'd like to remind you of another way that another culture, likely foreign to you, used story. I am not advocating for this method of using story, but I want to continue to bring your attention to the power and practice of storytelling in human history.

Keith Basso spent decades studying the Western Apache community. As he became increasingly familiar with their culture, he noticed a storytelling practice that was foundational to their way of being that had never been noticed by previous researchers. He wrote about his findings in his award winning book, *Wisdom Sits in Places.*

Basso found that, for the Western Apache, places held stories–important events that happened in specific locations still held lessons for the present. When a member of their community was violating a social norm, an elder would not resort to advice or admonishment. She would, instead, retell the story of a place. Instead of critiquing or advising the individual, she would tell the story of their ancestors, that place, and the folly that resulted in some misfortune.

Imagine this experience. The recipient is brought into an imaginary space–not one where she is uniquely bad–but one where she can imaginatively connect with her ancestors, her community, and her own current challenges.

Today, reflect on how story has shaped your life and how, in many different ways, it still can.

### TODAY'S AFFIRMATION

I notice how the way we tell stories has shaped my sense of self.

### TODAY'S JOURNAL PROMPT

This Western Apache way of storytelling would have been…for me…

# DAY 215

## *Notice your beginnings, middles, and ends.*

As you take this time to reflect back on your life, I'd like for you to try a new exercise. Instead of just thinking about when you were a mother, or an employee, or an active alcoholic, reflect on your changing journey throughout those experiences. Notice the natural rhythms that waxed and waned throughout the big experiences of your life.

Reflect on when the experience began (with pregnancy, employment, drinking, etc.). Who were you? What did you believe? Reflect on the moments in the middle. How were you different in this era? And reflect on the endings. What did closure from that time in your life look like for you?

Now reflect on your current life. Where are you with walking through your beginnings, middles, and ends? As we close in on the last decades of our lives, pay attention to how you feel about closure and endings. Pay attention to the endings you've experienced so far. See what you can learn from those journeys that might be useful to you now.

You will love the calm closure this rhythmic knowing can bring to your experiences and endings.

### TODAY'S AFFIRMATION

I accept the natural rhythms of beginnings, middles, and ends...

### TODAY'S JOURNAL PROMPT

My experience with endings is…This may shape my ideas about aging and dying in that…

# DAY 216

## *Having an ego is not a bad thing.*

Our egos have gotten a bad rap in this era of popularized mindfulness and meditation. There is an idea floating around that we need to destroy our ego in order to become an enlightened person. This is, as usual, taking a good idea too far.

Ego destruction is not the goal for most of us. A more measured approach of learning to take our ego-less seriously (or to stop letting our ego call all the shots) is better.

Your ego provides a way of being that allows you to interact in the world as a particular person, with particular likes and dislikes. Having this provisional sense of self is not a bad thing. When you grow spiritually, you don't destroy your particular ego. You simply stop taking your ego's stories so seriously. You are connected to something deeper that you know is more true.

Your ego is what is feeling the crisis when you lose things of physical or material value. Your relationship with your deepest self provides the comfort.

We get in trouble when we think the world we see from this ego perspective is the only way of seeing the world. Because the ego wants a certain measure of external comfort. Ego wants things to stay the same. Ego wants a predictable and fair world.

Today, pay attention to the balance between your ego and your spiritual self. Notice if you are over-focused on one or the other. Reflect on how you can honor your individual identity and collective connection.

### TODAY'S AFFIRMATION

I don't take my ego too seriously.

### TODAY'S JOURNAL PROMPT

My thoughts/feelings about my ego and
my deeper self tend to be...

# DAY 217

REST
REVIEW
REFLECT

*You don't get rid of your flaws to love yourself.
You accept your flaws and love yourself.*

The end of the therapeutic journey is usually different than we expect. Many of us start the process hoping that we will transform into a different kind of person. A person without all of our quirks and annoying flaws. We want to love ourselves. And we know when we change into a nicer person that we finally will.

But that doesn't happen. Deep work can bring transformative peace, just not in the way we expect. We can't escape the persistent reality of our shadow side—our repressed or 'dark' side that bugs us.

So, instead of finally transforming into a 'better' person who is easier to love, we learn to love ourselves with all of those quirks and annoying flaws. This process also allows us to more easily love others with theirs. This makes life much easier!

Today, pay attention to the parts of yourself you are still rejecting. See if you can open up to these repressed qualities in your writing, painting, or some creative visualization.

This work is hard work. Be especially patient with yourself as you explore.

You will love the self-acceptance this will bring you.

## TODAY'S AFFIRMATION
I will love myself with my flaws.

## TODAY'S JOURNAL PROMPT
When I imagine loving myself, I tend to think I need to...

# DAY 219

## *Failure is not a stepping stone to success. Failure is its own success.*

In the strange paradox of aging, everything gets inverted. We come to embrace things we used to consider anathema. Failure probably terrified you as a younger woman, but by now, you've accepted that failure is a part of your life. But, please remember, failure is valuable, not just as a stepping stone to a goal of eventual success. Failure is its own blessing.

Not everyone has experienced absolute, catastrophic personal failure. But after we do, we are granted an extraordinary new freedom.

Because trying to do everything right is exhausting. The women who are able to maintain that ruse end up the most depleted. Her success ends up being her undoing.

But after we have truly failed, we throw our hands up into the air–whether in a motion of exasperation or exultation–the experience is the same, "I can't do this."

After that moment, we are free. Because now it doesn't matter if we fail at something in the future. We've already crossed that bridge. We are not afraid of being humiliated because we've clawed our way back from those depths already.

Today, pay attention to your relationship with failure. Notice if it is still something that holds you captive. Are you afraid of failure? Do you still see it as a mere stepping stone to the comfort of eventual success? Or do you understand its innate, freeing value in its own right?

You will love the freedom that embracing (rather than fearing) failure will bring you.

### TODAY'S AFFIRMATION

Failure is its own blessing.

### TODAY'S JOURNAL PROMPT

When I think about my experiences and ideas about failure, I realize…

# DAY 220

## *Spirit doesn't reward you or punish you. You do.*

We so often project our unresolved issues onto the divine. If we feel guilty, we think God is mad at us. If we feel ashamed, we are sure the Universe wants to punish us. We imagine if we do a better job, Fate will reward us.

When we think about it more consciously, we realize this makes no sense. Your ineffable relationship with the spiritual world is not a behavioral reward chart like you had in kindergarten. You aren't discerning negative feelings from Spirit toward you. These are your feelings about yourself that you are projecting onto the divine.

When you are in that rut, piling on to yourself about how awful you think you are, I'd like to at least request that you stop adding ideas of supernatural condemnation into the mix. Every person who has had a profound spiritual experience knows that the mysterious spiritual reality is nothing except love. From near death to mystical union with the divine, the universal report is that it is love all the way down.

Today, pay attention to whether or not you are operating with this transactional idea for your spiritual relationship. Recognize these are old patterns, likely from your youngest years. If you can't believe it yet because of your own experiences, then borrow this belief from credible people who do.

Your relationship with Spirit is so much more than we can ever understand. Understand that you are loved completely and that you don't understand it.

You deserve the love this will bring you.

### TODAY'S AFFIRMATION
I am loved unconditionally.

### TODAY'S JOURNAL PROMPT
When I think of divine reward or punishment, I believe…

## *Know yourself and you will know the mysteries.*

We've all learned that Greek masculine imperative, "Know Thyself." So when our sense of self feels uncertain, it can feel like we've failed some early life exam of figuring out who we are.

But if we go beyond this ancient Greek imperative, we find an even earlier saying from ancient Egypt, "Know thyself, *and you are going to know the gods.*"

In this more ancient and *feminine* truth, we see that this statement is not imperative to arrive at a static knowing but is a call to know yourself and to then participate in an ongoing and mysterious relationship with the divine.

Because you will never completely understand the Divine, there is always more to discover. To know yourself completely would require a deadness antithetical to life. So, instead of the masculine mandate of Know Thyself, move into that more flexible, feminine, and sacred space of always knowing yourself and the mysteries more.

Today, notice how you feel about being on a continued journey of spiritual and self-discovery. See if you can allow yourself the freedom and flowering that your continued growth requires.

You will love the growth this will bring you.

## TODAY'S AFFIRMATION

I continue to grow and develop in every decade of my life.

## TODAY'S JOURNAL PROMPT

In the latter decades of life, I believe we are meant to discover...

# DAY 222

## *I can't imagine...*

As I try to make a case for the critical role of your imagination in your healing journey, I'd like to share a few examples of how the failure of imagination is possibly our most dangerous psychological state.

As a mental health therapist, I've worked closely with women who were profoundly suicidal. What I've noticed is that these women simply can't imagine relief. The inability to imagine has different causes, but the outcome is always the same–annihilating despair that makes life feel unlivable. Imagining death becomes the only soothing fantasy.

I see this in depression, where her brain is so slowed down that she has lost her ability to imagine that anything will ever change (she will usually assert an absolute feeling that her state or situation is permanent). I also see this in collectivist communities, where women can't imagine escaping from the oppressive culture she is in. I see this form of despair more frequently in the highest profile or wealthiest women; she is trapped in an oppressive, obsessive, and observing society that she can't imagine getting out of (my most brutally trafficked clients who can still imagine getting away from something or someone often have the imaginative capacity to feel more hopeful about their future options).

I also see this when women fail to imagine broadly enough. She may limit her imagination to concrete circumstances that likely won't change. She is unable to imagine that something else (her inner world, her perspective, or her spiritual growth) is what might change.

Today, pay attention to when or where you have experienced this failure of your imagination. This is usually a time or space where you feel completely stuck. See if you can reflect on how a rekindling of your creative imagination can open up a door you currently can't see.

You deserve the freedom.

### TODAY'S AFFIRMATION
I use my imagination to heal.

### TODAY'S JOURNAL PROMPT
Areas where I might have a failure of imagination
for healing or change might be...

# DAY 223

*Having wisdom doesn't mean you won't make mistakes. It means you forgive yourself when you do.*

We still mess up (especially when we can't remember things as well as we used to)! It is important to remind ourselves that being older and wiser doesn't mean we are striving for perfection. It means we are wise enough to stop striving for perfection.

As a wise woman, it is important for you to model that you can take responsibility for mistakes, feel and express sincere contrition, and be as compassionate with yourself as you wish for others.

Today, I want you to remember that your most important job is to continue to forgive yourself. Not just for the things you did long ago but for the things we all still do today. When we can accept our own fallibility and cultivate our own forgiveness, we are bringing that healing practice to a wounded world that desperately needs it.

Bring this healing into your world. For yourself and for those around you.

You deserve the peace this will bring you.

## TODAY'S AFFIRMATION

I am wise enough to still forgive myself.

## TODAY'S JOURNAL PROMPT

My feeling about still making mistakes tends to be…

# DAY 224

REST
REVIEW
REFLECT

*When you are brave enough to be yourself,
you give every other woman permission
to do the same.*

Women are so used to sidelining their goals that it is truly uncomfortable to imagine prioritizing them. It can be hard to focus on your growth when you are stuck in this rut, so I'd like for you to think of it in a different way. Your push to become who you want and need to be will give permission and inspiration to every woman who comes in contact with you for the rest of your days. Does that feel less selfish?

The truth is women tend to value community and cooperation over autonomous achievement, so they often feel 'selfish' when something seems to be just for themselves. When you understand that this growth isn't just for you but for your community, it can give you the extra push you need.

Today, reflect on how the fulfillment of your goals could positively impact others. Imagine the women it will inspire to do the same. As you visualize your intended work, keep this larger lens of how your purpose brings freedom and growth into the lives of so many others.

You will love the permission and purpose this imagining will bring you.

## TODAY'S AFFIRMATION
When I take care of myself, I teach all women to do the same.

## TODAY'S JOURNAL PROMPT
When I think about focusing on myself, I feel...

# DAY 226

*You use your intellect to think of solutions.
You use your intuition to choose your solutions.*

In our tendency toward black-and-white thinking, we often conceptualize ourselves as women who either "go with our head" (thinking) or "go with our gut" (intuition). As we mull over big problems or choices, we may struggle with which method is best.

The answer is neither and both. You've got a brain that has a lot of practical experience. You can think through the soundest scenarios. But you've also cultivated a connection with your gut feeling. You can 'know' without knowing why you know.

When you are frustrated by something, allow yourself to engage both faculties. Use your thinking mind to come up with various solutions. Then put your thinking mind away; its work is done. Allow yourself to be still and meditate. Now use your intuitive mind to select the best way forward.

Don't choose between being logical or intuitive. Use both.

Today, notice which of these methods you tend to use more–intellect or intuition. See if you can use this practice to allow more of the other faculty into your world.

You will love the balance this will bring to you and your decisions.

## TODAY'S AFFIRMATION
I can use all my ways of knowing.

## TODAY'S JOURNAL PROMPT
When it comes to thinking vs. intuition, I tend to be guided most by...
I could use the other more by...

# DAY 227

## *When you let yourself have an enemy, you let yourself become the enemy.*

You know that self-righteous anger. It can rise up against that person whose values don't align with your own. If we could just conquer evil people, then our world would be good, right?

Here is what I know, if your spiritual practice fosters hate against anyone, the problem is not with that person. The problem is with your spiritual practice. I know this is uncomfortable, especially when your most cherished values are being trampled upon.

But the truth is that when you are grounded in a deeply felt spiritual truth, you will disagree with their views, but you don't feel like they are the enemy. You might not like their beliefs, but you increasingly recognize your connection to all beings, including them.

Today, pay attention to who falls outside of your conception of 'good.' Notice who you think is 'bad.' Reflect on why you can't increase the space of your loving practice to also include them.

You will love the connected peace this will bring you.

### TODAY'S AFFIRMATION
I do not have any enemies.

### TODAY'S JOURNAL PROMPT
When I imagine that I can't truly have any enemies, I feel...

# DAY 228

## *Today, pay attention to everything that goes right.*

In most of our thoughts and interactions, we reflect upon and share the things that frustrate us. Whether this comes from our neurobiology or norms, you are probably familiar with this habit.

Let's say you've done something–cooked a large meal, organized a party, or ran a book group. Afterward, almost everyone tells you that you did a great job; a handful or fewer criticize you. Where does your mind go? Do you spend the rest of the day reveling in the kind words? Or are you, in the aftermath of obvious success, fretting over the few critiques?

This habit isn't just about evaluations by others. In general, we frequently ignore the good and focus on the negative. For example, most of us wake up most days with our homes upright, our climate control working, our electricity and water still functional, etc. But do we stop and reflect on all that is working wonderfully for us each day? Or are we frustrated that the dog chewed the plant or there are ants in the kitchen?

This habit of ignoring all that is good has a huge impact on how you feel each day.

Today, see if you can focus on everything that is going right in your world–from your functioning car to your relative safety in your neighborhood to the peace and quiet of your home. Anything and everything. See how many things you can discover that you've been missing.

This change in perspective will change your world. You deserve it.

## TODAY'S AFFIRMATION
I focus on what is going right.

## TODAY'S JOURNAL PROMPT
My focus each day tends to be on…

# DAY 229

## *What Kierkegaard didn't understand.*

Soren Kierkegaard was a nineteenth-century Danish philosopher most famously remembered as being the first existentialist–or as the famed *Christian* existentialist (later, existentialists were often associated with atheism).

Philosophers like Kierkegaard were concerned with the practical matters of the human condition. Basic questions about how we should live, act, or what we can or should believe. We can still look to his writings as we consider our own struggle to make sense of our world.

One of his most frequently shared quotes is, "Life can only be understood backward, but it must be lived forward," but this doesn't actually capture what Kierkegaard was exploring in his journal. The full quote shows him exploring these two already established claims and then using them to conclude that we cannot ever find a point in our life where we really have a moment of true understanding. He recognizes *he is always in the seat of not understanding.* He is wrestling with his recognition that we all have to live our lives without ever understanding it in our present-moment.

I bring us back to Kierkegaard because it is helpful to remember that the spaces we struggle with are the spaces we all have always struggled with.

Today, pay attention to where you feel frustrated by your own uncertainty as you move forward in your life. See if you can remember the nineteenth-century philosopher struggling similarly. Use Kierkegaard's confusion to recognize that your own confusion is something that even our most brilliant philosophers struggled with.

### TODAY'S AFFIRMATION
I can live without understanding.

### TODAY'S JOURNAL PROMPT
My belief about understanding myself and my world in this present-moment is...
When I feel a sense of uncertainty, I feel...

# DAY 230

## *You are developing the other side of yourself.*

No matter our gender identity, we are all on a journey to develop our masculine and feminine aspects. This is not a new age idea, but a very ancient one we've lost. You find this sacred value from East to West–from the Western ideas of logos and eros to the Eastern ideas of yin and yang.

One side is not more valuable than the other. Being overdeveloped in one or the other causes suffering. Everyone needs to develop both.

When we overemphasize justice, we become too rigid with our lack of compassion; when we overemphasize mercy, we become too accommodating with our lack of boundaries. We all need to develop both sides. Our cultural tendency to value our masculine aspects over our feminine is true across a number of domains–independence and connection, assertiveness and compassion, competitiveness and collaboration.

Your journey of healing includes the development of all of these 'opposites.' Today, explore where you fall on the spectrum across some of our masculine and feminine values. Notice if you feel that you are overdeveloped in one or the other. Ask yourself why you have a hard time expressing the underdeveloped side.

You will love the other sides this will open up for you.

### TODAY'S AFFIRMATION

I am growing in both my masculine and feminine dimensions.

### TODAY'S JOURNAL PROMPT

When I reflect on where I fall across some of these dualities,
I notice…

# DAY 231

# REST
# REVIEW
# REFLECT

## *Don't just think positive.*

I hear so many phrases intended to help that do more harm. Have you ever been told you just need to "think positive?" You know I am an advocate for practicing gratitude and for challenging our negative thoughts, but the mandate to "think positive" goes too far.

What does the call to "think positive" mean? Is it a mandate to hope for a particular outcome? Or is it an effort to control rather than be open to an unknown fate and how it might change us? Are we supposed to be perpetually courageous and optimistic in the face of pain and loss? Or should we embrace a more holistic view that includes all of our feelings of fear, grief, envy, rage, and/or whatever else might come up? What would it be like if we said we welcomed the whole experience? What would it mean if we stopped mandating optimism and afforded space for holding every part of our lived experiences?

Today, reflect on this phrase, "think positive." See what it means to you. Pay attention to whether or not you find it inclusive enough to guide the complexity of the life you are living.

You deserve to have everything included.

### TODAY'S AFFIRMATION
I let every part of my experiences be present.

### TODAY'S JOURNAL PROMPT
"Think positive" means to me…
this works/doesn't work for me in that…

## *A young woman adopts labels to find herself.*
## *A wise woman drops labels to find herself.*

When you were coming of age decades ago, you had to make sense of yourself in a confusing world. You started to make determinations, "I am this, not that." We all did this in interaction with our community, decoding or deciding things like, "I am a girl. I am loud. I am not very smart..." As we got older, this process continued, "I am a waitress. I am a single mom..."

This developmental process of adopting labels is one we can't avoid. It is a critical part of our ego development in the first part of life. The problem is when you get stuck with static labels and forget that you are a perpetually dynamic being. Some of these are obvious to you–you are no longer a young girl but an older woman. Others are more subtle.

It is okay to use labels loosely. They can be helpful grounding points to get along in the world. But it is dangerous to cling to them for your identity. Holding on to static labels goes against your natural, dynamic growth and everchanging pattern of living, aging, and embracing paradox.

Today, make a list of labels that you've used to define yourself–past and present. Notice how much has changed. Notice how, in some instances, your identity has run the spectrum from one end to the next. Notice where you have identified with one thing and then its opposite as you become increasingly inclusive of all things.

As a young girl, you clung to particular labels to identify yourself. Today, you let go of particular labels and find yourself.

Embrace your paradoxical existence. You deserve it.

## TODAY'S AFFIRMATION
I am more than the particular labels I gave myself.

## TODAY'S JOURNAL PROMPT
The labels I've used to describe myself are...
Areas where I have embraced opposites are...

## *Find your own source and go deep.*

As we struggle through our respective journeys, we often long for instructions from a teacher who can tell us exactly what we should do. When we are aging and on the precipice of the land of paradox, we can long to return to a childhood state where there is some expert who knows the way we need to go.

Anyone who has worked in the healing arts knows it doesn't work this way. A good teacher will function more like your facilitator or midwife. She has no idea what you should do, but she can help you to find and bring your creative self into this world. Every woman has to find her own practice for connecting with her deepest self.

Whether you meditate, pray, write, paint, or do something else, your job is to stay with the practice that resonates most with you. You can explore different traditions but don't stay on the surface by flitting around across a series of different practices. This is like digging a series of shallow wells and wondering why you never hit water. Find a practice and go deep with it. With a dedicated commitment, you will find what you are seeking.

Today, review the spiritual and personal growth practices that you've committed yourself to. Pay attention to whether they intuitively feel like the right fit for you. If they don't, keep looking. If they do, see if you can make an effort to push yourself to connect more deeply with them each day.

You will love the spiritual growth your dedication will bring.

## TODAY'S AFFIRMATION
I go deep into my spiritual practice.

## TODAY'S JOURNAL PROMPT
The spiritual practices I feel most drawn to are...

# DAY 235

## *Boethius' Wheel of Fortune.*

When we are exploring the challenging concept of how stories shape our identity and our worldview, it can be helpful to explore radically different times and spaces to see how different stories, in different eras, set different tones for what individuals might expect from themselves and/or their world.

One of my favorite ancient stories is one which was wildly popular for almost a thousand years in the Medieval Era but has fallen out of favor in our popular culture. It is the story of the "Wheel of Fortune" in Boethius' *Consolations of Philosophy*, written in the early sixth century and used as a text for study until almost the beginning of the Enlightenment era.

In this autobiographical text, Boethius is bemoaning his fate–unjustly imprisoned (he would eventually be tortured and executed) despite having lived a just and honest civic life. He meets with Lady Philosophy, who reminds Boethius of the "Wheel of Fortune," which randomly brings us up and brings us down. She reminds him this is in no way related to his behavior but the simple reality of our fate. Boethius is comforted by this, realizing he can be grateful for when he was living in comfort and freedom and can accept that his fate now is to live without.

I am not making a case for or against this as a life philosophy, but I am bringing your attention to how this foundational text (used as a primary educational text in medieval academic studies) offered a radically different view than the one we tend to hold today.

How would your expectations of the world be different if you completely let go of a causal relationship between your behavior in the world and your fate? How would you interpret your success or your failure? Again, I am not advocating for any particular view. I am using Boethius and his Wheel of Fortune paradigm as an example to illustrate how the stories we take in impact our sense of self, our world, and our deepest ideas about justice and the divine.

### TODAY'S AFFIRMATION

I pay attention to how the stories I learned shaped
my sense of self and the world.

### TODAY'S JOURNAL PROMPT

If I held this medieval belief in the truth of fickle fortune, I…

# DAY 236

## *You aren't denying yourself.*
## *You are freeing yourself.*

It is hard when we are trying to let go of habits that we know are self-destructive. Whether it is related to food, drinking, media, or something else, we all can get hooked on bad habits that we start to associate with pleasure and relief.

This association makes it doubly hard for you to lose the habit because it often feels like a denial of (often much-deserved) pleasure or relief after a hard day.

One thing we can do to help is to work on this association. Instead of feeling like you are denying yourself the pleasure of your habit, reconceptualize your attempt to quit as one of freeing yourself from your enslavement to it (anger can be helpful here)! It has so much power over you. It isn't a relief you are being denied, but a self-constructed prison you are going to escape.

When we reconceptualize our habit this way, we stop feeling deprived and start feeling empowered in the face of daunting change. Quitting is difficult, but we can make it easier if we change our thinking about what we are trying to let go of.

Today, pay attention to your attitude toward the habits you are trying to change. Do you imagine them as a reward or relief? What if you think of them as a prison? Notice if changing your perspective changes how you feel.

You deserve the empowering change this can bring you.

### TODAY'S AFFIRMATION
I am not controlled by my habits.

### TODAY'S JOURNAL PROMPT
The things I tend to go back to for comfort that I struggle with are...

## *Stop seeking a balance.*
## *Start flowing with your rhythms.*

At some point, you've probably set the goal of trying to find a better balance in your life. No matter what the polarities (e.g., work/life, personal/family, fitness/leisure), you probably imagine that this is an important but elusive goal that you've rarely been able to hit. This is another story that is making you sick.

The idea of balance is a terrible construct for you to use when thinking about the rhythms of your life. When something is in balance, nothing is moving. With balance, there is a perfect, static equilibrium. There is nothing about this stagnant image that resonates with the way you could or should live your life.

What you can do is embrace rhythms. Think about winter rolling into spring and spring rolling into summer. Imagine the celestial bodies that move away and toward you again and again. Reflect on the tides that go out and then in. These seasons and bodies are not seeking balance. Instead, they are moving with the natural rhythms of being alive–sometimes full, sometimes empty, sometimes close, sometimes far, sometimes cool, sometimes warm. They aren't seeking balance but are moving between ways of being.

Today, pay attention to where you are still hard on yourself for not finding the right balance. See if you can change your story from this measure of inactivity to a more natural one of your perpetually dynamic flow.

You will love the natural pace this will allow into your way of being.

## TODAY'S AFFIRMATION

I don't seek balance but accept the natural ebbs and flows of being alive.

## TODAY'S JOURNAL PROMPT

My experiences with seeking balance or allowing myself to flow
with the natural rhythms are...

# REST
# REVIEW
# REFLECT

## *Pay attention to the wisdom of your wounds.*

When you first start out on your healing journey, there is so much pain to process. Grief for what you've had to endure. Anger that this is your story. Envy of others who seem to be walking an easier path. We all need to stay in this space for as long as we need to be there, but please know that this is only step one of your healing journey.

After you've taken the time to feel your way through your grief, your anger, and your trauma, you move into a new space. Now, you notice that you are not so captive to the horrible things that happened to you in the past. You likely feel sad for the younger you who had to endure those things, but you are more grounded in a present-moment where you recognize those things aren't happening anymore. It's different to be in this space. It's easier.

As you continue your process of healing, you begin to notice the people who are still in as much pain as you used to be. You feel a deep empathy for what they are going through as you know how much it hurts. This is the next stage of your journey. Something purposeful and unique to you can come up here. You may feel called to new creative projects. You may feel called to speak, write, or paint. You may feel a need to be a healing presence for the younger people in your life.

It's not just that you are more than your pain. What you've overcome will become a central, creative resource for inspiring this next stage of your life.

Have the courage to move into and process your pain. Reconnect with the living, creative, healer spirit that is hidden there.

You deserve the healing and creative reconnection.

### TODAY'S AFFIRMATION

There is a purposefulness to my hard journey.

### TODAY'S JOURNAL PROMPT

Creative ideas, projects, or vocations that have recurred
in my imagination are...

# DAY 240

## *Gaman:* *Enduring the seemingly unbearable with patience and dignity.*

By now, you are starting to recognize that many of the stories you received in Western culture mixed you up. Many Westerners believe they should have a comfortable and easy life. If they do not, something is wrong, or someone is to blame. As we struggle to make sense of ourselves, it can help to look to foreign cultures to see how they have made sense of the universal trials we all endure.

One of my favorite terms is the Japanese word *gaman.* Often simplistically translated into English as "patience," the word has a much richer meaning. *Gaman* means to endure the seemingly unbearable with patience and dignity. Can you think of an American English word that comes close to such a beautiful and useful concept? We don't have a word for it because we don't ever think about our life this way.

Anyone who is aging has learned the experience of *gaman.* But every old woman who knows this likely learned it on her own because the stories and wisdom of elders are no longer passed on in our youth-obsessed culture. We don't honor the experience of *gaman.*

Today, reflect on what you've survived and celebrate that you have done so. Find meaning in your *gaman* and your ability to endure the hardships of life with dignity and grace.

Maybe we can pass this gift on to the next generation.

### TODAY'S AFFIRMATION
I endure with patience and dignity.

### TODAY'S JOURNAL PROMPT
My response to this word *gaman* is…

## *Trying again is how we all do it.*

It's easy for all of us to come up with reasons why we aren't more committed to our goals. Days can go by when we simply forget to do the things we intend to do. When we fall away from our practices, we feel less motivated to get back to them, starting a disintegrating trend.

My clients have taught me so much. One thing I've learned is that it isn't just me—we all screw up. We all fall away from our best practices. We all fall short of our goals for ourselves. We all are years behind on our projects.

But, as a therapist, what I also see is that some women are fiercely committed to keep trying. When this woman falls down, she gets back up. When she screws up, she tries again. When she loses her sobriety, she goes back to that meeting. When she misses her goal, she sets it again.

You can't make the choice to be perfect with your goals. That isn't realistic for any of us. Screwing up is part of all of our processes.

But, no matter how far away you've fallen, you can make the choice to return. To make the best choices for yourself today.

Today, make a commitment to get back to your best practices and goals, no matter how far away they seem.

You deserve the healing and health this will bring you.

## TODAY'S AFFIRMATION

Today, I return to my best practices.

## TODAY'S JOURNAL PROMPT

Am I expecting myself to be perfect in my practice? Or am I compassionate and responsible in understanding we all fall away and return?

## *Nature? Nurture? Mystery?*

Our scientific worldview degraded our spiritual worldview. Today, if you get a mental health assessment, you will likely answer a lot of questions that have to do with your genetic and environmental history (e.g., Did Mom also have depression? Was your father emotionally absent?).

There is nothing wrong with wondering about these parts of your story as long as you understand they aren't your whole story, as our assessments often suggest. If we were simply a mathematical sum of our genes and family environment, we wouldn't intuitively know and experience the absolute uniqueness of every individual.

Do you believe every individual is unique? Then you, too, believe in something more than our nature and nurture scientific worldview. Your job is to know your story but to always remember that there is also a mystery in your equation.

Today, pay attention to whether or not you consider yourself the simple sum of your genetic and family history. See if you can remember that, as a completely unique woman, you are also something so much more. Your task is to continue to connect with that mystery.

You will love the spiritual freedom this perspective will bring you.

### TODAY'S AFFIRMATION

I am more than the facts of my life.

### TODAY'S JOURNAL PROMPT

The facts of my life do not tell the full story of who I am in that…

# DAY 243

*A young woman wishes she could have had the life she always imagined. A wise woman doesn't compare a real life to an imaginary one.*

As I listen to older women tell the stories of their lives, I often hear the haunting of a parallel story of a life she didn't get to live. We can all get lost in this fantasy of another self who lived a better life. That other self with the better life is invariably happier, smarter, wiser, and more fulfilled than we currently are.

The problem is that this fantasy life is just that—a fantasy. It lives on in our minds, static and never subjected to the fluid challenges and frustration of a real life. Your imaginary life never got tested against the hardships and limitations of the world, so it can live on in this intoxicating, embryonic ideal that you forever mourn.

It is okay for us to mourn the things that we didn't get to do. But it is not okay to mourn an idealized and unrealistic fantasy.

Today, pay attention to whether or not you are allowing yourself to mourn a fantasy. Recognize its simple, static perfection and the unfairness of comparing such a thing to the real and messy lives that we all must live.

You deserve the present-moment peace this can bring you.

## TODAY'S AFFIRMATION

I won't mourn an imaginary fantasy.

## TODAY'S JOURNAL PROMPT

The unrealistic fantasy of how my life could have been is...

# DAY 244

## *If the space you are in isn't supportive, your responsibility is to find a space that is.*

In my women's groups and writing retreats, I get the chance to spend lots of time with resilient and wise women. These women always remind me of the importance of being with people who honor our truth and of searching out our spaces for healing, even, and especially when the people closest to us can't provide that for us.

So many women have walked a hard path, and yet so many women feel completely alone in their woundedness. When older women come together in writing, processing, and healing, I'm always amazed at the power of everyday women to heal each other. There are often tears and laughter among groups of women who were strangers to each other before.

Remember, you don't need particular people to believe you or support you to heal. The women I work with, often unable to find support in their immediate community, find new communities of healing–whether in twelve-step programs, pottery classes, synagogues, churches, or feminist groups. I am always in awe at how they have been able to carve out spaces of healing for themselves.

They remind me, and I want to remind you, if the people around you aren't supporting you in your healing journey, keep looking for your tribe until you find one that will.

You deserve the support. You deserve the healing.

## TODAY'S AFFIRMATION
I find healing spaces where I am supported.

## TODAY'S JOURNAL PROMPT
I do/do not have a group that I feel is supportive of me...

# DAY 245

# REST
# REVIEW
# REFLECT

# *Every irritation is an invitation.*

You may think that you can't find peace because there are too many things that are difficult in your current life. Maybe you are working long hours, in physical pain, taking care of someone with psychological or medical needs, or have some other chronic, pressing issue that interferes with your ability to find any moment of quiet for yourself.

But it is exactly the opposite. You might think you need quiet space to find quiet space, but you actually need to find it in the midst of this chaos. Think of Jesus in the wilderness. He wasn't sitting in comfort but being tormented by one distracting temptation after another. Buddha was tormented similarly in his spiritual quest.

Zen Buddhist priest Karen Maezen Miller shares how she used her difficult journey of depression and motherhood as her Zen practice. This is your journey–to find that inner stillness when the outside world won't bring any comfort.

Going forward, when you have a difficulty or something pushing you beyond the brink, instead of imagining it as an excuse for failing to do your spiritual practice, reconsider it as an invitation to turn inward and find your own inner quiet.

Don't wait for a moment of quiet to find yours. Your task is to still find it now.

## TODAY'S AFFIRMATION

I find inner peace in the midst of difficulty.

## TODAY'S JOURNAL PROMPT

I think I don't have time or space for my spiritual practices because...

## *We misunderstand detachment and how it helps us.*

The concept of detachment can be so confusing. If we are detached from the world, does that mean we don't care about the world or other people? If we are attached to a person or a cause, does that mean we are not letting go in the way we are supposed to?

Neither of these sounds like good goals, so it is no wonder we don't want to work toward them. But the problem isn't with detachment. It is with our understanding of the term.

Being detached doesn't mean you don't care. Being detached means you *let go of outcomes.* You see this ancient wisdom in so many sayings, "Let go and let God" or "Lower your expectations."

Being detached means you can still care deeply about fighting against injustice or exploitation, but you find peace in knowing the ultimate results are out of your hands. You find meaning in your present work, but you don't torture yourself over the outcomes you can't control.

The irony is that this detachment allows us to be more effective in the areas we are passionate about because we aren't so depleted by disappointment. We find fulfillment and meaning in the choices we make today but understand the rest is absolutely out of our hands.

Today, reflect on the things that feel important to you. Notice if you invest too much emotional energy in the aspects that are out of your control. See if you can find a more local and personal choice or action where you will find meaning that sustains, rather than depletes, you.

You will love the peace and meaning this will bring you.

## TODAY'S AFFIRMATION

I know the power and practice of deeply caring and true detachment.

## TODAY'S JOURNAL PROMPT

My belief about detachment and caring is…

## *Meeting our shadow.*

Have you ever had a visceral, gut-level negative aversion to someone? It is possible that you are intuitively picking up something that feels off in them, but therapists know and are trained to be immediately suspicious of ourselves. If you are doing any kind of depth work, step one is not to assume there is a problem with the other person but that we've tapped into something viscerally rejected in our own unconscious. This is what we call shadow work (and yes, we all hate doing our shadow work. In fact, that hate suggests you are on the right track!).

Shadow work is confusing and hard. Your shadow is, by definition, hiding from you, so these parts can be hard to find. You can get a surprise shadow exercise when you notice that negative visceral reaction to someone, but you can also try to play in this space more intentionally.

One exercise that I love is imagining our idealized selves. Who is it you want to be? What kinds of compliments mean most to you? Now, explore the opposite. How do you feel if you imagine yourself embodying the opposite of what you idealize? Go there and explore whether or not that material is in your shadow.

It is important to remember that not all of our shadow material is culturally negative. You might be attached to humility in a way that negates your success.

See if you can play with this with compassion. Shadow work is provocative. If you start having strong negative reactions, you are likely on the right track.

You deserve the compassion for yourself and others this work will open for you.

## TODAY'S AFFIRMATION

I have to courage to meet my dark side.

## TODAY'S JOURNAL PROMPT

The compliments I like most are…
the opposite of that is…

# DAY 249

## *Your individual creativity is the expression of the Universal Creator within you.*

So many women sideline their creative projects. You might consider working creatively to be too indulgent when you have so much to do. Or you may consider your creative project to be pointless because you have no idea where it could end up.

This is the wrong way to think about your creative impulses. Bringing your creation into the material world brings much-needed meaning and vitality to your life. It isn't indulgent. The end result of the project doesn't matter. The point is to delight in the life-affirming act of writing, quilting, painting, cooking, or whatever creative medium you pursue.

You know how you feel when you are in this zone. Deep inside, you intuitively know this is good for you. When you surrender to your creative imagination, you are closest to the Divine Creator and your truest self.

Today, reflect on the creative projects and hobbies you have set aside. Ask yourself why you haven't found time for them. See if you can find the time to reconnect with universal creation in your creation.

You will love the meaning this will bring you.

### TODAY'S AFFIRMATION
My creativity is the creator within me.

### TODAY'S JOURNAL PROMPT
I tend to think of my creativity as…

# DAY 250

## *Let's start telling each other our real stories.*

In our homes, we interact more with digital devices than with real people. In digital isolation, you can hide the parts of yourself you don't like, and you don't see those parts of others. We are losing our ability to be our real selves with other people. This lazy descent into the psychological comfort of avoiding our hard stories has come with a high price.

When we finally do interact with someone, we often wish for them to think well of us and are more likely to share the positive sides of ourselves and our experiences. This is a natural instinct, but the irony is that it doesn't cultivate the connection that we need. As lonely women desperately search for a nurturing connection, our habit of putting our best face forward is actually wounding.

When we find the courage to tell the whole truth about our journey–our success and our suffering–we transcend the superficiality that keeps us perpetually isolated and lonely. Together, we can finally laugh and cry and connect.

Today, pay attention to whether or not you have spaces to speak and hear real stories. Notice if you persist in putting up a wounding, positive front. See if you can find a space where you can stop. Notice how you feel when you imagine expanding the spaces in which you can express your true story.

We could all use the healing this will bring.

### TODAY'S AFFIRMATION

I find spaces where I can tell and hear true stories from real women.

### TODAY'S JOURNAL PROMPT

I imagine I am different from other women in that...
If I found other women were the same, I would feel...

# DAY 251

## *Aging teaches us to slow down.*

One good thing about aging is that there are so many new things happening that are helping us along on our spiritual journey. At midlife, we start to get the crash course on spiritual teachings.

If you are an older woman, you know your body has changed. You aren't moving as quickly as you did when you were younger. When you stand up, it might hurt, and it probably takes you a few extra moments to get going.

I'd like to ask you to use this extra moment as a spiritual touchstone. Your aging body is teaching you to slow down. You literally can't go as fast as you could when you were younger, and that is exactly what you need to learn. Slowing down is your psycho-spiritual task for this stage of life.

So, next time you stand up and are waiting for the stiffness to subside, remind yourself, "I am learning to slow down. I am learning to be present." Building this mantra into this moment will create a frequent spiritual touchstone for you.

You will love the present-moment practice this will bring.

### TODAY'S AFFIRMATION
I use my experience of aging as my spiritual practice.

### TODAY'S JOURNAL PROMPT
When I think about the process of aging, I feel…

# REST
# REVIEW
# REFLECT

# *The world doesn't need our help.*

"Are you worried about the world?" asked Chuang Tzu, the ancient Taoist master. "Do you think that it needs your guidance? Don't the heavens turn by themselves? Don't the sun and moon find their places?"

Stephen Mitchell, in his anthology, *The Second Book of the Tao,* combines ancient Chinese wisdom with both Greek mythology and Jungian psychology when he uses this ancient saying to ask us if we have an "Atlas Complex," a mistaken belief that the world can't get along without our help.

Have you ever watched the spring roll in? The leaves bursting from the branches? Have you ever woken up in horror to realize the world continues despite our tragedies? What does the world really need from you to keep going?

Many of us mistakenly imagine our words and actions are almost necessary for our world to function, but Mitchell reminds us that this is an ancient yet common delusion. The world continues without us. It doesn't need our intervention.

Today, pay attention to how you might be overtaxing yourself with beliefs about what you need to do or say in your world. See if you can watch the natural world and recognize that the world can and will continue, with or without our words and deeds.

As Mitchell reminds us, if we can learn how to govern our own minds, we will see that the universe governs itself.

You deserve the rest.

## TODAY'S AFFIRMATION
The world is okay without my intervention.

## TODAY'S JOURNAL PROMPT
I do/do not identify with this Atlas complex. I tend to...

# DAY 254

## *The story of stasis.*

Despite living in a completely dynamic body and world, we all drift toward the fantasy of a fixed and static reality. The world is in constant motion, but we often imagine we, others, and our world are unchanging in some capacity. This usually relates to the harder aspects of our journey, but it can show up anywhere.

My illness is unbearable. My child is unhappy. My grief is crushing. When we are faced with these present-moments, we usually can't get out of our painful, blinding bubble. We lose our awareness that we will change, that they will change, that the circumstance will change and that the world will change. It may be a movement toward ease. It may become more challenging. In this moment, we don't know.

This is an important truth to remember in your hardest moments. Whatever is good, bad, or indifferent in you, others, or your world will be different in a different moment.

Use this to let go of your present pain (to stop imagining your state is permanent) or to hold on more loosely to your pleasure (recognizing you can roll with the rhythms of life).

Nothing is static. You and our world are in constant process, learning to move through all the inner and outer experiences of this life. You are doing a good job.

### TODAY'S AFFIRMATION
Everything changes–me and my world.

### TODAY'S JOURNAL PROMPT
I am most likely to imagine things are stuck or permanent with/when...
When this comes up again, I will...

## *The Heroine's Aging Journey.*

You've probably heard of Joseph Campbell's Hero's Journey, but I'd like for us to think about Campbell's work a little differently. We often conceptualize Campbell's monomyth as representing the development of a younger person. Today, I'd like for you to explore the heroine's journey for a later stage of life.

I'm going to give you Campbell's summary of the monomyth, then ask you to apply this to your aging journey.

Here is Campbell's summary:

A hero ventures forth from the world of common day into the supernatural: fabulous forces are encountered there, and a decisive victory is won: the hero comes back from this mysterious adventure with new powers to share with humanity.

Let's explore this as an aging woman:

1.  What is the "ordinary world" you are leaving behind as you grow old?

2.  What challenges have you faced or do you fear facing on your aging journey?

3.  How might you be changed by those experiences (I encourage you to explore positive changes; if that is too challenging, think of someone you admire facing them in a way that you would admire)?

4.  What mysteries might be discovered in these trials? Even if this has not happened for you, what do you imagine might be a mystery you could discover and "bring back." Imagine the Wise Woman. What do you imagine she has discovered?

### TODAY'S AFFIRMATION
I am on a new heroine's journey.

### TODAY'S JOURNAL PROMPT
If I think about aging as a heroine's journey, I...

## *When the words cannot hold your pain,*
## *return to ritual.*

I get lots of questions about how we can heal ourselves outside of the time and expense of the therapy room. Therapy is helpful, but it is a luxury most older women don't have the resources to access.

When you are hurting, you know the regular go-to self-help practices–talk to a friend, write in your journal, cry, or rage to exhaustion. These are the first things you can do when you need to process your pain.

But sometimes, these simple practices are not enough. Sometimes, their simplicity can't hold our immense pain. When the experience is too emotionally complicated to share or write out of yourself, this is the time to return to ritual–an ancient and deep, symbolic language of the soul.

In our empirical and scientific world, we've lost touch with this healing, imaginative practice. Rituals embody experiences beyond words. When you need them, nothing else will do. Your ritual should be created by you. It should symbolically represent your experience in ways that only you know how to represent. Play around with your ideas until you find something that feels right.

Today, pay attention to any painful experiences that feel stuck. Reflect on whether or not some kind of ritual may help you find the processing space, peace, and closure that your previous work has not been able to do. Imagine what that ritual might look like. Imagine bringing it into the world through dramatic enactment.

You deserve the healing this can bring you.

### TODAY'S AFFIRMATION
I can process my pain.

### TODAY'S JOURNAL PROMPT
Experiences that I feel emotionally stuck on are...

# DAY 257

## *Audre Lorde's Erotic as Power.*

Audre Lorde was a black lesbian feminist/womanist poet in the 1970s Whether or not you've ever identified with any of her labels, we can all still learn from what she taught us about embracing feminine power.

One of her most famous essays is "Uses of the Erotic, The Erotic as Power," where she challenges a feminist position against the erotic. Advocating for embracing eroticism as a part of feminine power, Lorde reminds us that true eros is not about superficial sexual desire, but is the source of feeling that generates writing, cultivates connection and empowers all of our creative projects.

Lorde teaches us that when women go deeper, realizing that eros is not about superficial sexual desire, women will find the resource that connects them to their deepest power.

Lorde reminds us that when women truly connect with their eros, they are harder to control. She was speaking from the margins in the 1970s, but her claims hold true for all of us today. When you truly connect to this deepest feeling, you are alive. You can't be stopped (if you are having a hard time imagining this, imagine the feeling that comes up when you feel protective of someone you love; this is the same power).

Today, reflect on your attitude about the erotic. Pay attention to whether or not you've been duped into the story that this is just about shallow sexual desire. See if you can imagine going deeper with your understanding of your eros and reconnecting to your own power.

You deserve the energy this will bring you.

### TODAY'S AFFIRMATION
I recognize the power of my eros energy.

### TODAY'S JOURNAL PROMPT
My thoughts and feelings about the erotic and eros tend to be...

## *Sacred teachings are not moral laws to make you "good." They are spiritual truths to make you well.*

We are overwhelmed with a tidal wave of negative messages about ourselves and others. If we internalize these messages, we believe that we are not good enough, safe enough, or something-else enough. If we externalize these messages, we talk about how others are not good enough, smart enough, or something-else enough.

We all benefit when we are intentional about not participating in these messages of being not-enough. Every spiritual tradition teaches us to be kind to ourselves and others. Buddha said to practice loving-kindness. Jesus taught us to love our neighbor. Mohammed insisted that the best humans were those who never harmed others by word or deed.

These spiritual teachers did not bring us moral teachings to make us "good"–but spiritual teachings to make us well.

When you reject the dominant narrative of being not-good-enough, you stop this process; you are renewed and have more energy. Try it. Today, make a commitment to remember your spiritual practices are about learning to be well, not good. See how you feel.

You will love the clarity and energy this practice will bring you.

### TODAY'S AFFIRMATION
I am learning to be well.

### TODAY'S JOURNAL PROMPT
I notice I start to get judgmental of myself or others when…

# DAY 259

# REST
# REVIEW
# REFLECT

## *Simplify everything.*

Women in the West tend to think of simplicity as a material goal, but if you dig deeper, you will discover it is much more than getting rid of unwanted objects. Whether you hear it in a twelve-step program or an Eastern faith, the teaching to keep it simple is not just about minimalistic material life but a call to be disciplined against our tendencies toward complexity (which leads to a sense of chaos and/or overwhelm).

Keeping it simple means saying no to a lot of things–material objects, media noise, intrusive thoughts, or busyness and distraction. I will bet that few things in your life are calling you into this practice.

When you are living simply, you can sit quietly, doing nothing. When you live simply, you probably have few material objects. When you live simply, you are not filling your mental space with the chaos of other people's thoughts (television, media, news, etc.). When you live simply, you do one thing at a time.

Today, pay attention to where you can increase your discipline by keeping it simple. Notice if you are too busy. Notice if you are ever able to sit quietly with your thoughts. Notice if you have too many things to take care of and/or think about. You can't perfectly simplify your life, but you can take steps to hold back the constant creep of complexity.

You deserve the peace that your simplicity brings.

## TODAY'S AFFIRMATION

I bring the discipline of simplicity to many domains of my life.

## TODAY'S JOURNAL PROMPT

An area where I struggle with complexity is…

# DAY 261

## *Your mundane life is your sacred practice.*

Most of us have a repetitive loop in our heads telling us we 'should' be doing something more interesting. The things we are tasked with are 'wrong' for us. We should be working on something more important. We should have traveled more. We should have written more.

When we allow ourselves to be tricked into this idea that a more interesting life would have been a better life, then we are buying into a false story.

The truth is, for each of us, our mundane life is our practice. It is my job to find my spiritual work in cleaning up after an incontinent family member. I have to learn how to center myself when I feel overwhelmed with the repetitive tedium of my daily obligations.

When we embrace the actual experiences of our life instead of escaping into a fantasy of a more stimulating or interesting life, we find our spiritual practice everywhere.

Today, try to consider the most difficult or mundane experiences in your day as your assigned sacred practice. Instead of resenting them, use them.

You will love the inner peace this will bring you.

### TODAY'S AFFIRMATION
I find spiritual practice in the mundane.

### TODAY'S JOURNAL PROMPT
The activities I tend to resent are...
If I thought of them as a spiritual practice, I...

# DAY 262

## *I am flexible, not rigid.*

As you've aged, you've learned how to say no to things that don't work for you. You learned to set limits in at least some areas of your life. This is a healthy practice!

But we have to be careful that we don't allow our healthy ability to set limits drift into a rigid inflexibility. How do you know the difference? I am going to tell you one way to examine this question.

Limits that are coming from your inner self are almost always good for you. If you are an introvert, saying no to too many social gatherings is a healthy choice. If you have extreme social phobias, saying no to social gatherings might not be the healthiest choice.

As you can see, there is no single answer for what behavior is best for all of us. Only you can make the intuitive call on whether you are flexible with boundaries or becoming too rigid with fears.

Today, pay attention to areas where you think you may have become more rigid. Ask yourself if the limits you've set are inspired by an affirming inner experience or driven by a fear of something outside. Where you discover fear driving you into rigidity, see if you can imagine yourself pushing those limits in some very small way.

You will love the continued growth this will foster in you.

### TODAY'S AFFIRMATION

I am aware of the inner and outer motivations behind my actions.

### TODAY'S JOURNAL PROMPT

An area where I might like to become less rigid would be...

# DAY 263

## *You never lose your freedom to choose your response to any situation.*

There are times in our lives when we lose some of our freedoms. Wise women know that we can get trapped in our circumstances–maybe with an illness or a disability. Maybe in a role as a caretaker or a financial provider. Maybe in a situation without enough financial resources to be independent. It is easy to become resentful and envious when this happens.

These are the moments in our lives where we learn if we have built up any resilience or any spiritual depth during the easy times. If we haven't, this is our chance to finally do so.

Certain freedoms can be taken away from us, but we never lose our freedom to choose how we respond. During our difficult phases, we may not be able to feel happy, but we can feel good about the choices we are making. To not self-destruct. To meet our obligations to others. To not give up. To continue to work on our spiritual growth in spite of the immense obstacles.

When you've lived long enough–through illness, tragic loss, bankruptcy, disability, caretaking, etc., you learn that you eventually make it to the other side.

Today, if you are in a hard spot, make sure you are making the choices that you will feel good about when you do get to the other side. Your future self needs you to do that.

And you deserve it.

### TODAY'S AFFIRMATION
I can find inner freedom even with outer restrictions.

### TODAY'S JOURNAL PROMPT
When I feel trapped by my circumstances, I...

# DAY 264

## *Learning to tolerate conflict is learning to love.*

As you age, you might wish that people you care about would just get along better. But this fantasy has you trapped in the hope that can't fully manifest. The reality, for most of us, is that conflict will persist between people we care about.

When we are longing for an elusive peace, we misunderstand how that can manifest for us. It isn't that you won't have any conflicts; what changes is that now you can handle conflicts. Your grandchild may be distressing their parent, but you are not emotionally destabilized by the crisis situation. You can let it be present, loving everyone without reacting. You are learning to love the people closest to you–with the inevitable conflict that will always arise.

Today, remember that you are not trying to reach a place where conflict never arises in your relationships. You are learning that you are not knocked off your feet by them. You can tolerate conflicts as you learn to be a loving presence in your world.

You deserve the peace.

### TODAY'S AFFIRMATION
I can tolerate conflict.

### TODAY'S JOURNAL PROMPT
The conflicts that tend to distress me the most are...

# DAY 265

## *It isn't always projection.*

Is there a person or a personality that really gets under your skin? A type that immediately gets you angry or upset? You know where I am going with this–and it is so irritating, isn't it? You've already heard the self-help saying that what we hate in others is what we hate in ourselves.

Unfortunately, that popular phrase hasn't got it exactly right.

Yes, it is true that what I hate and deny in myself, I will project onto and loathe in others. But it is a huge leap to reverse the claim and assert that what I loathe in others is something I must harbor and hate in myself.

You may loathe injustice. You may loathe cruelty. You may loathe oppression.

There is a difference between a conscious awareness of our values and an unconscious triggering of our shadow. You will know the difference by your reaction. When we are unconsciously triggered, we feel like we've been taken over. Even the phrases we use, like, 'gets under my skin' or 'knee-jerk reaction,' indicates an automatic and unconscious process.

When we are consciously aware of our values being violated, we can remain calm in our distress. We can act against injustice without being destructively reactive.

Today, pay attention to your relationship to these two ways of responding to your interpersonal challenges. When you are bothered by someone, notice the distinction between your awareness of your conscious values and your reaction to your unconscious triggers.

You will love the conscious awareness this will develop within you.

### TODAY'S AFFIRMATION

I am always becoming more conscious.

### TODAY'S JOURNAL PROMPT

I am probably most reactive to...because...

# REST
# REVIEW
# REFLECT

## *Embrace your not-knowing until something new emerges.*

We are often under so much pressure to make decisions. In our get-it-done culture, we feel rushed to solve our problems quickly. But sometimes, your best choice is to sit with uncertainty without making a decision. Be still with your problem until something new arises on its own.

We see this wise guidance in the writings of our greatest teachers. In *The Tao*, Lao Tzu asks, "Can you remain unmoving until the right action arises by itself?" Carl Jung encourages us to sit patiently with our two irreconcilable choices until a 'third' thing emerges.

This concept is so foreign (even anathema) to our goal-oriented Western culture. In a world that celebrates taking action, being still in crisis is seen as being pathologically passive. But the reality is, your brain can't figure it out–or it would have already.

Today, take whatever you can't solve and allow yourself to sit with the irreconcilable conflict. Don't think. Don't consider alternatives. Just try to still your mind and let the problem just be there. Continue to do this until something else emerges on its own.

You deserve the respite.

### TODAY'S AFFIRMATION

I don't need to solve every problem.

### TODAY'S JOURNAL PROMPT

When there is a problem, I tend to...
I probably respond this way because...

## *Eve and Odysseus.*

You are probably very familiar with the story of Eve and how her taking of the apple caused the fall of all of humanity. You might not be as familiar with the story of Odysseus and his temptation by the Sirens.

In my view, these two stories are very similar, but we interpret them very differently.

A masculine god prohibited Adam and Eve from eating from the Tree of Knowledge of Good and Evil. Eve was tempted by the serpent and chose to eat from the tree, seeing that it was "desirable for gaining wisdom."

If we look at Homer's Odyssey, we see a very similar theme. In a perfect inverse, we now have a female goddess guiding a male hero. This goddess Circe warns Odysseus about the allure of the Siren's call. She teaches him how to avoid his own destruction by their irresistible temptation.

If you do any cursory research on the "Siren's Song," you will encounter descriptions of their seductive allure. The contemporary interpretation of the Siren is usually very superficially sexual. But do you know what the Siren's Song is? It isn't sexy women, but much more like Eve's Tree of Knowledge. Here is the Siren's Song that brings men to destroy themselves:

"He who listens will go on his way not only charmed but wiser…we can tell you everything that is going to happen over the whole world."

Just like the Tree of Knowledge, the Sirens were promising wisdom and knowledge. In both stories, our attempt to achieve this will result in our death.

We are tempted by knowledge. In both stories, the desire to know is irresistible.

Today, pay attention to how we tell and interpret these similar stories. Read them and make your own interpretations.

You deserve the wisdom.

### TODAY'S AFFIRMATION
We all wish we had more wisdom.

### TODAY'S JOURNAL PROMPT
When I see these similar stories of Eve and Odysseus, I think/feel…

# DAY 269

## *Wise old women are dangerous?*

The accusation of someone being a witch can still strike fear in some people, especially in conservative religious communities. As we cope with a culture that struggles with the existence of aging women, our Western history of witch trials is worth wondering about.

We know now that the majority of women tortured and executed for witchcraft were single women over the age of forty. You probably know (or identify with?) this single, over-forty woman. We may call her the 'crazy cat lady' or the 'crazy aunt,' but we are all familiar with the independent woman who is living her life going to the beat of her own drum. These were the women the authorities accused, tortured, and executed.

The rise of the printing press fostered a massive distribution of this story about the threat of these old, solitary women. Scholars estimated that tens of thousands of old women were tortured and killed (most historians also agree that the accused were likely innocent of devil worship).

I remember being sent a quote, "When did we learn to fear the witches and not the people who set them on fire?" We still hold negative attitudes toward and stereotypes about older women, but maybe we are starting to question this story.

Today, pay attention to your feelings about stories of 'witches' and quirky, solitary old women. Notice if you've adopted a story of fearfulness associated with this wise, older woman go who has learned to listen to the beat of her own drum.

### TODAY'S AFFIRMATION
I let go of negative stereotypes about independent, old women.

### TODAY'S JOURNAL PROMPT
When I think of the old women accused, tortured, and executed by authorities,
I wonder…

## *Returning to Erik Erikson.*

Our contemporary models of psychosocial development are dominated by the work of Erik Erikson. Whether you know it or not, what Erikson wrote has shaped your story of how you understand yourself, as his insights have traveled deep into our cultural understanding of what it means to develop as a human being.

Erikson's ideas became popular because they are good, but I'd like to reconsider how he considered the last stages of life. His developmental model rests upon a story of progress; I'd like to explore how we might revise his model with a more feminine and circular awareness.

Because I believe all of Erikson's psychosocial stages of early life are revisited in late life, and, importantly, we draw new insights from our return to these late-life psychosocial crises. According to Erikson, each stage presents a developmental task; I'd like for you to revisit some of his early tasks and questions, reflecting on how you might understand them differently in late life.

**Trust vs. Mistrust:** *Does the child find a world that is safe and predictable?* As we age, what happens when we stop expecting our world to be safe and/or predictable?

**Autonomy vs. Shame:** *Does the child feel competent?* What happens as we learn to cope with our inability to do things?

**Initiative vs. Guilt:** *Does the child feel guilty and that they are a burden?* What happens when we discover we are increasingly dependent upon others?

**Industry vs. Inferiority:** *Does the child feel her work is recognized by her society?* What happens when we realize we will not do all the things our younger self imagined she would do? Or that we can't do the things we used to do?

Erikson's model is a useful model of linear progress in early life. Pay attention to what you can add to your understanding of yourself if you use his model in a more circular method in your later years.

You deserve the new insights.

## TODAY'S AFFIRMATION

I return to old developmental questions
and find new answers.

## TODAY'S JOURNAL PROMPT

When I think about Erikson's questions in old age, I notice…

# DAY 271

## *Conspiracies and emotionally 'true' stories.*

How do you cope with friends and family that you think believe in unbelievable stories? The last few years have seen differences in beliefs tear apart our relationships. How can you cope with someone who seems to believe something that seems so absolutely absurd?

I am going to tell you how a therapist approaches this story, so you can try it out for yourself. The key is to understand, to absolutely know, that this 'absurd' story feels true to this person because it is emotionally true (stay with me!). The facts of their particular story may seem bizarre, but the understory–the emotional story–will be totally sensible. These are understories like, "I've been lied to," or "Powerful people are dangerous," or "I can't trust."

Because the truth is, what happens is that a person is walking around with this emotionally true story. When they find a specific, factual story that matches their emotional story, *that story feels true.* Think of the facts as the symbols they grabbed ahold of to express an emotionally true story they need to express.

There is absolutely no value in arguing about factual inaccuracies. Next time you feel frustrated and want to 'set someone straight,' see if you can go deeper. See if you can move beyond the symbols they've grabbed ahold of to express their emotional story. Instead of proving what is false, see if you can connect with what feels true for them.

We all deserve the connection and compassion this can bring us.

## TODAY'S AFFIRMATION

I know their stories are true in ways I don't always understand.

## TODAY'S JOURNAL PROMPT

When I encounter someone with beliefs that seem absurd,
I tend to…

# DAY 272

## *I can speak when I am afraid.*

As you imagine connecting to your own truth and speaking your own stories, I'd like to remind you of another muscle you need to build–tolerating others not liking what you have to say.

Many women get trapped by the thought, "I don't know if I can handle it if I get criticized or attacked for what I say or write." Here is what I know–you will be criticized and attacked. When we speak our truth, especially about our own dark sides, it is provocative. You are scaring people who are hiding from their own dark side; they are frightened and won't respond with kindness.

Audre Lorde reminds us, "When we speak we are afraid our words will not be heard nor welcomed, but when we are silent we are still afraid. So it is better to speak."

You can handle this. Remember, your goal is not to put yourself out there and hope that you won't be criticized. Your goal is to put yourself out there and know you can tolerate being criticized.

Today, pay attention to whether or not you are remaining silent because you think you can't tolerate being criticized. See if you can change your perspective from wishing you won't be critiqued to knowing you can handle it when it happens.

You deserve to speak.

### TODAY'S AFFIRMATION
I speak even when I am afraid.

### TODAY'S JOURNAL PROMPT
When I imagine being criticized or attacked for speaking my truth, story, or writing, I feel...I should probably...

REST
REVIEW
REFLECT

# DAY 274

## *Your Season of Return.*

You have moved from the visible to the invisible world. You are learning to live with loss. Your body is changing more rapidly now. Meaning and legacy emerge as keystone values.

Your body is starting to break down, but you are letting go of your attachment to your physical abilities. You are starting your season of *Return*, where you are an elder and a storyteller in body and spirit. You see, know, and welcome the reality that you are in physical decline and will ultimately return to the earth or your spiritual home.

Today, sit quietly with yourself. Reflect on the difficult and delightful path you've seen so far. Pay attention to your dreams and fantasies. Listen. Mediate on how all of these weave together into what you are losing and to what you are returning.

You will love the peace this knowing will bring you.

### TODAY'S AFFIRMATION

I am returning.

### TODAY'S JOURNAL PROMPT

My thoughts and feelings about loss and its presence
or function in my life are...

# DAY 275

## *Meet your inner ageist.*

Can you own your own negative biases about being old? Is the oppressor outside of you? Inside of you? Both? How does your answer impact how you will address ageism?

Connie Zwieg, a depth psychologist and author of, *The Inner Work of Age*, is one of the few authors who forces us to not just look outside of ourselves when it comes to ageism but asks us to do the inner work to meet our own inner ageist.

When we work from the perspective of Zwieg, we can't just blame the outside world for ageism. She asks us to take responsibility for our own internal rejection of this stage of life. When we recognize that parts of this oppressor live within, we have some power to dismantle its power over us.

How do you feel when you have to be truly present with someone who is elderly, dependent, or has age-related cognitive impairment? Are you open to this person? Or do you feel a sense of revulsion, rejection or fear? Pay attention to your mix of feelings and responses. Sit with them. Notice what it is about this human experience that you are still afraid of. See if you can bring more consciousness to your own inner ageist and take responsibility for your part in our collective rejection of our aging process.

You deserve the growth, compassion, and connection this brings you.

### TODAY'S AFFIRMATION

I can own, meet, and know my own inner ageist.

### TODAY'S JOURNAL PROMPT

When I see someone who looks old, dependent,
or impaired due to age, I feel...

# DAY 276

## *Medieval women mystics and the lifelong interpretation of story.*

You may feel frustrated by your lack of time or resources to pursue your own spiritual growth, but I'd like to remind you of the journeys of women with far fewer resources than us who cultivated extraordinary spiritual journeys.

In the medieval era, most women had very little access to spiritual education or texts. In this vacuum of education and literacy, women meditated on spiritual scenes they knew—the passion of their Christ was a common one. They would record their own responses to their meditation and reflect on its spiritual meaning.

Whatever spiritual symbol they felt drawn to, what is important for us to remember is that, in the absence of any text or teaching, these women were able to use their own imaginations to guide them to their own deepest spiritual truths—often eliciting visions and raptures that they would record and spend the rest of their lives interpreting. We still read many of these texts today.

In the fourteenth century, Julian of Norwich wrote two texts on her visionary experiences—the original version that described her experience and, later in life, a much longer version that included her lifelong interpretations (Carl Jung did something very similar with his own *Red Book*).

Today, see if you can take the time to reflect and meditate on your most powerful symbols. See what comes to you, recognizing that your interpretations may come over time.

### TODAY'S AFFIRMATION

I meditate on my most meaningful symbols of spirituality.

### TODAY'S JOURNAL PROMPT

I had a spiritual experience once. It was…
if I reflect on it now, I notice…

# DAY 277

## *Our hardest stories.*

When we think of healing work, we most often imagine a process where we have to face and cope with the terrible things that happened to us. We all have these stories, but, as a therapist, I've learned these stories of being hurt by others are not our hardest stories.

Our hardest stories are where we see ourselves as the ones doing the harm. Our hardest stories are the stories where we hurt someone (or ourselves)–out of ignorance, vengeance, or just a failure to cope.

Women who do the deepest work face these stories. She has to metabolize that she is not just a victim but sometimes a perpetrator. That it wasn't just a world that failed her but that she also failed others. This woman can more easily forgive others for their failures as she has faced her own.

A woman who has faced this story is at peace.

Today, pay attention to where you fall in this mix of stories. Notice if you have stories that you still need to tell yourself.

You deserve the peace.

### TODAY'S AFFIRMATION

I can accept all the stories in my history.

### TODAY'S JOURNAL PROMPT

When I imagine facing some of the things I feel bad about,
I feel...

# DAY 278

## *The violence of the truth.*

Have you ever read fairy tales or biblical parallels? Or ancient myths? If you have, you will recognize that our history reflects a tolerance for different versions of the same story.

Even one of our most sacred texts in the West, the *New Testament*, includes four different gospel narratives about the life of Jesus. Do you know why the compilers of the Christian bible included four slightly different versions of the same story? Because they recognized that each different version offered something important to their tradition. They weren't stupid and unable to see they were different; they were able to *tolerate* the obvious differences because of what each story brought to their understanding of their faith.

Our contemporary demand for a universal truth is killing you and all of us because none of us can hold, live, tell, or teach all of the perspectives of all of the stories. And the belief that one of us can is an act of violence to the other.

Any cursory review of our literature shows us that we can hold more than one way of telling, knowing, and feeling a story. We need to include all of them because each brings something different and important–even different parts of yourself can hold different perspectives!

Today, remember that there are multiple ways to know, feel, and tell the "same" story. Embrace this plural truth–for you and for everyone else. Her different story also deserves to exist. As you tolerate your own speaking voice in our spaces of difference, practice letting others do the same.

You will love the plurality this can bring into your own life.

## TODAY'S AFFIRMATION
I accept the plurality of our stories.

## TODAY'S JOURNAL PROMPT
When I imagine tolerating different stories about shared experiences,
I think/feel...

# DAY 279

## *When personal dreams don't come true, we find universal truths.*

You've heard the trite phrase, "It was the best thing that ever happened to me," spoken years after some terrible turn of events.

Almost all women learn to accept that many important dreams don't come true, but the wise woman also knows that this fate is not a tragedy. At some level, she knows that she discovered who she is and what she is made of in her hardest moments, not her easiest. And, as an older woman, this wisdom is more valuable than the manifestation of any childhood dream.

I'm not saying that any of us would willingly opt for our struggles, but I am saying we should remember that the failures of our wishes to come true were often the eras when we grew the most.

You discovered your resilience as you endured things you never believed you could endure. You discovered your compassion and empathy for others as you saw someone suffer and remembered that pain. The greatest spiritual traditions all speak of this journey of hardship, epiphany, and empathy.

It is easy to see the purposefulness in the past, but usually harder to do in the present.

Today, reflect on how your past trials have connected you to your current strengths. Use that reference point to reflect on the hardships you are facing today. See if this softens your perspective of the challenges you face today.

You deserve the comfort this can bring in the hard moments.

### TODAY'S AFFIRMATION

I know that hard times have fostered growth in me.

### TODAY'S JOURNAL PROMPT

When I think about challenges in the past, I see…
When I think about challenges in the present, I see…

# DAY 280

# REST REVIEW REFLECT

## *We reveal our true spiritual health in how we treat others.*

This statement can get women riled up. Many of us imagine ourselves to be good people. But what is this goodness? Is it expressing gratitude to the polite customer service representative? What about the rude or incompetent one? Are you good to him? Or do you match his rudeness?

When we have developed our spiritual self, our behavior isn't driven by these external factors. We don't need a specific response or validation from anyone (it is already coming from within). It is easy to be polite to the rude person and remain generous to the hateful one.

Please don't confuse this with being a doormat. You can be good to others and still say, "No, you can't live at my house anymore." Treating others well doesn't mean you don't have healthy boundaries. It just means you can implement your boundaries while still recognizing the inherent worth of others through your actions.

Remember, your actions are about your spiritual health, not about what others do or do not deserve. Reflect on your own behavior with regard to difficult people. Are they determining how you act? Or is your connection to your inner source determining how you act?

You deserve the control and inner peace this reflection and practice will give you.

## TODAY'S AFFIRMATION

My way of being in the world comes from within, not without.

## TODAY'S JOURNAL PROMPT

When I think of not letting their actions or responses affect my way
of being in the world, I think/feel...

# DAY 282

## *Nietzche's eternal return.*

Nietzsche gets a bad rap in contemporary spiritual circles, often only remembered for his "God is dead" quote that is always given without appropriate context (it was a critique of society, not the Divine).

This is unfortunate because, as a man who suffered terrible illnesses and tried to make sense of suffering and existing, he still has a lot to offer us. We could explore innumerable themes, but today I'd like to bring your attention to one of his thought experiments–the theory of eternal return.

Emerging from his own physical torments, Nietzsche proposed the thought experiment of eternal return–imagining that you must live this life, with every suffering and grace, over and over again, into infinity. He wants you to reflect on how you might approach your life if this were true.

Nietzsche ultimately lands at a place of *amor fati*–or love of fate. He chooses to embrace the entire journey with suffering joy.

Today, try this thought experiment presented by Nietzsche. What does it bring up in you? Horror? Delight? Despair? Pay attention to your response (all are okay!) and see how you can bring your responses and insights into how you choose to live your life today.

### TODAY'S AFFIRMATION
*Amor fati.* I love my fate.

### TODAY'S JOURNAL PROMPT
When I imagine living my own life, over and over again,
with every good and bad thing, I...

## *Learn to be with.*

So often, we feel inadequate when faced with the enormity of someone else's suffering. I've run women's groups for years and listened as women shared some of the worst, present-moment horrors–the unexpected loss of another child, imminent debilitation, or the onset of a new and unbearable chronic pain.

What do we do when her problem is too great to solve? What do we do when she shares something we can't fix? How do we sit with catastrophes that seem impossible to metabolize?

It feels Herculean, but there is something profoundly healing that you can do. I've seen it over and over again in my groups. And I've witnessed the joy and gratitude of women who have participated.

Your tasks are very simple but very challenging. You need to 'be-with' her and her story, let her pain fill the room, and just sit there. Hold her pain and her story as a group. She knows you can't fix it. You know that too. But the horror of her story often sends friends and family running (whether literally or just emotionally). The greatest gift you can offer is to hear and be with her, to not shut down, offer advice, or run away. Hold her sickening grief or fear as it fills the room. The peace this simple (yet very challenging!) action brings to her is immeasurable.

Next time you are stunned by the horror of someone else's story, remember this. Don't abandon her to suffer alone. Your most healing task is to stay with her, to just be-with her and her suffering.

Our world could use the healing.

### TODAY'S AFFIRMATION
I can be with her hard stories.

### TODAY'S JOURNAL PROMPT

When I hear something terribly tragic, I tend to…Imagining just being-with (not offering advice, blaming, problem-solving, etc.) feels…

# DAY 284

## *Letting go of doing it 'right.'*

The second half of life requires so much more from us than the first half as we grapple with the inversion of what we believe was good or expected.

After decades of trying to do it right, we had to learn how to go on with the recognition that we weren't ever going to get it exactly right–and that neither was anyone else.

Ultimately, we had to learn how to live with our failures and forgive ourselves. We had to learn how to live with the failures of others and forgive them.

Today, pay attention to how you still feel about things being "right"–in yourself or in our shared world. Notice if you are still expecting yourself to 'get it right or do it right." See if you can let go of these younger values and step into the paradoxes of your season of return.

You will love the self-compassion this will bring into your life.

### TODAY'S AFFIRMATION
I let go of trying to do things "right."

### TODAY'S JOURNAL PROMPT
When I imagine letting go of doing things 'right' or for others and
the world to do things 'right," I imagine/feel/think...

# DAY 285

## *Who are my role models of aging well? What have I learned from them?*

Life imitates art. My work with older women sometimes reminds me of the online games of kids, where each time the character advances a level, the game gets a little harder. The only way to meet the new challenge of the game is to continually increase your character's skills.

Just like this digital art form, as we move into the latter decades of our life, it is critical that we increase our skills to meet the new challenges of aging. But what are the skills required?

One way for you to explore this is to reflect on what you've learned about aging from others. We are all unconsciously impacted by the experiences of aging we've witnessed so far. I'd like for you to bring these lifelong observations into your conscious awareness.

Who were your best role models for aging? Not older people who aged without challenges but older people who aged well in the midst of extreme challenges. What skills did you recognize and admire in that person? What qualities did they possess that you would like to embody?

Who were people you saw age in ways you didn't like? What skills did they lack that you would like to possess (again, knowing we can't avoid challenges, but we can avoid certain ways of responding to them)?

Today, use your best role models to meditate on your vision of aging well. Imagine yourself embodying those same skills as you walk this journey.

You will love the inner wisdom this will bring you.

### TODAY'S AFFIRMATION
I meet aging with grace, curiosity, and resilience.

### TODAY'S JOURNAL PROMPT
A woman aging well is a woman who...

## *You are becoming someone you have never been.*

So many women in late life started their work with the complaint that they were too extreme in one area or another. She will lament, "I should have learned to speak up sooner," whereas another will mourn her failure to be more accommodating to others.

When we listen to women tell their different stories, we learn what is universal. In the last decades of life, women are developing the part of themselves that they neglected or rejected.

Jung spoke of our late-life development of our inferior aspects, and I believe we see his insight in both our individual experiences and when we span the centuries. In the medieval era, God was central, and individuals experienced themselves as terribly wretched. In our more secular era, the divine has fallen away as we deal with an epidemic of narcissism.

My point is that there is no correct way to move through these differences. The accommodating woman learns to be more selfish. The selfish woman learns to become more accommodating. Whatever we did or didn't do, we will find our way to its opposite in late life (maybe not in every aspect, but in many).

Today, notice if you are lamenting that you were too much or too little of something in your life. See if you can reimagine this experience as one where you are spending your life spanning the spectrum of these opposites, moving into an old age where you have become more things than you could have ever imagined.

You deserve the wisdom of old age.

## TODAY'S AFFIRMATION
I am growing into something I have never been.

## TODAY'S JOURNAL PROMPT
An area where I can see a development of an opposite way of being
in my journey (or still want to see one) is…

REST
REVIEW
REFLECT

# *Tragedy is our teacher.*

What do you think about illness, aging, and death? For most of us, these are the bogeyman of life–haunting us the most in our last decades. In our culture, this trio is almost always viewed as totally tragic. Women often respond with some variant of, "Oh, that shouldn't have happened."

But your season of *Return* reminds you that our experiences with illness, aging, and death are our next set of teachers. I don't mean to minimize the amount of suffering they bring us; this is the reason they are so terribly disruptive! But is it possible to reimagine that these disruptions can bring productive, developmental tasks?

The images of these three realities of life are what provoked the young Buddha to his journey of enlightenment. Do you think these things that initiated his spiritual journey are tragedies he shouldn't have seen or experienced? What about for you and your spiritual journey?

When we are coasting along unconsciously in life, there is hardly anything more disruptive than the birth of a child with special needs, the cancer diagnosis, or the loss of a partner, very slowly to dementia. In the immediate experience, of course, we are devastated. But, over time, as we are faced with living with the impossible, we change.

Let these experiences affect you. See what happens when you sit with what is. Feel the grief, the resentment, the devastation, and see what comes next.

You deserve the spiritual growth this will bring you.

## TODAY'S AFFIRMATION

My hardest experiences are my greatest teachers.

## TODAY'S JOURNAL PROMPT

When I reflect on my experiences with aging,
illness, and death, I realize...

# DAY 289

## *Everything belongs?*

Franciscan priest Richard Rohr reminds us that if we practice contemplative prayer, we will come to know that everything belongs. As a respected and studied theologian, his claims are worth wondering about, as most religious traditions push against these dualities that come so naturally to us.

Even if we are not yet in a space where this feels true, we can play with this concept as a thought experiment. Do you still get stuck in black-and-white thinking? Do you still find yourself thinking that some things are good and that others are bad?

The Buddha taught us that we are all part of a universal self (there is no other to loathe; she is me). Taoism states that the Tao "doesn't take sides/giving birth to both good and evil." The Christian New Testament encourages one to pray for her enemies, declaring that God is "kind to the ungrateful and the wicked" and that we should be, too.

Today, pay attention to the things that have happened that you don't think should belong. Wonder about the tension between your belief and these spiritual teachings. See what comes up.

It will bring you more peace than you have now. And you deserve that peace.

### TODAY'S AFFIRMATION
Everything belongs.

### TODAY'S JOURNAL PROMPT
When I imagine that everything belongs, I think/feel…

# DAY 290

## *Your hardest task is to forgive yourself.*

There are so many stages in our healing journeys. I see women do the hard work to process trauma, to forgive those who hurt them, and to engage in healthier behaviors. But, after all of that difficult processing, I wait for the last part of our work together–her forgiveness of herself.

Being able to forgive yourself takes time and is often the last stage of a therapeutic journey. This process requires a big-picture perspective where you see that you were living without the wisdom and skills you needed to do the job you wish you'd done. You move from anger or shame about the younger you to a wish that you could hug and protect that young girl.

Today, pay attention to where you are on your path toward forgiving yourself. Notice where you still feel shame or pain about things you wish you could go back and do differently. See if you can start to cultivate some empathy for that younger you.

You deserve the kindness.

### TODAY'S AFFIRMATION
I also deserve forgiveness.

### TODAY'S JOURNAL PROMPT
When it comes to forgiving myself, I notice...

## *You give from your overflow.*

You've learned to set limits in relationship and to adjust your expectations of what others can and will do for you. You've learned to stop sacrificing yourself in an effort to please or control others. But your goal is not to become a selfish automaton. How are we to make sense of holding our rhythm of valuing both autonomy and generosity? Our most ancient texts can offer us symbolic understandings to guide us.

Maybe you want to give more, but you feel like a dried-up well that has nothing left. When that happens, it means that it is time to return to your own spiritual practices.

In the Eastern sacred text, *The Tao*, the master tells us to turn inward toward the Tao, which "is like a well, used, but never used up." In the Western sacred text, *Interior Castle*, Teresa of Avila reminds us to connect to "the waters of grace near which the soul remains planted like a river." If the most sacred texts of East and West suggest we need to turn inward toward some infinite resource, we would be wise to stop and pay attention.

Today, make an effort to notice your sense of this inner resource. Are you feeling depleted? Then you don't have anything to give right now. Are you feeling a sense of plenitude and overflow? This is when you have something to offer.

We could use more wise women in our world, so please, as a gift to others, take the time to notice your own rhythms of depletion and overflow and respond accordingly. Soon, your well will be overflowing.

## TODAY'S AFFIRMATION

I give from overflow.

## TODAY'S JOURNAL PROMPT

When I imagine the plenitude that comes from connecting to this inner resource,
I recognize I am probably in the rhythm of (depletion/overflow?)…

## *Pride makes you fragile.*
## *Humility makes you strong.*

We've all felt that stinging moment of injured pride when we've been criticized. You feel small and defensive. You may wish that others would be consistently kinder to you so that you wouldn't have to feel that shame and shrinking. But there is another, more empowering, way to approach this that is far more freeing for you.

Pride is not self-confidence. When you are feeling pride, you are thinking only of yourself. You feel a need to prove yourself to the outside world. This isolation and self-absorption make you vulnerable to the cruel critiques of others.

When you are humble, you are thinking of yourself as an equal among others. You are able to take constructive criticism (and even reflect on the possible truths of cruel criticism). We aren't injured by the advice or attack.

Today, notice where you are feeling the need to prove yourself to another or the world. See if you can understand where that insecurity is coming from and, with that knowledge, start to let go of it.

Accept yourself with your strengths and weaknesses. Accept others with their strengths and weaknesses. Cultivate your humility and connection with your community.

You deserve the peace this practice will bring to you.

### TODAY'S AFFIRMATION
I know the strength of humility.

### TODAY'S JOURNAL PROMPT
When I am criticized, I feel...

# DAY 293

*We aren't afraid of growing old.*
*We are afraid of facing the truth of our total*
*dependence upon others.*

I work with older women, so I frequently hear the anxieties and angst that come with aging. The terror of the diagnosis or the recognizable onset of dementia. Like the young girls who feared being captured by the boogeyman, old women fear being caught by the inevitable decline of old age. And just like that little girl, she hides from him as best she can.

But just like she needed to face her fears to see what was real, old women need to explore what they are really afraid of when it comes to aging. There are lots to choose from–fear of pain, fear of loss, or fear of loneliness. But there is one common fear that hides behind all of these that really spooks women–her fear of being dependent.

We are terrified of needing help. Whether our memories or our bodies fail, facing the reality that we all might have to depend on some other person (or team of people) is the stuff of nightmares.

But this is a good time to realize that our idea of 'being independent' is an illusion. Maybe you had enough money or health in your youth to delude yourself into believing that you are 'very independent,' but the reality is you never have been. Drop your naked self in an isolated forest and see how well you do. You've always needed everybody and everything–dependence is your boogeyman.

Today, get real with yourself about your fears of aging. Make yourself explore, more deeply, what really scares you. Look under the bed. See if you can stop running from the elusive fears and find out what this dread is really made of.

You will love how much peace facing this fear will bring you.

## TODAY'S AFFIRMATION
I accept my total dependence upon others.

## TODAY'S JOURNAL PROMPT
My biggest fears of aging are…

# DAY 294

# REST
# REVIEW
# REFLECT

*When you feel connected with nature, you will protect and help nature. When you feel connected with all people, you will protect and help all people. Stop working on your behaviors. Start working on your connections.*

Do you feel guilty about your behavior? Are you trying to 'do' better but can't really stay with it? Maybe we need to rethink the way you are approaching the problem. Psychological models offer a variety of methodologies for helping us reach our goals, with the most popular ones being cognitive (change our thinking) and behavioral (change our behavior). But what do you do when those don't work? We go deeper.

Depth psychological models are less interested in changing your behavior and are more interested in exploring your deeper feelings, experiences, and motivations. What depth therapists know is that when we heal on a deeper level, our behavior changes on its own—without the requirement of all of that harsh self-discipline! You may wish that you were a better steward of nature. You may wish you felt motivated to be more generous (and less afraid of giving away resources).

The truth is, when you finally develop a deep connection to these things, your actions come easily. You are deeply motivated and not trying to force yourself to "be good."

Today, if you are struggling with any behavior (nature and people are just two examples), see if you can change from working on your behavior to working on your connections.

You will love the ease and generosity this will bring into your life.

## TODAY'S AFFIRMATION

I am connected to all things.

## TODAY'S JOURNAL PROMPT

I do/do not feel a sense of connection to all things...
If I did, then...

# DAY 296

*A young woman needs to prove her point.*
*A wise woman doesn't need to prove anything.*

As we move from childhood into middle adulthood, learning to find our voice is an important developmental milestone. As women, learning to set boundaries, say no, or address abuse head-on heals us.

But this journey of finding our voice can go off the rails when we add the mistaken belief that the other person must receive our words in some particular way. As we grow, we can learn to speak up for ourselves, but we also learn that our healing experience is not dependent upon how our words are received.

We say our piece and leave it at that. The other party can disagree. They can say we are crazy or too sensitive. We can even let someone else have the last word. We know we have found our inner strength to speak up, but we are not on a conquest to have someone else understand or metabolize our truth. As older women, we don't need to prove anything to anyone.

Today, pay attention to the difference between these two goals–speaking up for yourself but not having to prove yourself (or your ideas) to anyone.

This quiet will bring you so much peace.

## TODAY'S AFFIRMATION

I can speak, but I don't need to prove myself or my points to anyone.

## TODAY'S JOURNAL PROMPT

I get sucked into defending myself when…

*Your daily spiritual practice is a long-term investment, not a quick-fix scheme. I have the discipline and patience to invest in myself.*

After all of your work, it's frustrating when you are 'not feeling it.' Maybe you are meditating and reading and journaling and doing nature walks, but you still feel like you've lost touch with your spiritual centeredness. You are frustrated because you are doing your work but not getting any sense of connection.

This is the path for all of us. Our greatest spiritual literature speaks of those dark nights of the soul. When we feel lost, no matter what we do. In those moments, our job is to hold on and just return to our practice without the comfort that we wish it would bring us.

No matter how you feel today, every time you get back to your prayer, meditation, or nature walk, you are making an investment that will bring a return. You might not feel better today. You might still have a bad week, but I promise, over time, the commitment to return to the center will change the way you are psychologically and spiritually in this world.

In our quick-fix culture, we've developed this delusion that our effort should have an instant payout. It doesn't.

Today, pay attention to whether or not you imagine your spiritual practice as a long-term investment or a short-term gain. See if you can cultivate the discipline and patience for the long investment that will bring you the peace you seek.

You will love the peace this commitment will bring you.

## TODAY'S AFFIRMATION

I stay with my practices, even when I feel disconnected.

## TODAY'S JOURNAL PROMPT

When I am still struggling but doing my work, I feel...

# DAY 298

*You know you are on your path when you no longer need outside validation to keep you on track.*

So often, we feel confused about our path. What is your path? If you are like most women, you have spent so many decades thinking about others that this question can leave you with a blank. This confusion is normal.

As you may have seen in previous OMMs, we never arrive at our destination of finding ourselves; it is a continuous unfolding that changes through the seasons of our life. So, with that truth, you know you need to be flexible in your understanding of what being on your path means to you.

One tool I like to use to help women discern if they are on track is whether or not she feels fulfilled by the activity (or the fantasy of doing that activity) independent of what others think. This sounds small, but it is actually an enormous clue as we know the validation is coming from within.

Again, this can be hard to figure out because we spend most of at least the first half of our life paying close attention to what our culture and community want from us (this is not a bad thing, but a normal developmental stage). It can be confusing to move from society–to self-validating activities, but that is precisely what you need to do in this last part of your life.

You've walked a long road, and there is wisdom born from that journey. When your vocation is finally validated from within rather than without, you know you are connecting to your deepest and most transcendent self.

You deserve the validation.

## TODAY'S AFFIRMATION
My validation comes from within.

## TODAY'S JOURNAL PROMPT
The activity I derive the most joy from is…

## *The Divine wants you to stop being afraid.*

Where did you first start to feel afraid? This usually happens so early–when a young child's natural narcissism allows her to draw illogical conclusions about herself and her impact on her world.

When we construct these ideas about ourselves, we also project them onto the Divine. Long-standing misinterpretations of the sacred texts in the West haven't helped. In our Judeo-Christian tradition, many women grew to believe they weren't good enough, certain that something was wrong with them (fallen from grace) or their behavior (sinner).

As a woman of the West, you may be able to cite all sorts of Biblical references about how you are fallen or sinful. But Richard Rohr reminds us that the most frequent command in the sacred text of the Judeo-Christian tradition is not about sin but is an attempt to comfort you–"Do not be afraid." What a different environment we'd be living in if this true Biblical theme was the mantra of the West.

I'm not here to make a case for any particular faith, but I am here to show you where early childhood experiences combined with sociocultural constructs (made-up things that we think, by default, are true) might be worth deconstructing.

You are here to learn to love yourself and others. Every spiritual tradition ultimately teaches this truth.

Explore where you learned something different and ask why.

You deserve the love.

## TODAY'S AFFIRMATION
The divine wants me to not be afraid.

## TODAY'S JOURNAL PROMPT
When I think about God or the Divine, I believe…
I believe this because…

# DAY 300

## *You've had many winters.*

Years ago, indigenous cultures would say of old women, "She's had many winters." I love this phrase because it captures both our linear and circular way of being.

In contrast to our stories of improvement or preservation, this way of understanding our aging reminds us of a different perspective. When we think of the circular rhythms of nature, we are reminded of a different kind of beauty.

Many in the West grow tired of the temporary styles and trends, constantly replacing our old with 'new and improved.' But have you ever grown tired of the same old sunset? Or that repetitive aesthetic of snow-covered trees after a first snowfall?

We don't grow tired of these beautiful things. They remind us of our most ancient and natural aesthetic of loving the things that return again and again. Always imbuing us with a sense of aesthetic awe.

When I hear, "She's had many winters," it reminds me of this return in women. You aren't just on a linear path but are also on the spiral of constantly circumambulating your deepest self.

Today, think about how you conceptualize time passing in both linear and circular time. Pay attention to your attachment to the old, the new, and the constantly returning.

You will love the aesthetic and circular rhythm this will bring into your life.

### TODAY'S AFFIRMATION

I have had many winters.

### TODAY'S JOURNAL PROMPT

When I imagine myself in both linear and circular time, I…

# REST
# REVIEW
# REFLECT

# *We forgot how to die.*

We may have avoided our stories of aging, but we have completely annihilated our stories of dying. It is hard to know how to be with death and dying when we've lost the tale.

Our fear of decline and death has fostered a series of institutional systems that keep the dependent elderly and dying out of our daily lives. And there is money to be made in keeping you afraid of death. Others want to stay in control of an expensive, outsourced process that enables our avoidance of this psychological and spiritual threshold.

Instead of having family and children being a part of this natural process, we try to 'protect' them from the horror. This method is not working for us. Years ago, we couldn't escape it. The old and young died in our homes. We nursed, comforted, and mourned them in our living rooms.

Imagine how you might imagine your own death if you'd already walked through at least a half-dozen others? If death had visited your home over and again? What if you had been through the long process of dying–reduced eating, reduced bodily functions, increased sleeping many times since childhood. Watching someone follow her own circle into the return of total dependence on a body she can't control. Watching her move into the extended sleeping that precedes death. Surrounded by friends and family, holding her hand, alternately crying, laughing, and singing. A gathering, like a birth.

If we experienced death as this natural rite of passage, as we do a birth, we would have less fear about this perpetually taboo topic.

Today, pay attention to how you have been with the long decline and dying process. Notice if those experiences have felt natural or frightening. Pay attention to how those experiences shape your own views of death and dying.

You deserve the good death that more awareness and encounters can bring you.

## TODAY'S AFFIRMATION

I can embrace decline and dying as part of our process.

## TODAY'S JOURNAL PROMPT

My experiences with death have been...
this has shaped my views of death in that...

# DAY 303

## *St. Theresa's four ways of watering.*

Even if you are not Catholic, it can be helpful to explore the ways our medieval mystical women developed their spirituality (remember, the Catholic faith was the only option for most Westerners for centuries).

St. Teresa was asked by her superiors to write about her own spiritual journey and, in the rewriting of her book of her life, came up with a metaphor for her spiritual journey that many still find useful–the four ways of watering. I'd love to remind you of her imaginings and see if you find it useful as you reflect on your own spiritual practice.

St. Teresa asks you to imagine your spiritual journey as tending to a spiritual garden. Your continued and changing practices correspond to the four ways of watering your spiritual garden.

At first, you must do hard labor by manually drawing up water from a (sometimes dry well). Next, as you continue to tend to your spiritual garden, your practice becomes more akin to carrying water from a more plentiful water wheel. The process gets even easier with the third way of watering. St. Teresa imagined using the flow of natural waterways that now easily flow right into your garden. In the final stage, the rain comes, and you are no longer laboring but sitting in a totally receptive spiritual space as the water falls onto you and your garden.

This image of imagining spiritual plenitude as a receptive experience of rain is a recurring theme in ancient and medieval literature. Today, see if you can use this metaphor to imagine your own spiritual practice. Notice if it feels like you are still in the earlier stages, laboring, often with experiences of aridity, or if you are moving into an experience of receptive plenitude.

There is no correct response to this exercise. Your job is to imagine yourself in your own spiritual practice.

You deserve the receptive plenitude.

### TODAY'S AFFIRMATION
I water my spiritual garden.

### TODAY'S JOURNAL PROMPT
As I reflect on my spiritual journey and the four ways of watering,
I notice…

# DAY 304

## *Reflect and rediscover your not-knowing.*

We persist in our mistaken faith in our ability to predict the future, despite our poor histories of prophesying. We live in fear or hope of our projected futures.

As you reflect on your history, you recognize the lack of correspondence between what you hoped or feared would happen and what actually did happen. With this longer view, you can better see that you didn't know, don't know, and won't know.

This is one of the new gifts of old age. Reflecting on this reality facilitates your acceptance of your complete not-knowing of what is yet to come. As you do that, you are better able to let go of your expectations and stay present. When you let go and stay present, you become increasingly connected to your spiritual truths.

Today, reflect on the unexpected twists and turns of your life. See if you can use those experiences to help you let go of the mistaken belief that you have any control or knowledge about what the future will still hold. Practice accepting your not-knowing going forward.

You will love the relief your not-knowing will bring you.

### TODAY'S AFFIRMATION
I know that I don't know.

### TODAY'S JOURNAL PROMPT
When I imagine embracing 'not-knowing,'
I feel...

# DAY 305

## *See the world as yourself.*

Living in a difficult world with difficult people is a challenge, so I want to offer you different ways to cope so you can determine which method fosters your best practices.

One that I love is a cognitive trick. It is based on much deeper spiritual teaching (e.g., unitive consciousness), but my method is a bit more scrappy.

Whenever someone feels particularly irksome, impossible, or even evil in their actions, instead of resting easy in my outrage and horror, I remember Stephen Mitchell's translation of *the Tao* and the phrase, "See the world as yourself." I force myself to say, "I am..." whoever they are. This immediately deflates my outrage balloon–my quick rush to grab the stone to cast it.

My interpretation of this teaching might not be the deepest spiritual practice, as it really is functioning at a cognitive level, but I need all the tools I can get. It is easy for me to get lazy and move to my default delusion that they are 'bad' in contrast to me, who is relatively 'good.'

I am not asking you to completely identify with the worst of us. What I am asking you to do is use this cognitive trick to prevent you from lazily moving into the outrage that is ultimately set up to serve our own delusions of how much better we are. Our greatest spiritual teachers walked with the least of us. See if you can do this, too (at least in your mind).

You deserve the insight this can bring you.

### TODAY'S AFFIRMATION
I am everyone.

### TODAY'S JOURNAL PROMPT
When I imagine saying, "I am..." about...I feel...

# DAY 306

*Praying for gain brings you nothing.*
*Praying for nothing brings you gain.*

As you move into your deeper spiritual practices, you may start to notice a shift in the way you relate to your divine truth.

One way we see this is the difference between petitionary prayer and contemplative (or centering) prayer. In the first, we are asking some divine power to give us something. In the second, we are using our meditation and prayer time to improve our ability to simply be with the divine source.

Notice how you are relating to your divine practice. Are you still functioning with a petitionary model? Asking God to do some task for you? Or have you moved into a space of trying to be in a space of connection with the divine?

Today, see if you are still relating in a way that feels like pleading for specific outcomes or if you are learning to sit in a space of accepting all that is.

You deserve the contemplative peace.

### TODAY'S AFFIRMATION
I practice my connection with the divine in contemplative prayer.

### TODAY'S JOURNAL PROMPT
When I think about a prayer or meditation practice,
I notice my attitude (of petition vs. contemplation) is probably...

# DAY 307

## *I've earned and love my beautiful wisdom face.*

We celebrate the superficial, but only in a very narrow way. With normative standards of life, culture, and beauty being spoon-fed to us by popular media, we've been taught to exclude so much from the category of beautiful. This is tragic as the aesthetic of beauty has a much wider range than the repetitive images of sex-object models we see.

There is a part of you that knows this. When you see the deeply etched wrinkles on a wise old woman's face, something in you moves. You know she is beautiful, but this catches you by surprise or seems ironic as you filter your aesthetic experience through the debris of media brainwashing we've all received.

I want you to reconnect with your real experience and let go of the one you've been fed by a media culture trying to scare you into buying their ideas of who and how you should be.

Today, pay attention to this aesthetic of wisdom beauty. Notice the sun spots, sagging skin, and scars and the stories of our lives they tell. When we can see our faces and bodies through this lens, we can love the woman we are still becoming.

You deserve the self-love this practice will bring you.

## TODAY'S AFFIRMATION
I've earned and love my beautiful wisdom face.

## TODAY'S JOURNAL PROMPT
When I think about 'looking old,' I think that means…

# REST
# REVIEW
# REFLECT

# DAY 309

## *You are Nature.*

You remember that being more connected to the natural world is good for your mental and spiritual health, but I'd like to push you just a bit farther as you choose to spend more time outdoors.

A strange paradigm that entered our consciousness is a mistaken belief in our separateness from nature instead of remembering that we, too, are a part of this holistic system.

Imagine any indigenous woman or even a woman who is returning to the land as a homesteading gardener. How do you imagine she reacts to the bugs, the spider webs, and the dirt that touch her clothing and body? Is she in a constant battle to remove them in an effort to hold her boundary between herself and nature? Or is being in the dirt, the spider webs, or having bugs land on or near her part of her way of being in the world, as recognizing herself as another part of this holistic system?

Today, reflect on whether or not you are still imagining 'nature' as something you need to keep physically separate from your 'clean' existence. Wonder and imagine what it would be like to sink deeper into an awareness of your embeddedness in this world. Admire the spider web in the corner of your porch. Let the dirt be on your clothes. Watch the bug crawl across you.

As you turn inward and find your deepest self, loosen the boundary between your 'clean' world and your truest nature.

### TODAY'S AFFIRMATION

I am nature.

### TODAY'S JOURNAL PROMPT

When I think about being part of nature...
or about having dirt or bugs on me, I notice.

# DAY 310

## *You are not more than anyone.*
## *You are not less than anyone.*

Many of us say we believe this, but it is a challenge for most of us to truly take it in. As a mantra or affirmation, we can use this reminder to see where we are still stuck in our false hierarchies of better and worse people.

Every spiritual teacher taught about radical egalitarianism and the inherent dignity and worth of every person. In fact, almost every respected religious teacher from every tradition connected with the most marginalized persons in their communities.

But, I bet you, like most people, still see yourself as occupying some particular rung on a ladder of worthiness. Maybe you see yourself as not as worthy as someone you greatly admire. Or maybe you think you must be better than someone who has committed horrific crimes (I am not suggesting that all actions are good; I am citing the ancient spiritual masters who repeatedly assert that we are all absolutely equal in our worth and relationship to the divine, no matter what we have done). This false ranking of yourself and others keeps you from connecting. It is painful for you.

What is it like to tell yourself, as Jesus, the Buddha, or any ancient wise teacher taught us, that we are all totally equal? The person you admire is not better than you. You are not better than the incarcerated criminal.

Today, pay attention to where you are still placing yourself in some hierarchy of worthiness. Notice where this false ranking of yourself and others came from. See if you can start to let go of this isolating paradigm.

You will love the deep connectedness this truth can bring you.

## TODAY'S AFFIRMATION

No one is 'better' than me. I am not 'better' than anyone.

## TODAY'S JOURNAL PROMPT

My honest belief about people being 'better' or 'worse' is…

# DAY 311

## *How you faced your life is how you will face your death.*

No matter where you are in your process of aging, you still have one of your most important tasks ahead of you–dying. What is your death process going to look like? Most of us have no idea, but I can give you a clue.

You will probably die very much like how you live. When you've been faced with challenges, how do you respond? With anger? With curiosity? Are you open or fearful? Accommodating or resentful? Pay attention to how you have faced the challenges in your life today, as that is very likely how you will face your death.

Don't like what you see? There is still time to grow. How do you want to approach your death? With curiosity and connection? See if you can engage in some of those practices today.

You deserve the better death this will bring you.

### TODAY'S AFFIRMATION

I will approach my dying process with curiosity and grace.

### TODAY'S JOURNAL PROMPT

When I reflect on how I've approached challenges, I notice that I...
When I think about how I will approach my death, I want to be...

# DAY 312

## *Who deserves care?*

It can be hard to take care of a dependent, elderly adult who did not take good care of you. Maybe they were verbally or physically abusive to you when you were vulnerable. Maybe Mom or Dad abandoned you in your time of need. And now here they are, vulnerable and expecting you to take good care of them.

This can be a profound psychological crossroads for you. Something surges up in you, "But they don't deserve it!" Allow yourself to sit with this sincere psychological response as he or she looks to you in need. Imagine him or her as the vulnerable child who also did not receive good care. Imagine providing unconditional love to someone who has never received it.

This is hard. But it is the space where you grow psychologically and spiritually. He is still yelling at you, in his aged confusion. She is still melodramatic and self-absorbed in her cognitive decline. But you are able to see past their flawed humanity. You are spiritually still and no longer triggered by their difficult personality traits. You see the divinity in their lived experience, and you can care for them. You can hold the disgusting and exhausting journey of caretaking. Because if they don't deserve care, then none of us do. And if we deserve care, then everyone does.

Hold this knowing in those hard moments of caretaking. It can be a profound space of psychological and spiritual growth.

Who deserves care? Everyone? No One? Explore your feelings in response to this question.

## TODAY'S AFFIRMATION
Everyone deserves care.

## TODAY'S JOURNAL PROMPT
When I think about having to help people I resent,
I notice…

# DAY 313

*Instead of asking why God doesn't do more to alleviate the suffering of the world, ask yourself why you don't.*

Our frustration with the pervasive suffering in the world can raise our biggest existential questions. Why do they suffer? Why doesn't God stop this? These are some of our oldest theological wonderings that plagued even our most spiritual teachers.

But today, I'd like to turn this around for you. When you wonder about the suffering of the world and why God doesn't do more to end it, change your perspective. Wonder about the suffering in the world and why you don't do more to end it.

In many faith traditions, the most ancient mystical texts reference that we are in the image of God or that the divine kingdom is within us. If you submit yourself to this truth of being part of divinity, then what is your role in alleviating the suffering of the world?

Don't take on more than is appropriate, but notice what comes into your day. Is there one person in need that you encounter? Use your bit of divinity to make that bit of difference.

You will love how empowered compassion can change you.

## TODAY'S AFFIRMATION

I can be of service to the small needs I encounter in my life.

## TODAY'S JOURNAL PROMPT

My thoughts about the sufferings of the world and the role of divinity and the individual in alleviating those sufferings are...

# DAY 314

## *Free yourself from your likes and dislikes.*

It was so important to find your voice, to assert your existence and value in your earlier seasons, but as you age, your need to find and assert yourself lessens. We feel that the more we obsess over "my plans, my likes, my dreams' the more we separate from our community and the universal whole.

Your habit of interacting with our world from the lens of "I want" is something that will ebb away. It was very important to find that subjective "I" voice, but, like a novelty that becomes less important, you notice that your sense of "I want" falls away and an awareness of "what is needed?" rises up.

You are moving from a space of "I like" and "I don't like" to a more centered witnessing, connecting, and experiencing of your world.

Today, notice how much of your thinking and feeling is still dominated by your likes and dislikes (if you are still finding yourself and your voice, this might be exactly where you need to be!). See if you can imagine a space where you experience your voice as one among an equally valuable multitude of voices.

You deserve the cooperative rhythms this will connect you to.

### TODAY'S AFFIRMATION

I pay attention to what is needed, not just what I want.

### TODAY'S JOURNAL PROMPT

When I think about my journey of finding my voice, asserting my existence,
and then letting go, I notice I am...

# REST
# REVIEW
# REFLECT

# DAY 316

## *Be more curious than cautious.*

It is so easy for us to get spooked when things change. We all have our strange human tendency to cling to the familiar.

Sometimes change is scary, so I am not asking you to go from feeling cautious to being naively optimistic. I think an easier and much more productive method is to approach the inevitable changes with more curiosity than caution. More like, "I wonder what it will be like to use a mobility scooter?" instead of, "Oh my god, I won't walk through the grocery store ever again!"

When we approach new situations with curiosity, we let more aspects of the new experience into our life. We aren't narrowing our lens to just the hardships but opening our perspective to all the changes that might come.

Approaching the inevitable changes that come with growing old can push us to grow in ways that we never expected. Today, you don't know what that experience will bring to you–spiritually, relationally, etc. Today, with regard to whatever big change you might be facing, see if you can open yourself up to more curiosity than caution.

You will love the bigger experiences this will bring into your journey.

### TODAY'S AFFIRMATION

I approach change with curiosity and grace.

### TODAY'S JOURNAL PROMPT

When I start to feel afraid about things changing, I tend to think...If I were to approach change with more curiosity, I might open myself up to...

## *A patient mind is a calm mind.*

If you've continued to practice your patience, you may have noticed a new sense of calm entering your life. When a crisis happens in your family, you are not too quick or urgently reactive. You are able to address immediate emergencies and be still with the discomfort and uncertainty of what remains unresolved.

If you are caretaking, you notice increased comfort in allowing your loved one to wait for you as you finish up other tasks. Everything isn't an emergency. You have more patience and calm.

You may notice less urgency to speak as you have the patience to let everyone be exactly where they need to be.

As you've aged, you've accepted that you simply can't juggle as many things at once. You are more patient with the fact that things are not getting done.

In your hardest moments, you have the patience to wait for your dark night of the soul to lift.

Today, notice where you have become more patient. Pay attention to where you are still growing.

You've earned the calm.

## TODAY'S AFFIRMATION

I am more patient than I have ever been.

## TODAY'S JOURNAL PROMPT

When I think about the role of patience in coping with my challenges,
I imagine…

# DAY 318

## *Bear witness to the confusion of individuals and remember they are a part of the whole.*

In Stephen Mitchell's translation of *The Tao*, we find the verse, "Watch the turmoil of beings, but contemplate their return."

This simple phrase holds almost the entire mystery and method for how to be with difficult people. When we are stuck with someone who seems impossible, this reminder offers us a spiritual strategy for being with them and their actions in a way that can actually bring us more peace.

Because when we get really worked up (triggered, irritated, etc.), we can lose our footing. We might want to fix it, tell them off, do something to change the situation, help, or speak up. But in some cases, all of those actions are fruitless (you've probably tried all of them before). Returning to this new method actually helps you in your spiritual practice.

Today, if you are beyond your tolerance, if you feel like you are losing your connection to your centering practice, try this method. Stop reacting or planning any action or words. Instead, observe them and contemplate their return to the universal whole. Let everything else fall away.

In your most challenging moments with your most difficult people, remember these words from *The Tao*, "Watch the turmoil of beings and contemplate their return."

You deserve the peace.

### TODAY'S AFFIRMATION
I watch the turmoil of beings and contemplate their return.

### TODAY'S JOURNAL PROMPT
When I am dealing with a difficult person, I tend to...

# DAY 319

## *Julian of Norwich and the grace of bodily illness.*

If you've not already met our teachers, disability, and illness, late-life will almost certainly introduce them to you. As we wrestle with our grief and fear over the unwanted challenges they bring, it is worth exploring how other spiritual teachers approach them. Our ideas about illness aren't the only ideas about illness.

Julian of Norwich wrote some of our earliest English writings by a woman. A medieval mystic of the fourteenth century who chose a life of spiritual seclusion, she prayed for the 'gift of illness' as a method of growing deeper into her spiritual practice. In her subsequent near-death delirium, Julian experienced a number of visions that she spent a lifetime interpreting. Her spiritual insights are still some of the most popular writings of medieval women.

I am not arguing for seeking out a near-death illness or even for the Catholic faith of the medieval era (though, I repeat, it is always worth remembering it was the only option). What I am asking of you is to see that our stories about illness are not the only stories. Smart and spiritual women have imagined illness in very different ways. Their stories are still available to us.

Today, pay attention to whether or not you have a simplified view of illness as an error. See if you can think of Julian of Norwich and be open to what some of our hardest experiences might bring.

You deserve the comfort this can bring.

## TODAY'S AFFIRMATION

I am open to new interpretations of our hardest experiences.

## TODAY'S JOURNAL PROMPT

When I think about illness, I think…

## *Be with the spaces in between.*

We pay so much attention to things and activities that we can hardly conceptualize anything else. In a world obsessed with objects and action, it can be a profound spiritual practice to pay attention to the spaces in between.

This applies to both your physical and mental awareness. On a physical level, notice the objects you interact with. When you hold your coffee cup, notice that it is the empty space that holds your coffee. When you are in your home, you are surrounded by walls and windows, but notice that it is the empty space that you use.

When you come to the end of something, see if you can be with the emptiness. Don't try to immediately fill the gap with junk. When you are waiting, see if you can just wait. When you are done with your activities and tasks, see if you can do nothing (this is a good time to notice the empty spaces around you!).

Today, notice what you do with the spaces in between. Are you able to notice the emptiness and be with it? Or do you rush to fill the space with something else?

You will love the inner stillness this can bring you.

### TODAY'S AFFIRMATION

I pay attention to the spaces in between.

### TODAY'S JOURNAL PROMPT

When I think about my relationship to objects and activities as compared to my relationship to emptiness or stillness, I notice...

# DAY 321

## *We need to hear from old women who have walked the path from wounds to wisdom.*

As you know by now, our community has lost its connection with our wise women storytellers. Our for-profit story model doesn't include stories like yours. Over the course of these last several months, you have paid more attention to your story. You have discovered the aspects you are still hiding from yourself. You have felt the hard parts. You have told the hard parts. You have felt and heard the hard parts from other women in the safe spaces that you discovered.

Part of you may still wish you could travel back to your younger self and whisper guidance in her ear. You still can. Because, as you've discovered the paradox and enigma of ancient stories and explored your own, you now find yourself in a space where you have something to return.

You resurrected this ancient process. You are now an elder and a storyteller. You both know your own story and aren't so attached to it. You have owned it and let it go. The comfort and sharing of your story bring you full circle as you function as a guide for the young women who aren't there yet.

Today, make a commitment to be open to how you can return your wisdom to your community. It may be in showing up for your grandchildren, by participating in a volunteer project, a creative project, or in writing your own story for a wider audience.

You've walked a long path. You've learned so much on your hard journey. Today, be open to how you are called the share your wisdom with others.

You will love the full circle meaning giving your healing gift to your community can bring you.

### TODAY'S AFFIRMATION
I am open to being a healing guide in this world.

### TODAY'S JOURNAL PROMPT
As I imagine being a healing presence in the world,
the space I imagine I might find to do that is...

# REST
# REVIEW
# REFLECT

## *Unconditional love.*
## *That means everyone.*

So many of our complaints are about not getting the unconditional love we wanted. Most women can quickly recount situations where they felt judged, unlovable, or unworthy by another person. We can spend much of our life trying to heal from that emptiness.

The pain is real, but I'd like to reverse the paradigm on you for a moment. I'd like to challenge you to go through your day trying to express *unconditional* love for everyone (hint: It won't be easy).

Try to see others through the eyes of Spirit–completely worthy of love, no matter what. If you feel particularly challenged by a difficult person, imagine that person as they may have been loved (or should have been loved) as a child or by their own family.

I am not suggesting that you should be able to easily do this. It is a challenge. I am suggesting the practice of pushing yourself to see the world through this lens will bring more love into your life.

You deserve the healing this will bring you.

### TODAY'S AFFIRMATION

I love everyone unconditionally.

### TODAY'S JOURNAL PROMPT

When I imagine trying to express love for everyone unconditionally,
I feel…

# DAY 324

## *Practice saying 'yes' to the unbearable.*

By now, you know that your life continues to include the hard days and also the really hard days. You've had (or will have) those moments that almost break you as you conclude, "I can't take this anymore! This can't be my life!"

On those days, you know you need to stop fighting the hard situation. You can allow it to be the case (remember, even if you hate it, it is the case, so you may as well accept it). You know you can't demand that you find happiness in these moments. You know that you are learning to be with your hardest experiences.

I'd like to offer you a visualization to help. In these moments, start visualizing your body as fluid and capable of flowing with this painful experience. Lao Tzu reminds us, "The soft overcomes the hard. The gentle overcomes the rigid. Everyone knows this is true, but few can put it into practice." You can put this into practice.

Notice the tension in your body and try to release it. You are increasingly flexible, not rigid. You are practicing saying 'yes' to the unbearable.

You may not need this message today, but you have needed it before, and you will need it again. Today, remember this practice so that you have it when you need it.

You will love the comfort this will bring to your hardest moments.

### TODAY'S AFFIRMATION

I accept the natural rhythms of ease and difficulty.
I can be with both.

### TODAY'S JOURNAL PROMPT

The experiences that feel beyond my ability to endure are…
When I visualize myself being able to be with them I…

## *Tell the stories you can't find.*

So often, I hear women share that they feel like they are just a bit different from others in ways that they experience as negative, positive, or neutral.

The gift of women experiencing our world from a space of difference is that they have a perspective (and potentially valuable critique) of our shared culture. Where she didn't 'fit' reveals the missing pieces of our collective story. All of our greatest spiritual teachers inhabited this space. This is the freedom and perspective of the outcast.

If you don't see your stories reflected in our stories, it is your responsibility to bring that story to all of us. We are all standing in and speaking from a particular space, and yours is missing. It isn't a hierarchy but our shared kaleidoscopic image, and we need your story.

Today, instead of thinking about how you are persistently different from the family or world you are in, see if you can make an affirmative claim for what you know. Reflect on what is different for you and true for you. When you do this, you are expanding the story of all of us.

We could use the stories.

### TODAY'S AFFIRMATION
My story is part of our story.

### TODAY'S JOURNAL PROMPT
I have always felt different in that…

# DAY 326

## *Our physically aging bodies are a spiritual teaching about the impermanence of this world. Honor this wisdom.*

We misunderstand the last years of our life. In a culture that celebrates doing, making, and gaining, we only honor the vigorous youthful body. As we've lost the wisdom of detachment and impermanence that informs all spiritual faiths, we've disconnected from the deep spiritual meaning of aging and declining bodies.

Our physically aging bodies are a spiritual teaching about the perpetual impermanence of this world. In this stage of life, we lose the superficial attachment to self-images. We gain the wisdom that we are infinitely more than our physicality.

As we lose the physical and intellectual strength of youth, our bodies remind us that we will all learn how to let go. We were weak. We were strong. We are weak again. Ultimately, our bodies will die; this is the final letting go that awaits everyone.

Befriend your aging body. Love her and the deep teaching of impermanence and detachment that she is bringing you.

You will love the self-acceptance this practice will bring.

## TODAY'S AFFIRMATION
My body is teaching me the sacred truth of impermanence.

## TODAY'S JOURNAL PROMPT
My feelings about my aging body (the aches, pains, loss) are…
If I reconceptualized this as a spiritual teaching, I…

# DAY 327

## *We are remembering how to slow down.*

In this season of life, you may have noticed a move toward new recreations. It might be painting, gardening, genealogy, or something else. What I will guess is that you've developed a new interest in longer and slower projects.

When you start a plant from seed so that you can have broccoli a few months later, you are in a slower time than when you buy a frozen bag at the grocery store for tonight's dinner. When you take three months to knit a sweater, you are in a slower time than when you click "buy now" online for the birthday party this weekend.

This is a change in rhythm as you feel your natural draw into longer and slower creative projects. It doesn't matter if a different method is faster. Something in you connects with the labor of writing or with the slow process of stripping and refinishing your grandmother's table.

The way you want to be in the world is changing. You are moving into slower time, longer time. You don't need things to be in a rush. You are more like the slow-moving tortoise who eventually wins the race. The younger and faster hare may ridicule the tortoise, but you already know who wins this game in this ancient tale.

Today, pay attention to the new types of creative projects that attract your attention. Notice if your rhythm feels closer to the creative rhythm of slow time.

You've earned to time to do this.

### TODAY'S AFFIRMATION

I pay attention to what my creative energies are drawn to.

### TODAY'S JOURNAL PROMPT

Some of the projects or hobbies that have started to appeal to me as I age are…
I think I like these because…

# DAY 328

## *What is there possibly left for us to be afraid of?*

We are so lucky to have the stories of wise women who shared the most intimate aspects of their hardest journeys. It is easy to idealize these revolutionary women as somehow stronger and wiser than we are, but Audre Lorde, in her raw honesty, doesn't let us off so easily.

In, *The Cancer Journals*, she tells us the painful truth of her experience, lamenting, "I don't feel like being strong, but do I have a choice?" Sharing her journal entries, she walks us through her experience of pain, suffering, rage, and her commitment to keep speaking and writing in the face of it all.

Ultimately, Lorde asks, "What is there possibly left for us to be afraid of, after we have dealt face to face with death and not embraced it? Once I accept the existence of dying as a life process, who can ever have power over me again?"

In her worst experience, she found new courage. Facing her own mortality, she actually found a space that transcended her fears. We are so lucky that Audre Lorde, who died at age fifty-eight, chose to share her story with us before she left us.

Today, remember Audre Lorde. Remember that you don't know how your hard journeys are going to change you. Find courage as you bear witness to her courage. Find the space to engage with the raw, complicated influx of feelings that comes up. And remember the importance of women, outsiders, telling their stories.

You have the courage to do the same.

### TODAY'S AFFIRMATION

I have the courage to face my real feelings and tell my true story.

### TODAY'S JOURNAL PROMPT

When I think about being strong and not wanting to be...

# DAY 329

# REST
# REVIEW
# REFLECT

# *You must see divinity in everyone.*

No matter what faith tradition you dive into, you will find some iteration of this teaching. In the Eastern faiths, you see it most explicitly in the mysterious concept of Brahman. One way of understanding Brahman (which can't be understood) recognizes that everything that manifests in our world comes from this divine, universal presence. No one thing can effectively represent the infinite divine reality, but we are always encountering one aspect of it when we encounter anything.

This idea shows up again and again. In the Sufism of Islam, God is the only thing that even exists. The Christian faith reminds you that the Kingdom of God is within you. Dig deep enough into any tradition, and you will find this mystical claim about the divinity of everything.

These concepts can make us feel like our head is going to explode. Or rage in fury that certain things or people could ever also be from the Divine. I admit, I don't understand it. But what I have learned is that if every faith tradition has this teaching, then even (and especially) if we can't understand it, it is worth reflecting on why we encounter it everywhere.

Today, try to remember that every faith tradition ultimately teaches that divinity is in everything. When we can't see this, it is worth wondering if the problem is not with them but with my own spiritual understanding.

See the divine in everyone. You deserve the peace.

## TODAY'S AFFIRMATION

I see the divinity in everyone.

## TODAY'S JOURNAL PROMPT

When I imagine that everyone is an expression of divinity, I...

# DAY 331

## *Things fall apart.*

As you move into your season of *Return*, the increased rate of loss, change, and challenge for you and the people you know can feel dizzying. You are in the advanced class now. If you haven't learned to let go yet, you are going to now.

Things are falling apart. The world you knew is starting to feel out of your control. Do you throw your hands up in despair and conclude this is too much? Or do you throw your hands up in surrender and recognize you never had any control over any of this?

When the world begins to feel so out of control that you fear you are going to collapse in despair, remember to use this moment to practice your knowing that all things have always been out of your control. When we live with the illusion of control, we don't get to practice this truth. You are only reminded of this reality when it gets really scary.

Today, use your specific challenges of aging and physical decline as a reminder that the world was always out of your control. When you let go and return to your spiritual practices, you will discover that you are and always will be okay.

You've earned the inner peace.

### TODAY'S AFFIRMATION

I use the chaos to remind myself that I was never in control of the world.
I can still find peace.

### TODAY'S JOURNAL PROMPT

When things get too chaotic, I usually…
It might be better if I…

## *Feminine spirituality is an embodied spirituality. You can love this world.*

The holy feminine hasn't fared well in the more recent monotheistic religions. Despite her presence in the sacred texts of every religious faith, she has been repeatedly snuffed out in religious practice by those in power. Her unrelenting resurgence has always been a grassroots growth coming up from the people.

We've seen her return in the devotion to our Our Lady of Guadalupe in the turn toward Sophia in the Old Testament and in the resurgence of goddess theology in the new age movement.

We are seeking a more natural rhythm when we call the lost feminine back into our faith practices. We move away from the shaming of our physical body to a connection with our creative body. We move away from a focus on another spiritual world to a connection and desire to protect this earthly world. We move away from the goal of a reclusive union with the divine to an inclusion reunion with the world.

Today, pay attention to your beliefs about the divine. Notice if you feel the presence of both the masculine and feminine or if you have prioritized one over the other. Pay attention to how the alienation of the feminine may have alienated you from the truth of your deepest faith.

You will love the embodied spirituality this will bring you.

### TODAY'S AFFIRMATION

I connect with the holy feminine, this earth, and my body.

### TODAY'S JOURNAL PROMPT

My experience with divinity imagined as masculine
and/or feminine has been...

# DAY 333

## *Be brave enough to ask for the help you need.*

Women usually don't need any encouragement to help others. If you are like most, this habit was both born and bred into you through a one-two punch of nature and nurture. Your hormones drove you toward caretaking behavior, and your culture rewarded you for it.

Helping does feel good. And it does even more good for our homes and our communities. But being the hero asks so little of us compared to the journey of being the supplicant.

One of the greatest challenges we can encounter as we age is being in a position where we must ask people or programs to help us. Having to engage fully with our vulnerability, humility, and interdependence crumbles our fantasies of beneficence and autonomy.

Being truly dependent upon the charitable acts of others will forever change your experience of being charitable. You deeply understand the courage and humility it takes to turn to your community and say, "Please help me. I need you. I can't do this by myself." This is a sacred journey.

Today, pay attention to where you are still trying to be a hero. Allow yourself to imagine what it would be like to recognize our interdependence and be the supplicant (hint: This probably won't feel good at first!). Explore why being so independent might be important to you (for example, feelings of safety, control, or something else).

You deserve the support this can bring you.

### TODAY'S AFFIRMATION
I can ask for help.

### TODAY'S JOURNAL PROMPT
Asking for help makes me feel…

## *You are like water. Formless, flexible, and unrelentingly strong.*

We have so many recognizable symbols for spiritual growth, but a simple one that doesn't make its way into popular references as frequently as it should is one of my favorites–water.

Water shows up in every spiritual tradition. In *The Tao*, the master reveres the humility of water, which flows to the lowest points. To the charity of the water, which nourishes all things equally. To the flexibility of water, which adjusts to whatever form it finds itself within. To the strength of the water, which wears away majestic mountains.

In the Hindu and Judeo-Christian-Islamic traditions, water has powerful cleansing properties for sacred rituals. Catholic mystic St Theresa of Avila repeatedly spoke of water as her favorite metaphor for spiritual nourishment.

I could continue with religious references, but my goal is for you to reflect on the incredibly powerful meaning held by this ubiquitous and almost invisible resource. It is so simple but so powerful.

Today, your exercise is simple. Try to notice water. Notice its properties. See if you can be more like the water you see–humble, flexible, and strong.

You will love the peace this will bring you.

## TODAY'S AFFIRMATION

I am like water, humble, flexible, and strong.

## TODAY'S JOURNAL PROMPT

Water, as a symbol, feels to me...

# DAY 335

## *The purpose of life is to experience life. You are doing a great job.*

We can all fret over whether or not things should have happened in our lives, feeling distressed, guilty, or envious of those walking what looks like an easier or better path. Today, I'd like to propose a thought experiment (I am not asserting this is true; I just want to see how you imagine your life with this exercise).

What if the only purpose of life was to experience a life? What if, like the Hindu Brahman concept, you are merely one aspect of one spiritual thing, that is, having every experience of every possibility?

How "successful or unsuccessful" has your life been if the only point was to experience a variety of good and terrible things? How does holding that belief make you feel about regrets and "failures?"

Today, imagine you are one aspect, one manifestation, of divinity. You are here to experience one particular life. Notice how this thought experiment impacts your interpretations of your life.

### TODAY'S AFFIRMATION

I am one aspect of Divinity, living one particular life.

### TODAY'S JOURNAL PROMPT

The thought that the only purpose of life is to experience life feels…

# DAY 336

# REST
# REVIEW
# REFLECT

# DAY 337

## *Feminine courage.*

The word courage gets thrown around pretty quickly and easily in the self-help world. But oftentimes, its presentation is a particularly masculine version. You see this in the inspirational 'courage' posters that invariably show some heroic physical feat or a display of incredible bravery in the face of grave physical threats.

That is courage–masculine courage. Feminine courage is quite different–and not so easy to present in an inspirational photo. Because women value community over conquest, and feminine courage reflects that distinction.

An example of feminine courage (which can be embraced by either women or men) is the courage to continue to say yes to a world that has, *and still can*, hurt you. You are old enough to have been hurt terribly. You are old enough to know you can be hurt again. Your feminine courage is your commitment to stay relationally open in the face of these very real threats.

Today, reflect on what courage means to you. Notice if you recognize the distinction between how courage has typically been presented and how that is different from the feminine courage of embracing our vulnerability but still saying yes to your community and this world.

You will love the love this will bring into your life.

## TODAY'S AFFIRMATION

I have the courage to stay open in an imperfect world.

## TODAY'S JOURNAL PROMPT

When I think of masculine vs. feminine courage and my beliefs
and experiences with courage…

# DAY 338

## *Be an example for the world.*

There are so many people out there telling us how we should live our lives. Some mean well, some are trying to make a living, and some sincerely believe they know what you need to do.

In a world with so many competing experts, it can be a reprieve to free ourselves from the burden of knowing. Instead of trying to demonstrate that we are wise, we can show what we believe to be true through our quiet actions.

In conflict, a wise woman is fair and kind. In relationships, a wise woman is present and courteous. In living, a wise woman is receptive and flexible.

Today, instead of trying to heal the world with your words, see if you can bring healing to the world through your deeds. Be an example for the world.

You will love the quiet peace this will bring you.

### TODAY'S AFFIRMATION
I show my values through my actions.

### TODAY'S JOURNAL PROMPT
When I imagine myself living out my values,
I imagine that I would be more…

*A young woman learns how to fight.*
*A wise woman knows how to yield.*

Your paradoxes of development can feel surprising as you circle around from one important value to its complete opposite. In this process, we discover that there is no 'correct' position but a variety of truths and realities that work for different times and spaces.

One that I see so often is the discrepancy between what feels necessary for a woman in her responsibility years versus a woman in return. In our younger years, we need to find our voice. We need to set those limits. We need to stand up and say, "This is not okay."

The surprising shift is how, late in life, this urgency can ebb away. As you become increasingly centered in your own truth, you feel less and less compelled to convince or assert anything in relationship to another struggling soul. You are more inclined to allow her to float along on her own path, navigating her certainty and her opinions about you or the world.

As you enter the season of Return, you are increasingly able to let everyone be exactly how they need to be in that moment. As a young woman, you needed to learn to fight. As an old woman, you find peace in the yielding.

## TODAY'S AFFIRMATION
I know how to yield.

## TODAY'S JOURNAL PROMPT
When I reflect on my own journey of needing to speak up and
no longer needing to speak up, I notice...

# DAY 340

## *Caretaking as a spiritual practice.*

If you have cared for a dying person for any period of time, you came away changed. The longer we stay with such a process, the deeper we need to go with our spiritual practices.

Because caretaking a declining and dying person is hard–across every domain. But, I'd like to remind you of something available to you that might help make the suffering feel more purposeful.

Your caretaking journey closely parallels one of the deepest spiritual practices in the East–the death meditation. In the death meditation, monks are required to bear witness to the death and decay process in order to facilitate their own spiritual growth. Watching the decay, the monk remembers that she, too, will face such a fate. Her body will follow the same pattern.

When you are sitting with this dying person, possibly exhausted from a sleepless night. Maybe revolted by the intimate maintenance of uncontrolled bodily functions, see if you can look to her and turn your weariness for this task into a recognition that we all need to have, "This too is my fate. What am I still attached to that doesn't make sense? What can I see, in this moment, that offers me clarity about my own life?"

You know that your life is your spiritual practice; this is the master class.

### TODAY'S AFFIRMATION

I use the visibility of decline and dying as a spiritual practice.

### TODAY'S JOURNAL PROMPT

When I think about caring for a declining or dying person,
I feel...

# DAY 341

## *Redeeming the goddesses.*

Academic and social critic Camille Paglia can hold big historical surveys in her mind and offers us important reminders and corrections to our sometimes idealized and naive attempts to reconnect with the lost feminine.

Paglia reminds us that, as we moved away from our connection to nature, the feminine, and her associated goddesses, that all of these things were relegated to the bin of "things we've conquered." New age feminists tried to redeem these earth mothers, but it seems most have only redeemed the benevolent mother and not always the destructive one.

The Goddess Kali of the Hindu tradition reminds us that these feminine goddesses were far more complicated than the simple, loving mother we want to find.

In discussion with Paglia, psychologist Jordan Peterson questions why we are living the half-myths of a tyrannical father (our critique of patriarchy) and benevolent mother (idealized feminine). He asks, where is the other half of these sacred images? Where is our story of the benevolent father or tyrannical mother in our current collective understanding?

It seems our stories should be more complicated. Today, reflect on the stories we lost. Remember the wise old man. Remember the terrifying Baba Yaga. Don't simplify our masculine and feminine into something 'bad' or 'good.' Remember that these ancient sacred figures held both our creative and destructive truths.

As you move into your last years, you need these more complicated stories.

## TODAY'S AFFIRMATION

I can hold the complicated truths of our sacred images.

## TODAY'S JOURNAL PROMPT

When I imagine masculine and feminine values,
I tend to think/feel...

## *Let them let go of you.*

Do you know how to be with a dying person? It can be hard to let her walk through a process that is so foreign to our ways of being. Friends and family often say things that are not, in fact, being with the dying process but denying the process. This makes the process harder for everyone.

Too often, we can't tolerate the dying person's feelings about her process. Maybe she is angry. Maybe she is sad. Maybe you wish she weren't. Don't equate 'keeping up hope' with your expectation that she needs to want to keep living. This is unfair to a dying person if she has moved past this stage. Tolerate her misplaced rage as she lashes out inappropriately in her anger and confusion. She will get where she needs to be with her own process, not by you controlling or being reactive to how she feels. Listen to her words about her experience–whatever they are. You know now that your task is to learn to be with suffering without trying to change it.

This task of being with the dying is hard. But this is her rite of passage. It is not about our needs. It will go exactly as it is supposed to go. Bear witness.

Today, reflect on your feelings about letting another person die. Reflect on your ability or challenge with letting the dying person go through her range of emotions. Notice if you can be with these hard feelings. See where you still have room to grow.

We all deserve the good death.

### TODAY'S AFFIRMATION

I don't idealize the dying process, but allow the dying to experience dying
as she experiences dying.

### TODAY'S JOURNAL PROMPT

When I imagine embracing the real, and not the idealized,
experience of being with someone who is dying, I feel...

# DAY 343

# REST
# REVIEW
# REFLECT

## *Express your gratitude for everything.*

We've touched upon the practical use of incorporating gratitude into your daily rituals (for running water, climate control, etc.), but today I'd like for you to take this practice a bit further.

Today, I'd like for you to practice declaring your gratitude for as many things and people as you are capable of. When you turn on the water, express gratitude for the water, the plumbing, and the workers at the utility center. When you brush your teeth, express gratitude for being able to have a toothbrush and toothpaste and the truck driver who brought those items to your store.

See how many things you can both bring to life by imagining the journey they took (and the people involved) to get to the place where this experience is with you. This deeper practice not only cultivates our gratitude but our awareness of our total interdependence and gratitude and compassion for all beings.

Maybe that truck driver is a jerk that blocked your entry on the freeway, but when you remember him as the person bringing you the goods you need, you open yourself up to a different way of being–with everyone.

Today, try to see how many things you can wake up with gratitude for the process and the people that brought them to you. Notice how this changes your relationship with those things and with all people.

You will love the gratitude and compassion this will bring into your life.

### TODAY'S AFFIRMATION

I am grateful for everything.

### TODAY'S JOURNAL PROMPT

When I think about practicing gratitude for everything in my day,
I feel...

# DAY 345

## *You will learn to be with everything.*

You are in an invisible world. A world that young people don't see or understand. You are in a world where the opposite of everything you believed before becomes true. You are holding the beautiful paradoxes of the last decades of life.

One of the most important things the last stages of life teach us is the power of being with the things we cannot change. Because as much as the thirty-five-year-old tries to learn to be with what is, there is nothing quite like the master class of aging to fully embrace, embody, and live out this truth.

You will experience the transformative experience of being with whatever is the case when you sit with someone suffering from the pain and confusion of physical or cognitive decline. You truly can't fix it. But you can be with them in this present-moment. You don't leave. You can witness and hold the suffering and stay.

Our bias of fixing and solving falls away naturally at this crossroads, whether we try to or not. You, and the people you love, are walking into experiences that won't get fixed. Instead of trying to fight this truth, see how walking into them, being with them, accepting and feeling them can transform your psychological and spiritual world.

You deserve the peace this can bring you.

### TODAY'S AFFIRMATION

I am capable of being with all things.

### TODAY'S JOURNAL PROMPT

When I think of all that I have been able to endure, I realize...

## *Keep our dignity of dependence.*

As a therapist who works with aging women, one of the newest stories that harm women's aging process is this belief that we should attempt to and allow others to "keep her dignity and independence." Linking dignity to independence is so pervasive in our culture, but one only has to reflect for a moment to realize how destructive this myth is.

You know by now that independence is a myth–an especially popular one for the West. You know that the wish to maintain our independence is an effort to feed the needs of our ego and is an avoidance of our fears.

There is more dignity in asking for help. There is more dignity in allowing someone to help us with our most intimate tasks.

Please stop saying that the goal is for any of us to keep our 'dignity and independence." We can all live the tale of exhibiting the *dignity of our total dependence.*

### TODAY'S AFFIRMATION

There is dignity in honoring our dependence.

### TODAY'S JOURNAL PROMPT

My response to the phrase, "Keep her dignity and dependence," is…

## *When you truly connect with the sacred, you will stop fighting over its symbolic representations.*

Have you ever been under the thumb of someone trying to convince you of the absolute truth of their religious belief? And maybe the falseness of yours? Their intention is usually good. They often want to share the healing they have experienced in their own faith.

This is a both/and situation. Their experience is usually very deep and very true. But other, very different experiences are also true. We get tripped up when we think our symbol has an exclusive hold on Truth.

If you study comparative religions closely, you see some parallels. If you study the mystical traditions of those same religions, you see the complete overlap. Faiths are founded by spiritual teachers who tried to explain that ineffable divine. But the experience is beyond words and matter, so they often use parables, symbols, koans, and myths.

We don't need to fight over these conflicting symbolic representations of things we can't ever completely understand. When you have a deep encounter with the divine, you see its truth everywhere.

Commune with your divine source wherever you feel most connected. And honor theirs, too. Your effort will bring you more peace than anything else.

You deserve that peace.

### TODAY'S AFFIRMATION
I accept what is true for me and what is true for others.

### TODAY'S JOURNAL PROMPT
With regard to the sacred truths, I believe…

## *My awareness of my mortality cultivates my compassion and connectedness.*

Illness and death frighten most people, but that is because most people don't reflect deeply on death. Research repeatedly proves that when we try to keep a distance from our awareness of our looming mortality, we become less compassionate and more likely to protect people most like ourselves.

But when we take a deeper, more contemplative, conscious, or meditative look at our mortality, the exact opposite happens. Research repeatedly shows that deep meditations on our own mortality improve our sense of connectedness and compassion for ourselves and others.

If you are feeling frightened by illness or mortality, it is likely that you are letting it sit at the edge of consciousness—tormenting and terrorizing you. Instead of distracting your attention from death, deepen your attention toward death.

We find this practice across all philosophies and faiths—from existentialism's death anxiety to Catholic Thomas Merton's call to 'consult your death' when determining your life priorities.

Meditating on your own mortality helps you to focus on what matters in this moment. It frees you to prioritize your actions, to speak your mind, and to stop wasting time on things that aren't in alignment with your values.

Today, instead of letting illness and death terrorize you from the sidelines, see if you can turn your attention toward this meditative practice that will bring you peace. You deserve it.

### TODAY'S AFFIRMATION

I am comfortable facing my mortality.

### TODAY'S JOURNAL PROMPT

When I think about my own decline and death, I feel...

## *Your life is your answer.*

What is your meaning of life? I can tell you. Look at your life. How are you choosing to live in this moment? This is your answer to what you believe the meaning of life is.

Whether you are broke and living in a difficult situation, sick, or caretaking alone and exhausted doesn't matter. How are you choosing to be in your impossible circumstances? Is this brutal life your spiritual practice?

What is your relationship to your resources (or lack of)? Are you still as kind as you want to be?

How do you spend your days? What are you doing with the challenges you have been given? What do you allow yourself to imagine?

Do you take responsibility for your life and your growth? I think you probably do.

Today, reflect on how the way you live your life is your expression of your belief in the meaning of life. See what you like and see where you still see room for growth.

You deserve the meaningful life.

### TODAY'S AFFIRMATION

I feel good about the way I choose to live my life.

### TODAY'S JOURNAL PROMPT

When I think about how I've chosen to live my life, I notice…

# DAY 350

REST
REVIEW
REFLECT

## *A young woman seeks power.*
## *A wise woman embraces powerlessness.*

In the face of our own death, or loss, or death or loss of someone close to us, we become fundamentally in relationship with our total powerlessness. Your lifetime of being unable to face this truth is over. You are, with powerlessness, the most powerful spiritual lesson of your life.

When we were young, we imagined that we just needed to get the upper hand, to have more control in a relationship, or to get people to do what we knew was best for them. In short, as young women, we believed what we really needed was more power.

These are the fantasies of a young woman because every spiritual tradition teaches us exactly the opposite. We may seek more power, but power is not the spiritual journey we need to take. From Jesus to the Buddha to the twelve-step programs, we learn that our journey out of darkness is one of embracing our powerlessness.

Today, pay attention to where you are still in the grips of trying to gain power or control. See if you can change your perspective. I am not asking you to abandon healthy efforts, but I am asking you to do your work and embrace your powerlessness.

You will love the burdens this will lift from you.

## TODAY'S AFFIRMATION

I am powerless over others, the world, and outcomes.

## TODAY'S JOURNAL PROMPT

For me, the word powerless means...

# DAY 352

## *What if we allowed the decline of our Return season to be visible?*

We tolerate some stages of life better than others. You've thrown the sympathetic glance at the mom with the screaming child in the grocery store. You don't bat an eye at the young mother wrestling with her toddler on a bathroom changing table. But do we have the same attitude toward a caretaker with an elderly or disabled person?

How do we respond to the old man yelling profanities or the disabled mom who needs a diaper change? Are we okay with these people being visible and moving through our world? Or do we imagine caretakers need to 'protect' everyone else from having to 'see' this truth of our lifespan?

How would our world be different if our grandmothers could scream in frustrated confusion and our grandfathers could need a diaper change in our shared community spaces? What if this stage of life was allowed to be present with all the others? What if we didn't hide this? How different might our world be? For those living that journey, for those caretaking that journey, and for those wondering about that future journey?

Today, reflect on your ideas about the decline in the last part of the season of return and how you feel about letting that part of our journey become a part of our shared spaces.

## TODAY'S AFFIRMATION

I can let the season of return be visible.

## TODAY'S JOURNAL PROMPT

When I imagine allowing an elderly or cognitively impaired person to be visibly needy or difficult in public, I tend to think/feel…

## *Your task is to connect with nondual reality but to act in dual reality.*

If you are studying any spiritual texts, you may have come across the descriptions of dual vs. nondual reality. Nonduality is basically a belief, experience, or understanding that everything is actually just one thing (if you study the mystical theology of any faith, you certainly encounter this concept). Duality is the belief, experience, and understanding that we are all separate beings. This is the way most of us experience our world.

As you become increasingly aware of this strange paradox, you might wonder about your rhythm between contemplative practice and awareness of unity (nonduality) and your experience of being a particular woman, living in a particular place with particular circumstances.

This is where I believe it is useful to accept the important role of our ego. Our ego feels like a separate and particular being with its own likes and dislikes. Your ego stories are your experience of dual reality. This is where we act in the world "as if" we are separate beings.

You can live and act from the seat of your ego stories, but your increasing connection to a sense of spiritual unity allows you to experience your ego stories almost in the spirit of play. You are connected to unity and don't really believe in the duality that you experience in your life, despite living, feeling, and acting from the place.

Today, pay attention to your intuitions and feelings about nondual and dual reality. Notice how this paradox lives in your life.

You deserve the playfulness.

## TODAY'S AFFIRMATION

I accept the paradox of nonduality and duality in myself.

## TODAY'S JOURNAL PROMPT

When I reflect on my beliefs and nonduality and duality, I…

## *When you aren't attached to anything, you don't fear losing anything.*

As you fully embrace your season of *Return*, you are more challenged by loss than you probably have ever been, but if you are continuing to connect to your sense of unitive consciousness or nature, you are becoming less and less attached to your particular circumstances having particular outcomes.

You know that your journey is learning that you can learn to be okay, no matter what challenges come into your life. You might be more connected to Eastern ideas like Dharma, where we accept that we must live out our responsibilities, despite our dislike of them. You now have more patience to sit with the terrible, knowing something will change.

In short, you are living in less discomfort and fear. You are living out the experience of detachment and letting go. Experiencing perpetual decline and loss in this context is easier.

Today, notice where you are on this path. Pay attention to where you might have more room to grow. Take action to connect with your best practices in getting there.

You deserve the peace.

### TODAY'S AFFIRMATION

I am living out my practice of nonattachment and letting go.

### TODAY'S JOURNAL PROMPT

When I reflect on this concept of nonattachment,
I notice/think/feel…

## *We are Nature.*

As you become more connected to your deepest self, you will start to feel that you are connected to everything. Your return to nature feels different.

You no longer simplify nature into a one-dimensional, idealized beautiful thing. You've experienced creation and destruction in your own life, and you see this same rhythm mirrored in nature–her creative growth and her destructive power. You are reminded of our lost nature goddess. Reflecting on your own life, you better understand the ancient expression of benevolent mother and cannibalistic hag.

You are nature. We are nature. You aren't good or bad. Nature isn't good or bad. You recognize the rhythms of development and decay, and you don't assign hierarchical value to either one. They are all part of your same circle.

As you move into your stage of return, reflecting on your own losses, the decline, and the death of people you love, you know that this is all part of the same circular rhythm.

Today pay attention to your sense of nature. Is she good? Bad? How does the story of her natural rhythm of the natural world better mirror the life you live?

### TODAY'S AFFIRMATION
We are nature.

### TODAY'S JOURNAL PROMPT
When I reflect on my own life, its growth and decay, and meditate
on the natural world, I feel/think/notice…

# DAY 356

## *I embrace the changing seasons of my life.*

You've explored the stories of your growth and development this year. You think about your life in a new way that returns you to more ancient ways of understanding. You recognize your life includes four seasons, *Receptivity, Responsibility, Reflection,* and *Return.*

**Receptivity:** As a young girl, in the spring of your life, you were open and receptive to the ideas and stories of those around you. As you engaged with your community (whether positive or negative), you constructed your own interpretations of yourself, others, and your world.

**Responsibility :** When you went into the world, you started the summer season of responsibility. Maybe you were a mother or a worker, or both. Laden with the responsibilities (or chaos) of this season, you didn't have much time to think deeply about your stories and your journey.

**Reflection :** In the fall of your life, something happened. You discovered some shortcomings, experienced some failure (a divorce, death, or just inexplicable despair). Now starts the season of turning inward. In this third part of your life, you are forced to reflect in ways you've not reflected before.

**Return :** And finally, you return. With the wisdom you've gained from your reflection, you become a teacher. You are now a wise woman in the winter of her life, stepping into an invisible world and learning how to completely let go.

This year you gained a greater awareness of why you made the choices you made in your earlier seasons. You stopped blaming yourself and started intuitively knowing that the way you were was exactly how you needed to be in that moment.

You embraced the purposeful change that comes with aging into the wise woman you were always meant to become. You are a wise woman who remembers all of her seasons as she looks to her moment of return.

## TODAY'S AFFIRMATION

I accept and love the changing seasons of my life.

## TODAY'S JOURNAL PROMPT

When I think about this season's model now, I...

# REST
# REVIEW
# REFLECT

*A wise woman can find peace in the storm. Because she has seen storms come and go before.*

You've seen the truth of older women's resilience presented in so many ways. A mother stressed with her first child at ease with her fifth. A devastating diagnosis better tolerated as the years go on. A great-grandmother as a calming presence for a family in extreme crisis.

We forget that being young was difficult. When we experienced hard things for the first time, they completely devastated us. When we are old, we know people can endure long periods of hardship and come out on the other side. We know that nothing is permanent, good or bad. We know things change.

When we are younger, we look at the world in naive frustration. We want to save the world or remove the burdens from the people we love. We want to change things and sometimes believe we can.

As we age, we discover that impossible situations don't necessarily change but that we do. Maybe our child continued to struggle, or the caretaking lasted years longer than we ever expected. Maybe we had to learn how to live on less money than we ever imagined we could.

We adapted. If we were able to let go of our expectations and accept our situation, we would experience profound internal shifts. We found peace in situations that others may have found impossible.

Today, reflect on your wise woman's resilience. You've earned it.

## TODAY'S AFFIRMATION

I am a wise, older woman.

## TODAY'S JOURNAL PROMPT

An area where I can see I have more wisdom is...

# DAY 359

## *Die in relationship.*

As you come to the end of your life, my wish is that you will share openly about your experience of coming up to this threshold. We stopped telling our stories about dying, but you can restart the process by including your experience in our shared stories.

I am not asking you to sugarcoat your struggles but to continue to be real about what the experience is like for you. If you are sad, angry, tired, or ready to go, it doesn't matter. What does matter is that our diverse stories of dying get told.

Let this be another process we do in our relationship with each other. When you share your whole experience, you allow those you are leaving behind to imagine their own death with less isolation, more courage, and less fear. It is an extraordinary gift you can leave behind for a world that is still very frightened of decline and death.

Your only job is to be real together. No masks of courage or cheerfulness. Let them walk through the real experience with you.

We all need these stories.

## TODAY'S AFFIRMATION

I can talk about my experience of dying when the time comes.

## TODAY'S JOURNAL PROMPT

When I imagine speaking openly about my thoughts, feelings,
and experience of dying, I feel…

# DAY 360

## *You connect with our most ancient stories.*

You have spent a year or more exploring your own stories and remembering our forgotten ones. You recognize that you have used stories throughout your life to help you imagine who you are and how you can be in your community.

You know where these stories come from. You now can connect with the ancient art of storytelling, the sacred way we pass down our traditions, our values, and our understanding of how to live, love, lose, and grow old.

You better connect with the paradoxical and confusing wisdom myths of our elders and laugh at the easy stories provided by our story dealers. You are nourished by how these old stories better hold your complicated life.

This year, you stopped listening to the for-profit storytellers and started exploring, discovering, and telling our own truest tales.

You are a more complicated story than they know. And now you are telling the tale.

## TODAY'S AFFIRMATION

I know my story and our ancient stories.

## TODAY'S JOURNAL PROMPT

Reflecting on this year, I notice...

# DAY 361

## *What are you imagining now?*

As you come to the close of your *OMM 365* journey, I'd like for you to reflect on your changing relationship with your imagination. What did you think about imagination, eros, and creativity when you started this journey? What do you imagine now?

Can you recognize the forgotten role of our eros energy and her role in fueling our creative and healing imaginative experiences? Do you recognize the spaces in between, where you are always constructing a story between you and your world? Have you realized this is a space where we can get stuck or creatively find our way out?

What are your thoughts about your imagination as you move into this last phase of your life? Are you more protective of her? Are you less likely to let outside media influences manipulate your imagination?

Today, reflect on how you have opened up your creative imaginings. How you have fueled them with your stronger connection to your own eros energy. Wonder (without knowing!) how she will continue to accompany you on your journey.

You deserve the imaginings.

### TODAY'S AFFIRMATION

I know the power of my own imagination.

### TODAY'S JOURNAL PROMPT

When I reflect on how I thought about imagination before and now,
I notice…

# DAY 362

## *You found your story.*
## *You lose your story.*

You embody the storyteller. You've learned to share your true story with a holistic and accepting attitude that includes all the darkness and all the light. You've lived through many deaths and rebirths as you see you are coming to the ending chapters of this tale. Like our ancient and sacred teachers, you recognize your story includes your creation and destruction.

As you feel increasingly connected to everyone, you feel decreasingly attached to your own story. Your story feels like part of all the stories. And all the stories feel like part of you.

You feel the purposefulness of coming into this life, finding a sense of self, living out that particular existence with her joys and sufferings, wounds and wisdom, but then, in an unexpected and ironic twist, you let go of that, too. Like the song, "Row Row Row your boat, gently down the stream, merrily, merrily, merrily merrily, life is but a dream."

You worked hard to find your own story, and you recognize that, like a dream, you can also let it go.

Today, notice how you found your stories. Feel how you have embodied the wisdom of the storyteller. Now recognize your connection to all the stories and let yourself let go of this, too.

You are already connected to the eternal spirit that this brings you.

## TODAY'S AFFIRMATION

I am a part of all the stories. All the stories are a part of me.

## TODAY'S JOURNAL PROMPT

When I imagine letting go of my attachment to my own story,
I think/feel…

# DAY 363

*A young woman finds her ego identity in the material world.*
*A wise woman discovers her wisdom in the spiritual world.*
*A healing woman brings her wisdom back to a broken world.*
*A dying woman teaches us how to let go of this world.*

As you come to the end of this year, you've learned a new way of understanding women's development across the lifespan. Letting go of the story of our traditional developmental models of identity and material achievements, you rediscovered and included the seasons of aging and dying that unwound those earlier projects.

Hopefully, this perspective has cultivated compassion and understanding for the younger you who moved through the earlier phases. Hopefully, this perspective has cultivated curiosity and acceptance of the purposefulness of what is still ahead.

You were a *Receptive* girl who tried to discover what the world wanted of her. You became a *Responsive* young woman who tried to take care of herself and others in a confusing world. You became a *Reflective* older woman who, often in crisis, let go of the projects of youth, turned inward, and brought back new gifts from within. And you are becoming a *Returning* old woman who will decline and die with us and teach the next generation about truly letting go.

Today, take a big picture look at how you have walked this journey so far. Imagine how you will enter the season of declining and dying in relationship with curiosity, grace, and a knowing of the full purposefulness of that journey. Notice the feelings that come up for you.

You've earned the growth and wisdom.

## TODAY'S AFFIRMATION

I embrace all the seasons of my life, even and especially the *Return*.

## TODAY'S JOURNAL PROMPT

When I reflect upon my own long journey,
including declining and dying, I feel…

# REST
# REVIEW
# REFLECT

# DAY 365

## *Your **OMM 365** Journey*

We've spent a year together as you've explored your life through your stories, imagination, healing, and aging journey.

How are you different today from the woman who started this exploration? What do you still want to explore? I encourage you not to rush, but to allow yourself time to reflect on how different you are from the woman who first picked up this text. Be still and pay attention to where you feel called to go from here.

We are all always forgetting and remembering these practices, so you will be gentle as you accept that rhythm for yourself. You might want to start the *OMM 365* again, from the beginning. (You will be surprised how different your journal responses are the second time through!) You might want to facilitate your own group. You might want to write or create your own project that reflects who you are and what you know.

There is no right answer for where you go now. What I do know is that you have the courage, patience, and intuition to take the next step on your own winding path.

You are a gift to our world.


Thank you.

# *OMM 365* Group Structure and Guidelines

You are welcome to use the structure and guidelines I use in my *OMM 365* groups if you find them helpful.

## Structure:

- Keep groups limited to six-week sessions. This allows women to join or leave as they feel comfortable.
- Six to nine women is a good number for groups.
- A quick fifteen-minute consultation is good to see if a woman is a good fit for group.
- Most women won't remember names, etc. I remind women this is a memory-fail-friendly space.
- I estimate about ten minutes per member (if six women are present, a sixty-minute group, etc.).
- A mandatory fee (whether she is present or absent that week) dramatically increases weekly commitment and participation.

## Basic Process Questions for each week:

- I prefer unstructured questions where the group members bring in the content; being too specific in my questions shuts things down to my narrower view. I open with questions like:
  1. What OMMs did you connect with?
  2. What OMMs did you not like?
  3. What came up for you in your Rest, Review, and Reflection?

## Group Guidelines:

I provide a copy of the group guidelines to each member before group starts. We discuss it in the first group. I refer back to it when someone is struggling to stick with the guidelines. The most frequent challenge is the desire to offer advice or problem-solve. Learning to simply be present with her in her struggle is the exercise and goal for the *OMM 365* group.

# Group Guidelines:

**The purpose of this guideline is to create a group culture that feels safe and useful for all participants. By participating in the group, you agree to help co-create a safe and useful group by adhering to the following guidelines:**

**What is said in group, stays in group.** Don't discuss what others share outside of group.

**Share your own experiences and feelings.** Statements like "I feel…" or "I remember when I…" work well.

**Do not problem-solve, offer advice, or ask questions to others.** Questions or statements like, "Have you ever thought about…?" or "Maybe you should…" to other group members <u>are not appropriate</u> for group.

**Remember to do the processing exercises.** This group is for women who want to share these experiences, so please read/review them so we have a common point of discussion.

**Be mindful of privacy.** As we are working online, we are all responsible for cultivating a private space. Please make sure people are not walking behind you, talking to you, etc. If you will have a caretaker present (or are caretaking someone who may interrupt you), please just let the group know.

**The group can hold our differences.** We can let other group members hold important views that are different from our own. We do not share in an effort to persuade or convince others.

**The group can hold our hard feelings.** If a member feels sad, hopeless, angry, or depressed, we do not try to rescue her or change how she feels. We can **be with** these hard feelings.

**Be mindful of how much or little you are sharing.** I am a very good facilitator to balance this, but it helps if you are able to be thoughtful about sharing more or less depending on how much you have already shared.